A FOOLISH ODYSSEY

AN INSPIRATIONAL STORY OF CONFORMITY, AWAKENING AND ESCAPE

NEIL HAWKESFORD

Published by

ISBN-13: 978-1985604674

ISBN-10: 1985604671

A special mention of appreciation and thanks to:

Richard, Charlie, Malc & Paul at Manor Farm
Mike & the team at Weir Quay Boatyard
Ben & Alex at Messack Farm

James & Hanneke for inspiration and making it all possible

CONTENTS

Part III
ESCAPE

FREE BOOK OFFER

As a thank you for buying my book I'd like to send you a gift.

It's a small collection of anecdotes about my time in the Royal Navy.

Just visit www.neilhawkesford.com and you can download it completely free.

I hope you enjoy it.

PREFACE

The story told in my first book 'A Foolish Voyage' ended in late 1984. 3 years of youthful adventure that finished with me leaving the sea and returning to a 'normal' life again.

If you've read it, I thank you. If you haven't, then I suggest you do.

Reading 'A Foolish Voyage' first will give you a better appreciation of what's to come here. You'll enjoy this book more.

Just search *A Foolish Voyage* on your countries Amazon Store

Of course, if you'd just prefer to start here that's fine too. This story stands alone.

Society conditions and pressures us to conform doesn't it?

As young adults, many of us had freedom and a desire for adventure. Some of us even managed to escape for a while, as I did on my Foolish Voyage.

But sooner or later normality and conformity suck us back.

We're encouraged to find the job, find the partner, buy the house, have the kids. To do what everyone around us is doing. The groove becomes the deepening rut and escape becomes less and less likely.

Our dreams fade. Our urge to fight wanes. We accept our lot. Our last hope gets pinned on the weekly lottery ticket. Most never make it out. That's tragic.

I remember watching a film years ago. It was a tale of survival in the wilds of Alaska. One man lost in a vast snow-covered forest. Darkness was falling, the temperature plummeting. He had no shelter, he was shivering with cold and fear. His only hope was to build a fire.

He searched for kindling and wood. Carefully he built a little pile of the driest material, striking his knife on a flint trying to set it alight.

He tried and tried his desperation increases. Suddenly a spark flashed, a wisp of smoke appeared. He put his face close to the little pile, cupped it with his hand. Blew.

More smoke appeared, then a tiny flame, the tinder started crackling. He delicately placed some twigs, more flames, more crackling. Within minutes the fire burned strongly.

Soon he had logs roaring and spitting. He sat close, basking in the heat and bright orange light. He smiled, his face glowing. He was saved, he was going to be OK.

Eleven years ago I too was lost and fearing for my survival.

Conformity was my wilderness.

The kindling for my fire was a dream I thought lost.

A spark flashed.

The fire caught.

It saved me.

PART I
CONFORMITY

A TWENTY YEAR ITCH

Conformity is dangerous

— ADAM GRANT

*Conformity is the jailer of freedom and the enemy of
growth.*

— JOHN F. KENNEDY

PART I
INTRODUCTION

Just when every ray of hope was gone
I should have known you'd come along
If sleep don't take me first, you'll come around
I know I can always count on you
Lovers leave and friends will let you down
But you're the only sure thing that I've found
No matter what I do I'll never lose
My old friend the blues

— STEVE EARLE

It had been dark, cold and raining when I'd stepped outside at 5:30 that morning.

It was dark, cold and raining now, 14 hours later.

Ten hours of driving and 4 hours of meetings. Truth be told they hadn't really been meetings. Rather just opportunities for various people to complain, demand and shout at me.

A bunch of pricks.

I fumbled for the key to my rented flat, trying not to drop my takeout chow mein onto the doorstep.

Opening the door, I hit the light switch and dumped the food on the table.

Grabbing a beer from the fridge, and a fork from the cutlery drawer, I walked into the lounge, pulling the ring tab as I went.

I collapsed on the sofa and slugged a mouthful from the can, eyes closed. My stomach rumbled. That Burger King lunch had been hours ago.

Ripping the lid off the foil container I forked a mouthful of noodles into my mouth and punched the TV remote.

Adverts, how do they do that? How is it possible to catch the commercial break every fucking time you switch on?

I switched channels, more ads. Unbelievable.

I kept pushing the button again and again, faster and faster. Channel after channel of shit. Shit, shit and more shit, everything's shit.

I hurled the remote across the room.

It hit the wall, the batteries flew across the floor.

The girl on the TV carried on rollerblading, apparently very happy with her sanitary pads.

I took another swig of beer and pushed my head back into the sofa, staring at the ceiling. Thoughts swirled.

Why did she do this to me?

How can I have lost everything again?

Is this how it's going to be for the rest of my life?

Is everything I ever do always going to go to shit?

It's all been for nothing.

What's the point?

Maybe I should just end it.

Tears welled up.

My old friend the blues was back.

The year was 2005.

Let me tell you how I got there.

BACK TO THE FUTURE

*N*ineteen Eighty-Five, I was 28 years old and back living with my parents in Lichfield, a small city in the Midlands of England.

My dream of sailing and living a life of adventure had ended. I'd come close to losing my life. And 'Mor Gwas', the little boat that had been my sanctuary for the past two years now belonged to a Frenchman in Brest.

The previous months had drained me physically and emotionally. I was running on autopilot, going through the motions, saying I was OK; I wasn't.

I'd lost everything except my life, and lost was how I felt.

I started working with my Dad. I needed money and I needed something to do. His company needed a van driver. I liked driving and it seemed like a good way to keep me busy.

In 1969, with a background in asphalt and timber flooring, my Dad had started a small flooring distribution warehouse. It was doing OK. Dad worked hard and took his reward, but most of the profit got ploughed back into the business. The warehouse was in the city of Birmingham, an hours drive away.

It wasn't easy slotting back into normality.

Everyone seemed to know what had happened to me. I'd introduce myself to a customer and they'd respond with, "Oh yeah, you're the one that got shipwrecked". They'd ask questions and I'd try to answer, but they were from another world. For them, the sea was something you saw twice a year when you went on holiday. They didn't understand. I felt like an alien on my own planet, trapped and lonely.

On 'Mor Gwas' I was isolated from everyday 'normal' life. Now I'd been thrust back into it without any chance to acclimatise. I wondered how people couldn't see what I could see. Normal it was not. It seemed the world had gone mad.

Violence dominated the news.

The coal miners strike had just ended after a full year. It had been a war.

National Union of Mineworkers leader Arthur Scargill had said. "The policies of this government are clear – to destroy the coal industry and the NUM".

Prime Minister Margaret Thatcher had said. "We had to fight the enemy without in the Falklands. We always have to be aware of the enemy within, which is much more difficult to fight and more dangerous to liberty".

The strike had torn communities and families apart. Bloody battles had taken place between police and pickets. Not least at a place called Orgreave in Yorkshire, where 5,000 police had fought with 5,000 miners.

Afterwards, Scargill said. "We've had riot shields, we've had riot gear, we've had police on horseback charging into our people. We've had people hit with truncheons and people kicked to the ground. The intimidation and the brutality displayed are something of a Latin American state."

Thatcher won. In 1983 Britain had 174 working pits. The industry was privatised and by 2009 there were 6.

There was violence and death in the national sport too.

A fire at the Bradford City Stadium killed 56 people. On the same day, a young lad was crushed to death under a collapsing wall at Birmingham City's St Andrews ground.

A few days later rioting Liverpool football fans caused a stampede in the Heysel stadium in Brussels. It left 39 people dead. British clubs were banned from European competitions as a result.

In just 16 days in May, 96 football fans died.

That year there were riots in the streets. Brixton and Broadwater Farm in London. Toxteth in Liverpool and in Handsworth Birmingham, only a few miles down the road from my Dad's business. Social injustice & police racism the justification. Destruction of property, loss of life and injury the result.

We were halfway through a decade during which Britain was becoming more and more divided. As Andrew Marr pointed out in his 'History of Modern Britain'. "During the 80's the rich got richer but the bottom 10% saw their incomes fall by about 17%".

Farther afield terrorists were hijacking planes. Most notably TWA flight 847. For over two weeks the passengers were held hostage. One American was shot dead. The news showed images of his body thrown out onto the tarmac.

There were other kinds of madness.

In the US an ex-movie actor called Ronald Reagan was President.

He was talking about getting laser weapons into space to shoot down Soviet missiles.

A guy named Steve Jobs was asking $2,500 (that's about $5,700 in today's money), for something called an Apple Macintosh. I really couldn't see why anyone would buy such a thing.

On the radio, 'Madonna' was getting into the groove. Some lads calling themselves 'Foreigner' wanted to know what love was. And Bonnie Tyler was holding out for a hero.

It wasn't all bad though.

In July, I and about 1.5 billion other humans sat and watched one of the most monumental music concerts in history - Live Aid.

Mr Geldof and Mr Ure raised some £150 million ($245 million) to relieve famine in Ethiopia.

It was a historic event.

It's believed 95 percent of the world's television sets tuned in to Live Aid at some point.

What's more amazing is that this was before the Internet, cell phones, e-mail, and text messaging.

There was no disputing its most important effect though. It brought people together at a time when it seemed that the world was tearing itself apart.

All I knew for sure was that I felt disconnected with time and place. Like Marty McFly in that year's biggest movie. I was going back to the future.

Any thoughts of returning to my life afloat were instantly crushed by cold hard reality. I'd let myself and my boat down. I'd failed, I'd shown I wasn't up to the job, I'd nearly died and I'd lost my boat.

My self-confidence had been destroyed, I had no choice but to accept it.

So I gave in to it. I followed the path of least resistance. I did what everyone else around me was doing. I conformed.

Within a few months, the old conditioning had regained all its power. Any thought of a return to the sea had been erased.

The temporary job turned into a permanent one, I knuckled down.

ON THE UP

*R*oll forward a year and my return to normality was complete.

I'd met a girl called Paula at the local motor club. She was sexy, sassy, and into cars. I was in love. This was it, I was sure.

Things happened fast after that.

By early in 1986 we'd bought a semi-detached house, in the little Staffordshire village of Austrey. It was right on the borders of three other English counties. Derbyshire, Leicestershire and Warwickshire.

We settled into the country life. I commuted two hours a day into Birmingham, going via Lichfield to drop Paula at work. In the evenings we'd snuggle down in front of the solid fuel burner and listen to Dire Strait's 'Brothers In Arms'. Played on our brand new state of the art CD system.

The world outside intruded now and again. Not least in April when a reactor at the Russian nuclear power station in Chernobyl exploded. Within days sheep in North Wales, Cumbria and Scotland were eating radioactive grass.

We married in the village church on October 25th, 1986.

The reception was at a countryside Victorian mansion called Moxhull Hall.

Our wedding cake had a little wooden model of my boat 'Mor Gwas' on top. I'd known nothing about it. I smiled and said how wonderful it was. I was lying. It dredged up too many memories. It reminded me of what might have been.

During the reception, the cake started leaning like the tower in Pisa. Paula got stressed and angry. I thought it didn't matter. I should have paid more attention to that omen.

That first year of married life was filled with work. I left home before dawn. It was usually dark when I returned.

At weekends I'd be working on the house. I fitted a new kitchen, decorated every room and put some mock oak beams in the lounge to make it more 'olde worlde'.

We spent many a cold evening snuggled up next to the fire in our little sanctuary. We needed to that winter.

There were two major weather events in the UK that year. In January we had a record-breaking two weeks of freezing temperatures and snow. All the pipes in our utility room froze solid.

One afternoon the snow started falling hard. So I left work early to pick Paula up and get back home before things got too bad. I stopped on the way to pick up a big sack of coke for the fire. I figured the coal man wouldn't have been able to make his scheduled delivery.

By the time we left Lichfield the snow was falling hard. The main roads were all jammed, so we took to the pristine snow-covered country lanes to get back to Austrey. I'd lived and breathed rallying for years. Driving on surfaces with not a lot of grip was something I knew. Rallying had bought Paula and I together and she trusted me. It was a blast, and we almost made it.

Then, a mile from home we found the lane blocked by a huge snowdrift and had to abandon the car.

I couldn't risk getting back to the house to find we had no fuel for heat. The sack of coke had to go on my shoulders.

It took an hour of trudging through knee-deep snow before I collapsed on the doorstep exhausted. Paula opened the porch door and there on the mat was the receipt from the coal man. The bunker was overflowing.

It was two days before I was able to recover the car and we were mighty glad of that coke.

Later in the year, the 16th of October to be precise. I opened the front door and stepped outside.

It was very early morning, all was still. Then it struck me. It was too still, too calm, too warm. Something felt odd. It had been very windy all night but now the air was completely calm, not a breath, almost humid.

I got in the car and turned on the radio as normal. There was only static. Strange I thought, and turned the dial to find another station. I picked up BBC news. The announcer said the broadcast was coming from an emergency facility outside London. It seemed the South East was being battered by hurricane-force winds. Most of the area was without power.

It became known as the 'Great Storm'. The previous evening a BBC weatherman had said. "Earlier on today, a woman rang the

BBC and said she heard there was a hurricane on the way. Well, if you're watching, don't worry, there isn't".

That weatherman was Michael Fish, and that moment defined his career.

120 mph winds felled an estimated 15 million trees. The National Grid was severely damaged. Hundreds of thousands of people were without power for weeks. The storm caused £2 billion worth of damage. Eighteen people lost their lives. Home Secretary Douglas Hurd called it the "worst, most widespread night of disaster since the Blitz".

I'd stepped out of the front door just as the low-pressure centre was passing over on its way north.

Life moved on.

Our beautiful daughter Nicole was born in January 1988.

It should have been plain sailing after that.

Nineteen Ninety-Eight, and house prices were rising steadily. We'd paid £23,500 for our little semi-detached and now, only a couple of years later, it was worth a lot more.

Paula had spotted a gorgeous chocolate box cottage for sale in the next village. Slate roof, rose garden, white rendered walls, oak beamed ceilings, 220 years old. What Paula wanted Paula got, we sold and moved across the border to Warwickshire.

'Well Cottage' was tiny. Open plan living and kitchen downstairs, two small bedrooms and bathroom upstairs. The low front door was the only door. We had no back garden because next door had bought the land decades before and the back door had been bricked up. The front garden was long and narrow leading to the road. We'd moved from a three bedroom with garage, it was a squeeze. I screwed a big hook into the huge ceiling beam and hung up a baby bouncer. Nicole spent hours in that thing.

We loved the place. Our new village, Appleby Magna seemed stuck in time. A couple of pubs, a shop, a church, stream running through the centre, great community.

The place was full of history. We found a book called 'Son of The Rectory' written by a gentleman called Aubrey Moore. It was the story of his Victorian and Edwardian childhood in the village. In it were old photos and descriptions of life back then. Most of the buildings still stood. The Sir John Moore School, the old post office, the pub and the rectory itself.

I did some research and discovered Well Cottage was one of a few built for workers by the local landowner who lived in Appleby Hall. The timber used for its construction had come from The New Forest on the South Coast. The wood had been destined for shipbuilding but the order got cancelled, so he'd got it cheap. Maybe that's why I felt so at home there. Land-locked as it was, the place still had some connection with the sea.

At work, I may have been the boss's son but it was no easy ride. I worked hard, proved my worth and started managing the warehouse. I worked six days a week. Paula stayed home looking after Nicole and enjoying the country life. She got a horse and stabled it at the farm just up the lane. I loved coming home after a hard day at work. Opening the front door and smelling the wood smoke from the open fire. Dinner would be in the oven, Paula and I would sit down in front of the burning logs with a glass of wine. Nicole gurgling and giggling beside us in that bouncer I'd screwed into the ceiling beam. Life was good.

In June that year, we went down to London to watch Dire Straits at the Hammersmith Odeon. It was a small intimate gig for fan club members. They hadn't played together for a few years but had agreed to play at the Nelson Mandela 70th Birthday Tribute in Wembley Stadium. They used the Hammersmith gig as a rehearsal.

Paula and I sat in the second row of the circle behind Mark Knopfler's mom and dad. He played Romeo and Juliet with his chromed steel guitar reflecting a single spotlight around the audience. His parents were in tears. We were spellbound.

Midway through the set, they called an old mate on stage. It was Eric Clapton. They played 'Wonderful Tonight' together. It was a memorable night.

The property market was still going crazy. Between May 1988 and May 1989 house prices in the UK rose 28.8%. No, that's not a typo, almost 30% in a year. Once again we found ourselves sitting on some healthy equity. Nicole was getting more active, we realised Well Cottage was too small, it was time to move again.

We found a new little development of houses a few miles up the road in a Leicestershire village called Heather, (pronounced Heether). It was a corner plot detached, three bedrooms, downstairs cloakroom, ensuite master.

Asking price was £78,000. We made an offer and began the race to get contracts exchanged.

These were the days when 'gazumping' was commonplace. Gazumping, as far as I know, is unique to England and Wales. Ancient property laws mean that a buyers verbal offer is not legally binding, even after acceptance by the vendor. In practice, this meant that until contracts were signed and exchanged the vendor could raise the price. He could accept a higher offer, or decline the sale completely. Huge demand for property combined with fast-rising prices made gazumping far more likely back then. It just added to what was already a stressful process.

We'd made a profit on our last two properties, I was earning decent money, a mortgage was no problem. Lenders were throwing money at folks. 100% mortgages were common, it was possible to borrow 4 or 5 times your annual salary. They'd tell you what figure you needed to write on the form to make the numbers work. We weren't stupid, but we still stretched ourselves to the max. If we got gazumped we'd lose the place.

As we prepared for our last Christmas in the cottage it was hard not to worry. But on December 21st things were put in perspective. Pan Am Flight 103. A jumbo jet en route from London to New York was blown apart by a bomb in the skies above Lockerbie, Scotland. All 243 passengers, 16 crew and 11 people on the ground were killed. The TV showed unforgettable images of a vast crater in the town and the plane's severed cockpit lying side down on a misty wet hillside.

Unbelievably, just a few weeks later, a Boeing 737 crashed on the embankment of the M1 motorway at Kegworth, less than 30 minutes up the road from us. It was a bad month for air travel.

Back on the ground, our sale went through without a problem.

We moved into the delightfully named Belcher Close at the beginning of 1989.

The year nineteen hundred and eighty-nine. What was that like then?

Well, for a lot of people in the UK everything was great. The economy was booming, unemployment was low and they felt good about the future.

Maggie Thatcher had been in power for almost a decade. We'd survived a recession and won a war over the Falklands. OK, strictly speaking, it was a 'conflict', but for the lads and lasses that were there, it was a war.

Maggie had come to power on the back of the 'winter of Discontent', when strikes and walkouts had paralysed the country. Now the Trade Unions, in particular, the National Union of Mineworkers, had been castrated. Workers were working. More than that, 'working class' people were becoming 'middle class'. Buying their council houses for a song, and investing in newly privatised utility companies. It seemed everyone was making money, everyone was 'on the up'.

The year before there'd been a song in the charts called 'Loadsamoney'. 'Loadsamoney' was a character created by comedian Harry Enfield. It spoofed the attitudes of Thatcher-era Britain. Search for it on YouTube if you like but be warned, it's painful. Watch as much as you can bear and then consider this.

There was an exchange in the British Parliament between Thatcher and the leader of the opposition Labour Party, Neil Kinnock.

Kinnock accused the government of creating a "Loadsamoney economy". Thatcher stood up and said: "We've been accused of creating a 'Loadsamoney economy'. Well, what's wrong with that!"

I think that tells you all you need to know about how it felt in 1989.

George H.W.Bush became President of the United States that year. During his inaugural address, he said this. "I come before you and assume the Presidency at a moment rich with promise. We live in a peaceful, prosperous time, but we can make it better. For a new breeze is blowing, and a world refreshed by freedom seems reborn.

In November the Berlin Wall came down. It looked like he was right.

Five years had passed since losing 'Mor Gwas' and leaving the sea. The change had been dramatic.

I was a husband and a father. I was in a steady job earning decent money. My company car was a brand new white Mazda 323 fastback, with one of the new fixed carphones. Early one morning on a deserted motorway I maxed it out at 130mph. We had a Land Rover to tow the horse box at weekends. Our daughter was now a gorgeous toddler. We hosted parties and BBQs at our new house. We jetted off for holidays in the sun. I kept track of everything in my Filofax. We were deep in debt but so was everyone. Anytime I got near my credit card limit they just raised it. It wasn't a worry, the house was already worth more than when we'd bought it. We were, without a doubt, on the up.

DARK CLOUDS

*N*ineteen-Ninety started well. It really did seem that things were changing for the better. In February Nelson Mandela was released after 27 years in jail.

I'd lived and worked in South Africa during 1979/80. I knew what a momentous event that was.

We'd settled into village life. Paula had trained as an aerobics instructor. Step aerobics was the new thing. We had a stack of 'Reebok Steps' in the garage. Many an evening the Land Rover would trundle through the lanes to a local village hall so that Paula could teach a class.

At weekends we'd tow the horse box to a show jumping event somewhere, so Paula could compete on her horse 'Stella'.

We got involved with the community. Not least, by joining them to fight British Coal. They'd made an application to dig a massive open cast coal mine in the countryside outside the village. The existing mine had just closed down. They'd already taken some eight million tons of coal out of the ground. The village had been blighted and scarred enough.

The local MP David Taylor was a regular visitor to our house and Paula threw herself into the battle almost full-time. It wasn't just a case of 'not in my backyard'. We'd come to love the ancient hedgerows, the copses of trees, the space. We fought with a passion and we won.

The buoyant mood of the country started to ebb in March.

Terrorists were targeting the UK. The IRA (Irish Republican Army) bombed Wembley and the London Stock Exchange. They blew up a member of parliament and shot and killed a soldier in my old home town of Lichfield.

The longest prison riot in British history took place at Strangeways in Manchester. It lasted 25 days and the prison was virtually destroyed.

Mad cows were making headlines. Fears of BSE/CJD led to the EU banning cattle exports. The Agriculture Minister and his young daughter ate beef burgers on TV to 'prove' it was safe.

The government tried to introduce a new tax called the 'Community Charge'. It was meant to replace domestic 'Rates' tax on property. It would mean every individual in the property having to pay.

It was a step too far. The 'Poll Tax' as it became known, sparked violent protests across the country. On 31st March some 250,000 people joined a rally in central London. It turned into the most serious riot London had seen for a century.

In August Saddam Hussein decided to invade Kuwait. We had no way of knowing that we'd still be living with the consequences of that decades later.

By November of 1990, Maggie Thatcher had resigned. She'd defined the 1980s. So much had changed. So much was yet to come.

In December there was another blizzard. It was a Saturday morning. I was at work in central Birmingham. The snow started and kept coming, getting heavier and heavier. There was no way I was going to get stuck in the city.

I sent the lads home, locked up, and headed for home myself.

The journey took nearly five hours instead of the usual 45 minutes. I dug the car out three times. Once again it was only my rally driving skills that allowed me to get as far as I did.

Many others didn't make it. I passed a group of lads beavering away with shovels trying to extract their Vauxhall Nova. They stopped and stared as my Mazda slid past them at 30mph completely sideways.

A few miles from home I was defeated though. You can't drive through snowdrifts 6 feet high and once more I had to abandon the car and wade through snow drifts to get home.

I was lucky. Hundreds spent the night trapped on the M42 motorway. Hundreds more had to sleep in the National Exhibition Centre. They'd gone there to see a fashion show called 'The Clothes Show Live'. At least they had plenty to keep them warm.

We lost power and a few days later the water. The big freeze disabled a vital pumping station in our area.

Once the snow ploughs had cleared the roads I drove Paula and Nicole to the in-laws at Lichfield. Without power, we had no heat. Without water, we couldn't use the toilet.

Our expensive newly built house ceased to be a home, and I couldn't help but think back to my days on 'Mor Gwas'. A little fibreglass box that had been my home. Self-sufficient, off-grid, reliant on no-one. I'd have been fine.

It was a long cold winter, and I couldn't shake a feeling of anxiety about the year to come.

THE STORM HITS

*N*ineteen Ninety-One - The shitstorm arrived.

Inflation went up to 9.5% - Today (the UK, 2017) it's less than 1%

The Mortgage Interest rate hit 15% - Today (the UK, 2017) it's at 0.25%

House prices collapsed. They wouldn't recover for another 10 years.

The economy started sliding into recession.

That was only the start.

Here are a few of that year's highlights;

In January the country was at war. The news showed rolling coverage of Operation Desert Storm, the US led operation to free Kuwait. There were Scud missiles hitting Israel. Hundreds of oilfields were burning. There was talk of the smoke causing a 'nuclear winter' in Northern Europe.

February saw a period of record-breaking freezing temperatures in the UK We wondered if Saddam Hussein was to blame.

The country was on the brink of what was to become the longest recession since the Great Depression some 60 years earlier.

We'd had the boom, now came the bust, and one of the many casualties was my Dad's business.

Twenty-two years of hard work destroyed by an accounting firm that couldn't add up.

12 months before, they'd produced a set of figures showing that the company was breaking even. Given the state of the economy that seemed OK. We just had to hang in there.

Early 1991 the same accounting firm handed over a set of figures showing a huge 12-month loss. It made no sense, it didn't feel right. The figures were questioned.

It turned out that 12 months before, they'd made a mistake. The company had actually made a significant loss. They'd corrected the error in this most recent set of accounts. Sorry.

End result? Instead of having months to try and turn things round, Dad had a few weeks to try and save the business

It wasn't possible.

The company went bust.

Liquidators arrived, the gates were chained, assets impounded.

I spent hours standing outside explaining to customers through the fence what had happened. Dad spent hours inside trying to salvage something from the wreckage.

After a few days, all the staff including me, got laid off and sent home. I joined the fast increasing ranks of the unemployed.

With the job gone hope of hanging onto our home looked bleak. House prices were plummeting and now we and many of our neighbours were in 'negative equity'. In other words, our mortgages were bigger than the value of the property. A few had been unable to keep up the payments as mortgage rates went up. We'd only managed because I'd taken a fixed rate at 12.5%. Now the rate was 15%. Some people had cleared out, posted the keys back through the letterbox and crawled away, dragging a prison ball of debt behind them.

At the end of the year, we went to see Chris Rea's 'Road To Hell' Tour at the NEC in Birmingham. We'd booked the tickets months before.

The show started with the venue in complete darkness.

Then the huge speakers rumbled to the sound of thunder.

Strobe lights flashed like lightning.

A single spotlight hit the stage. The man himself in silhouette, his long overcoat touching the floor.

His harmonica wailed. Steel slid down guitar strings, and that gravel-scoured voice sang out the words we knew so well.

> Stood still on a highway
> I saw a woman
> By the side of the road
> With a face that I knew like my own
> Reflected in my window
> Well she walked up to my quarterlight
> And she bent down real slow
> A fearful pressure paralysed me in my shadow
> She said 'son what are you doing here, my fear for
>   you has turned me in my grave'

I said 'mama I've come to the valley of the rich,
   myself to sell'
She said 'son this is the road to hell'

The words of a prophet.

THE STORM CONTINUES

*P*aying the mortgage with your credit card isn't a long-term strategy. We had no choice. The house had to go. The market was saturated but somehow we managed to sell, for £30,000 less than we'd paid 2 years earlier. Who knows how much more we lost in carpets, curtains, light fittings etc.

The good life we'd had back in Appleby now seemed a distant dream. Everything had fallen apart. Constant worry and stress piled on the pressure. Something had to give.

Paula decided she'd had enough. She took Nicole and headed back to her parents. I'm not going into detail. It happened, and we are both culpable.

Fast forward another year and once again my life was in tatters.

Paula and I had separated. Her Dad had set her and Nicole up in a little bungalow back in Appleby Magna.

The place was a mess.

I helped as much as I could, decorating, building a kitchen, trying to make the place a home for my daughter.

It seemed the least I could do as a failed father and husband.

Home for me was a caravan.

Dads business had been bought by another flooring distributor. Dad and I were re-employed to run it as before. Except it wasn't like before. It was a mistake for both of us.

Dad went before I did. He'd managed to hang onto the house and a small pension. It was a poor reward for decades of work. He retired and tried to forget.

I stayed on for a couple more years running the whole place. The new boss was a hard-nosed bastard. He didn't understand the business and he didn't understand our customers. I eventually resigned a few minutes before he sacked me.

There was only one reason I stayed for as long as I did.

I needed the money. Most of my salary went on paying off credit card bills and supporting Paula and Nicole.

These were desperate times. The company car had gone and now my old Land Rover was my sole means of transport. It developed a gearbox problem. No way could I pay to have it fixed in a garage, I'd have to do it myself. But I couldn't take it off the road because then I wouldn't be able to commute from my caravan to the warehouse in central Birmingham.

I had to get creative.

The warehouse immediately next-door to where I worked was empty. It had been on the market for months and there was no prospect of it being sold anytime soon. I knew the boss of the company that owned it. After a short conversation and the gift of a bottle of whisky, he handed me the keys.

Next morning before dawn I nursed the Landy and caravan through the shutter doors and parked up inside.

That night I stayed late at work. When all the other staff had gone I drilled a hole through the connecting wall and ran a power cable through it. I filled up my water containers from the outside tap and 'commuted' next door.

For the next couple of months that big empty warehouse was home. I took the opportunity to strip the Landy down completely. I renovated the chassis, re-built the engine and repaired the ailing gearbox. It gave me something to do and took my mind off the mess I was in. I hardly saw daylight.

My boss came into the office really early a few times, trying to catch me out. He never did figure out how I always beat him in.

I remember a song repeatedly played on the local radio station BRMB, as I worked alone in the evenings. It was D:Reams 'Things can only get better'.

Every time I heard it I hoped they were right.

They weren't.

DOWN & OUT

Once the Landy was back on the road, I got the caravan onto a nice little site just outside Lichfield and was back to being a commuter. I had two work colleagues at the time who were also good mates and lived in the same area.

We fell into the habit of stopping at the local pub on the way home each evening.

One of the mates, John, had a wife and family, he never stayed long. The other, Brian, was like me, separated and on his own. The landlady was friendly, the beer and company were good. Neither of us had anything to go home to.

Before long the 'swift halves' on the way home turned into several slow pints, sometimes many slow pints. Back then the licensing laws meant pubs shut at 11.00pm. More than a few times I got back to the caravan well after that. Some nights we had a 'lock-in' and I didn't get back until the early hours. I know there were nights when I slept in my work clothes.

It was only a few miles on back roads from the pub to the caravan, but I was driving drunk. Somehow I got away with it.

It sounds pathetic now. It was pathetic. But the Shoulder of Mutton public house became a sort of home. A hateful day at the office was made bearable by the thought of that first pint. It gave me something to look forward to, it made me feel better.

Had I become an alcoholic? To some degree, I guess so. But I never touched spirits and I never drank during the day. It was no less dangerous though.

I can't remember how long this habit went on for. The bulk of 1993 and 1994 has been wiped from my memory. Truth be told it's unlikely there's much worth remembering. I worked a job I hated. I lived alone in a caravan. I worked, I drank, I slept, I repeated. What's to tell? What I do remember is that drinking stopped making me feel better. It started having the opposite effect.

For no particular reason, I was seeing less and less of my daughter. I spent working hours going through the motions, hating every minute. Evenings and weekends were empty except for the pub. This left many hours in which to sit in my crappy caravan, listening to the rain hammering on the roof. Pondering the depths of my fall. Blaming the world and everyone in it. Feeling completely useless, totally worthless.

My life was a sinking ship. Me trapped inside.

I need to pause here.

This is where the writing gets tough. This is where I have to tell a part of my story I've kept secret for 23 years. I'd planned to keep it that way.

Then I remembered these words from Gail Tsukiyama's novel 'The Samurai's Garden'

.... what you're telling is just a story. It is not happening anymore.........The story you're telling is just words. "Sometimes you can't let go of the past without facing it again."

I learnt the truth of that when I wrote 'A Foolish Voyage'.

This time it's different though. This time my words may cause pain to those I love. But I write them with a hope. My words might save a life. It's my duty to write them.

So now, I have to recall and relate how Depression nearly killed me.

One night I got back to the caravan late. It was autumn I think, anyway the weather was typically wet, cold and windy. The caravan was freezing inside. I lit the little gas fire and sat watching the blue and orange flames dancing.

Suddenly a crushing wave of emotion completely overwhelmed me. Darkness, sadness, shame, despair. It felt physical. I started sobbing, struggling for breath. I slid to the floor and curled up, I started shaking.

I don't know how long I was there, maybe I passed out, but I woke with one crystal clear thought in my head. This had to end.

I went to the bathroom locker and took out every packet of pills I had in there. Paracetamol, Codeine, Aspirin, I don't know.

I filled a glass of water, sat down at the table and started ripping open the packets. Swallowing the pills as fast as I could. I kept going till they were gone.

The weight lifted. I felt calm. I'd made a decision, I'd taken control, I'd beaten the bastards.

I lay down on the sofa and closed my eyes, completely at peace.

Soft light. Pinkish, blue-tinged, orange.

Pain, above my hips, around my waist.

I opened my eyes, breaking the gum sticking the eyelids together.

My lips cracked, dry as sandpaper, numb. The air in the caravan was stifling. The gas fire must have burned for hours before the cylinder ran out.

I swung my legs to the floor, reached down and turned the fire off. The pain in my back doubled. My whole body ached.

Brain cells stirred. Memory returned.

The sun shone brightly through the curtains, I looked at the clock. Nearly 2 pm.

I shuffled to the door, opened it and sat on the step breathing in the cold fresh air.

I was still alive.

Over the next few days, I slowly recovered. The pain in my kidneys told me my body was still working to flush the poison out. I slept, I drank water, I ate soup and I reflected.

I'd failed. Of course I had. I should have felt worse. But I didn't.

I felt differently, dare I say it? Better.

It felt as if some of the poison in my head had been flushed out along with the drugs.

For the first time in months, I started thinking about the future. My future. It was a big step. A few days before I hadn't believed there was one.

* * *

So NOW IS a good time to stop and talk about suicide. Some might question if there's ever a good time to talk about it.

That's part of the problem. It's a taboo subject for many. It shouldn't be.

All I can do is talk about what happened to me. I know that suicidal thoughts and actions can have many causes, and I'm no expert. My experience is a very personal one and it relates directly to Depression. But I believe the lessons I learned can help others feeling as I did back then. So here's my take.

Did I do what I did because I was mentally ill?

Well, using the definition of 'mental illness' ; *health conditions involving changes in thinking and emotion,* then yes, obviously.

Depression is most certainly an illness.

The first symptoms are minor. You start to feel a bit low, you start to think that maybe you've just got a case of the blues. Yes, that's it. Life's a bit shitty right now, it'll pass.

But it doesn't pass, you keep sinking lower. People notice, they ask if you're OK. You say 'Yeah I'm fine, thanks for asking". But you're not fine at all.

Ebola starts with minor symptoms and ends up killing you in the worst way imaginable. Depression will do the same if it's not stopped.

But you don't think you're ill. You fear telling friends and family how you're really feeling because they'll just think you're being soft. They won't understand anyway. In any case they'll probably only tell you to 'snap out of it' to 'pull yourself together'. No, better to keep it to yourself eh?

That's Depression at its evil worst. Tricking you into keeping quiet, fuelling feelings of shame, and depriving you of any power to fight back. Even if you have people looking out for you Depression keeps you blind to the fact. It fools you into thinking that you are completely alone.

If you really are alone, then Depression has a head start.

So you try to find ways of escaping the pain. Alcohol, drugs, sex.

All temporary, all end up making it worse.

Depression is an illness that poisons your mind. It stops it from working normally. It creates thoughts that are the antithesis of reality.

'Nobody cares'

'I'll never be happy again'

'I'm a worthless piece of crap'

An endless stream of poisoned thoughts flowing backwards and forwards. Killing you, slowly.

You have no idea this is happening. For you, these thoughts are your reality. You have no power over them.

Depression ups its game. New thoughts join the gang.

'There's nothing worth living for'

'They'll be better off without me'

'End it'

That's how I felt.

My attempted suicide wasn't a cry for help, it was made with clear intention. I'd had enough and I wanted it to end. The poison had done its work.

But I made a huge mistake. I took physical action based on an illusionary reality.

The biggest con Depression plays is to convince you that you're powerless. You believe that you feel as you do because of all the bad things that have happened to you. People have said things, done things, not said things, not done things. Everything that's happened to you was beyond your control. THEY'VE made you feel worthless. THEY'VE bought you to this point. How could you be expected to feel anything but depressed given all the shit that's rained down on your head? Anyone would.

It's like you're a passenger in the backseat of your own car. You know it's your car, you were proud of it once, you looked after it, you drove it everywhere, it made you happy. You called it 'Life'. But somehow the car got hijacked. Now you're locked in the back and crazy people are fighting over the steering wheel. The car careers this way and that, slow and fast, sometimes out of control completely. You've no idea where you're headed. Pretty soon the inevitable happens. It crashes.

All the while you sit in the back, hanging on, waiting to die.

I was lucky. I survived the crash. Something happened while I was out of it though. Because when I woke up I realised something. I realised I could have grabbed that steering wheel back anytime I wanted.

So here's the beautiful truth. Those feelings you have, all of them. They're created in your head, they're created by you, created by your thoughts. How is that beautiful? Because once you accept that as a truth you discover another one. YOU are not powerless. YOU can decide to clamber over that seat push the crazies out of the door and get back behind the wheel. It's YOUR damn car. It's YOUR damn life.

I'm a big Steve Earle fan. Here are some of the lyrics from one of his songs 'It's All Up To You';

> No one said it would be easy
> But it don't have to be this hard
> If you're lookin' for a reason
> Just stand right where you are
> Now there ain't no one out to get you
> They've got to walk in their own shoes
> It's all up to you
> No one else can get you through
> It's all up to you

Earlier I talked about the fear of telling others about your true feelings. I talked about the fear of having people telling you to 'snap out of it' or to 'pull yourself together'.

Is that what I've just done?

No. I'm not telling you to do anything. In fact I'm doing the exact opposite. I'm telling you to do nothing. Let me explain.

Please pay close attention. This is important.

You're not actually depressed. You just think you are.

Read that line again. Please.

OK. If you've done that you're probably thinking no. You're probably thinking it's a ridiculous idea. Bear with me, read on, let's look a bit closer.

I started out by describing Depression as a mental illness. I stand by that.

But I believe that treating it as a 'medical' illness doesn't work. Treating it from the outside-in doesn't work.

Drugs, electric shocks, therapy. Perhaps there are some short-term benefits, I don't know.

What I do know is that my own mother suffered with Depression for decades. She was 'treated' using all of these methods. None of them ever worked.

I don't believe any external treatment can provide a long-term 'cure'. Only an individual can do that, from the inside-out.

I discovered this accidentally. It saved my life and changed my life. It was years before I found that what I'd stumbled across wasn't new.

In the 1970s an ordinary working man named Sydney Banks made the same discovery. And a few months afterwards he quit his job and dedicated the rest of his life to showing others what he'd found.

Although he was living and working in Canada at the time, Syd was Scottish and a welder by trade. Folks don't come much more down to earth than that.

It's fascinating to know that like me, Syd wasn't looking for anything. Like me he had no idea there was anything to look for.

Like most of us, he shared the view that life is what it is, and there's not much we can do about it.

But Syd made a startling and amazing discovery.

Everyone already has mental health. We just don't know it.

That might seem a little crazy, so let's use an analogy.

Our mental health is like the sky. A clear blue sky where the sun always shines.

Our thoughts, our feelings, our behaviour, are like the weather.

Clouds cover the sky, storms roll in. Thunder crashes, lightning flashes. It feels like the world is ending. But it's only weather. It'll pass. The blue sky is still there, the sun is still shining.

That's all we need to get us through. To believe that it's true.

So know this.

Your feelings are coming from Thought, NOT from other people or circumstances.

Your thoughts are not YOU. They're simply thoughts passing through.

Back to Steve Earle;

> No one said it would be easy
> But it don't have to be this hard
> If you're lookin' for a reason
> Just stand right where you are

Once you realise this. For yourself, through your own insight. You start to have your experiences without your experiences having you.

If you are reading this and feeling suicidal, convention is clear. As a responsible author I should tell you to get help. I'll keep it simple. Talk to someone, preferably someone trained to deal with Depression. Most countries in the world have a charity dedicated to helping. You can talk, text, chat online, anything. Find someone and do it. I talked to no one and I should have.

Just get stable enough to start thinking straight. Be cautious about taking prescription drugs. They're not a long-term solution.

Think about taking a natural drug like St Johns Wort. Stop watching shit TV and read books.

I recommend starting with 'Somebody Should Have Told Us!: Simple Truths for Living Well' by Jack Pransky.

Seriously, get hold of a copy and read it. Get outside, walk, bike, sit. Breathe some fresh air and start noticing the world around you. Look at the sky, the clouds, the ocean, the mountains, the forests. Get away from the city on a clear night and find somewhere to gaze at the stars.

This planet and the Universe beyond are amazing and beautiful. So are you. Realise you're part of it. Realise that you're amazing and beautiful too. Realise that there's nothing wrong with you.

Take each day as it comes and do something every day to help yourself.

The dark thoughts will pass. Better ones will come. That blue sky is still there. Trust me.

It was 48 hours before my phone rang. It was the office wondering when I was going to turn up. I apologised, told them I was sick and that I'd be back in a week. That night my mate Brian called by the van to see how I was. He said I looked like shit, asked if I fancied a pint. I said no.

When I next saw Nicole I nearly broke down. The shame of what I'd done hit me like a punch to my still sore kidneys. I'd come close to shattering her life. I thought about my parents, my brother. We're not close, that's just the way it is, but there's love there. I don't think my Mom would have been able to live with the thought I'd gone.

Gradually I came to realise that what had happened had been a watershed. I'd sunk as low as was possible to go and I'd survived. The experience had made me stronger, and much much wiser.

45

The words of that D-Ream song came back into my head; 'Things can only get better'.

This time they would. It was time to stop being a victim.

NEW JOB NEW GIRL

*A*part from the major events of the first few years of that decade, my memories of time and place are vague.

I recovered enough to realise that I had to find another job and a better place to live. I needed a new start.

In 1995 I managed to get another mortgage and bought a small new-build townhouse in the Derbyshire village of Overseal.

Overseal was just a few miles up the road from Appleby. I was close to my daughter again and I was able to see more of her.

Moving to Overseal meant I'd now lived in all four of those counties I mentioned a while back. Four houses in four villages, in four counties, all within a few miles of each other. Something kept pulling me back there.

My new place in Squirrel Walk never felt like home. It was a new-build. No carpets, no curtains, every wall painted magnolia. Bare light bulbs hanging from the ceiling fittings. I've never been one for design and decor. I painted the lounge bright white with black gloss woodwork and laid a timber laminate floor. One easy chair and a black Ikea bookcase later and it was job done.

I couldn't afford a proper bed. I slept on a camp bed on the floorboards, eventually upgrading to a mattress on the floor. The other rooms stayed as they were.

Basic it might have been but after a caravan it was luxury. No more sleepless nights feeling the wind rocking my bed. No more wearing earplugs to lessen the sound of rain hammering down.

With a roof over my head thoughts turned to my job. Dad had retired, I'd been made General Manager. Two warehouse guys, a van driver and a sales assistant. I knew the business inside out, I knew the customers well, we were doing OK again. But my relationship with the new owner was going downhill fast. It'd never been good. Maybe I didn't have the full story. But from where I was sitting his demands became more and more unreasonable, more and more impossible. I touched on it already. Eventually the inevitable happened and I left.

I remember driving away from the place for the last time. Sadness had long faded, all I felt was an immense sense of relief. It was the right time to move on. I was out of a job but full of optimism, I just knew things would be OK.

Within a matter of weeks, I was back in work. One of my business contacts suggested I apply for a role as Technical Assistant at a French flooring manufacturer by the name of Gerflor. They had a distribution centre in Warwick and offices in London. After interviews at both, I was in. There was a company car and petrol included in the package. Commuting from Overseal was 45 miles each way but that was fine. I settled in, enjoying the work, making new friends.

1996.

Life was better but I was still alone. I figured it was better that way, the split from Paula had left me damaged. The decree absolute had come through. I was now officially divorced. Why is that by the way? Why is it that you can't go back to being single? Why are you expected to tick the divorced box for the rest of your life? Anyway, I digress.

I wasn't socialising outside of work so it seemed unlikely that I'd meet anyone in any case.

There was one girl at the office that attracted me, but I wasn't sure if she felt the same. There seemed to be something there, but I wasn't then, and still aren't now, any sort of Casanova. One of Gerflor's regular sales conferences came around. The evenings after dinner were always a laugh, free drink flowed, gossip and jokes abounded. I, along with most of the other managers and on the road sales staff lived a distance from the office. We got to stay over in the hotel. Office staff had to taxi home. Alcohol gave me courage, I asked the girl to stay, spend the night in my room. She turned me down. I wasn't surprised.

The following day in an office full of hangovers we chatted. She'd been right to refuse. Neither of us was the type for one night stands. We started again, taking it easy. Occasional evening drinks after work. It was nice to have someone in my life again.

Not long afterwards my old mate John from Lichfield, persuaded me to meet him at a pub near him for a drink and a catch-up. When I arrived he was sat at the bar with his wife and another girl I didn't know. Her name was Alison. There's an old saying about opposites attracting. She was bubbly, extrovert, full of life. She never stopped smiling or laughing. It had been a long time since I'd been in such good company. John knew her as she was working behind the bar in his local. She'd just broken up with her partner. John gave me a sly look and I twigged. He'd set me up.

I wondered what planet he was on. My self-confidence around women was almost non-existent. Whatever I thought, there was no way a girl like Alison would be attracted to someone like me. Thinking that way took the pressure off and I relaxed. For the next hour, we chatted, laughed, and generally had a good time.

Soon it was time to leave and we walked out to the car park together. As I opened the back door of John's car so that Alison could get in, she leaned over and kissed me on the cheek. 'Lovely to meet you' she said. I glanced over at John. He winked.

I drove back to Overseal in a dream, feeling like I had when I'd first met Paula years before. Maybe there was hope that I could have someone in my life again. I was all over the place.

My memory of the exact sequence of events over the following months is vague. I remember a site visit took me past the pub where I knew Alison worked. I decided to drop in on spec. Sure enough, she was behind the bar and she seemed pleased to see me again. One evening a while later I made a deliberate visit and asked her out. She knocked me back. She said the breakup with her other half wasn't going well, and by the way, she'd got a son Jamie, a boisterous 11-year-old.

I think she thought that what she'd told me would freak me out and send me running but it didn't. I sympathised, I could see she was suffering. My own breakup wounds were still raw, and although Jamie was a good few years younger than Nicole I could easily draw comparisons. Despite our differences, Paula and I had always prioritised Nicole. It was obvious Alison was trying to do the same for Jamie,but from what she said her other half was being a bastard. I told her it would work out, told her to call me if I could do anything. Truth be told I thought that was that.

Around the same time, I went on a couple of proper dates with the girl from work. Distance made it harder as Overseal was an hour away, but I'd stay late, we'd go eat. She was a really nice girl. She made me feel better about myself, but somehow things just didn't seem to be leading anywhere.

I'd settled at Gerflor but my life still felt as empty as my house. At work I was fine but on my evenings alone I could feel myself sliding back towards Depression. There was a pub around the corner. More than a few times I thought about strolling round. Then I'd remember the Shoulder of Mutton. I wasn't taking that road again. I knew I was weak, I knew it was just my thinking, but I still feared the future.

Then Alison called. She'd got some free time. Jamie's Dad had taken him away for the weekend, she didn't have to work. Did I fancy doing something together.

As I put down the phone it felt as if I'd been injected with an instantaneous acting dose of joy. I jumped around the lounge punching the air.

As I calmed down it dawned on me that Alison could save me.

We spent the weekend together. She stayed over. I drove to work Monday morning feeling as I'd done driving home from that first meeting.

Alison was 13 years younger than me. Paula had been about the same. She was sexy sassy and smart just as Paula had been. It seems obvious now, but I was falling into the exact same trap.

This sad loner now had a problem. In effect, I had two girls on the go. This wasn't something I was equipped to deal with, and I made a right hash of it.

Things were moving slowly with my office girl and fast with Alison. Folks say that office flings rarely work out. Geography came into play. I was trying to compile a pros and cons list for a matter of the heart. That just doesn't work. I let my heart decide and told my office girl it was over.

Embarrassing as this might be, I now have to lay bare the extent of my romantic incompetence.

In a ridiculous attempt to ease the obvious sadness of the rejected party I modified a well known UK phrase about buses. I said "girls are like buses, aren't they. You wait for ages and then two come along at once". Apparently, that didn't help. Neither did the gift of a 5lit plastic keg of scrumpy cider recently purchased on a site visit to Somerset.

I felt like the bastard she rightly thought I was.

HAPPY DAYS

$\mathcal{A}$lly and I started seeing each other regularly.

She'd been working hard for qualifications as an accountant. She passed her exams and was offered a job at an IT firm. There was a problem though. She wanted the job badly but it was too far away. Her car wasn't up to that kind of commuting and she wouldn't be able to afford the petrol. She was upset. She told me where the place was. I couldn't believe it. It was just outside Warwick. I literally drove past the gate on my way to and from my office. Problem solved. It felt like fate. She took the job.

An offer made without thought resulted in some craziness.

I would leave Overseal at silly-o-clock and blast through the lanes to Lichfield. I'd then pick Allie and Jamie up, we'd drop Jamie at the child minders and then I'd drop Alison off on the way to my office. In the evenings the whole trip was reversed. Sometimes, depending on wether Ally's ex was around or not, I'd stay for something to eat. More often than not I'd head home. On the weekends when Jamie was with his Dad Ally would come stay with me at Overseal.

Needless to say, this routine had to stop at some point. I loved driving and it meant we got a couple of hours together every day, but this was silly.

The solution seemed obvious. I asked her to move in with me. She'd already put her house in Lichfield on the market and she liked the area around the four counties. We hatched a plan. We'd start looking for a house together, we'd use Overseal as a temporary home, then, once hers was sold, I'd sell mine.

Ally and Jamie moved in during 1996, and in 1997 we all moved to a new place in Appleby Magna. We were the opposite side of the village from Well Cottage and just round the corner from Paula and Nicole.

The house we bought ticked those three important property boxes; Location, location, location. But it was far from perfect. It had been self-built in the 60s and on the face of it a fairly standard 3 bed detached. But out back the garden was completely overgrown with a selection of derelict sheds. Every room in the house had polystyrene tiles on the ceiling. The kitchen was all orange and green Formica. It was like time-travelling back to the 1960s. Basically it needed gutting. I threw myself into it with relish. I was deliriously happy. Back on my feet, back in a place I loved, building a real home for my new family.

It really did feel like the start of a new era. The Conservatives had been in power for 18 years.

Now the Labour Party under Tony Blair had won a landslide victory in the general election. Blair became the youngest Prime Minister since 1812.

Another major news event that year was the death of Princess Diana. On the morning of Sunday 31st August I walked into the kitchen to make a cuppa and turned on the radio. Instead of the usual cheery pop music, I heard an announcement that Diana, Princess of Wales had died after a late night car crash in Paris.

The following year a more personal emotional shock hit me. Paula told me she'd accepted a job as a farm manager. The farm was in Cornwall, right down in the South West of the UK. It wasn't just Cornwall either, it was farthest Cornwall, only a few miles short of Lands End. She was taking Nicole far away from me.

Once again I found myself powerless. I could have ranted and raved but it would have been pointless. A mother and daughter should not be parted. I thought about the quality of life Nicole would have living in such a beautiful part of the country. Even if I'd been a bastard and ignored all of that, fought to keep her near me somehow, it was an unwinnable battle. At least Paula hadn't done it a few years before. I couldn't imagine having dealt with it in the state I'd been in back then.

It was what it was. I had to learn to live with it. In the coming years we visited a few times during annual holidays. Each time I could see that Nicole was happy and healthy, and I did all I could to let her know that her Dad was still there for her.

It wasn't all a bed of roses though. Unbeknownst to me Paula had got into a bad relationship and there were problems. Things came to a head as I sat alone in a hotel room one night after a particularly difficult day on site. I opened up an email and saw one from Nicole. As always my heart leapt. Hearing from her was just the tonic I needed. I started reading and nausea gripped me. She said she never wanted to see me again, that I wasn't really her Dad. It was a short dagger straight to my heart. I got Paula on the phone, told her about the email, and demanded to know what the hell was going on. She said there'd been some domestic problems, that I needn't worry, she'd talk to Nicole. I told her I was coming down, she said there was no need. I ignored her, drove down that

Friday night and spent time with Nicole. All went well, I drove home a Dad again. But it scared the crap out of me.

For the most part the next seven years were magical. I was promoted to Technical Manager, more money, a better car. Alison had got her accountant qualification and landed a new job not far from home. She was earning good money. She got a Mazda MX5 drop top. We poured money into the house and I spent every evening and weekend working on the place. I got on well with her family. Her Dad helped me with the work. Her sister and kids spent time with us. The garden was cleared and I built a pond for the Koi Carp Ally loved. Most of the sheds were demolished and cleared. I re-roofed the remaining one and the garage so I had a great workshop. All the rooms were re-decorated, we completely gutted and re-designed the kitchen. I built a conservatory onto the back.

The house was in the centre of the village. The church was on one side of us, the pub on the other. Jamie went to school a short walk away across the fields.

We took holidays in Cornwall and to the South of France, Nicole came with us a couple of times. Once again life was good.

It had taken seven long years, but I'd made it back almost full circle. A home, a family, a good life.

I started to think as I'd never thought before. This was it. We were sorted. We'd live here forever, Ally and I would grow old together.

THE GOOD LIFE

My job as Technical Manager at Gerflor meant I was primarily a trouble shooter. Floor coverings are one of the last things on the list of construction projects. If things go wrong months, even years of cumulative delays all come to a head. Huge sums of money and huge pressures. It was down to me to establish what had gone wrong and provide solutions.

A normal day might see me leaving home before dawn to drive a couple of hundred miles for a site meeting. The meetings would last a few hours. A circle of suits looking at me for answers and a big clock ticking. Most of the time I enjoyed it.

My title may have had Technical in it, but to me most of the solutions involved nothing more than some basic knowledge, logic and common sense. To some extent it amused me. I was an unqualified poorly educated odd job dealing with highly qualified professionals. Architects, chemists, arbitrators, you name it. Despite that, there were many times when it seemed I was the only one able to see the obvious.

On other occasions things would get nasty. Tempers would be

lost, language would be used, toys would be thrown from the pram. When that happened I just zigged as they zagged. The louder and angrier they got the calmer and quieter I got. It always worked. Instead of escalating the situation to a destructive culmination, the one shouting loudest would quickly realise they were making a fool of themselves and go quiet.

I was no Zen master though. The mask would stay in place only until I was back in my car driving away. Then it would fall, and I'd be banging the steering wheel and screaming at the windshield. Woe betides anyone that cut me up or drove too slow blocking my way home.

12 hour, 400 mile days were not unusual. My brand new company cars went back after a couple of years with 90,000 miles on the clock.

There were many highlights though. Gerflor manufactured Sports Flooring. We landed some prestigious installation contracts. The Commonwealth Games in Manchester in 2002, and the Special Olympics World summer Games in Dublin in 2003, to name but two. These were 'failure not an option' jobs with the reputation of the company on the line, not to mention a lot of money. I had sole responsibility for project managing them.

The Dublin Games were a highlight. Not least because it served as an antidote to news in the Middle East.

We'd been told that Saddam Hussein had Weapons of Mass Destruction with the potential to impact the UK - Chemical weapons, maybe even nuclear weapons. George W Bush and Tony Blair shook hands and declared war. In March they invaded Iraq. Dublin felt like a different world.

It was a huge event. 7,000 athletes with learning disabilities. 28,000 family and friends, 3,000 coaches and officials, 30,000 volunteers.

My right hand man was taken ill just before we were due to start the installation phase of the project. This meant I had to spend nearly a month living on site in a hotel. The weight of responsibility was heavy on my shoulders, but Guinness helped.

I learned a lot about Guinness during that month. It got to the point where, after a long day of graft, I'd walk into the hotel lobby, glance into the bar as I walked past, and get the nod from Kieran the barman. He'd start pouring my pint. I'd go up to the room, have a shower and get changed. By the time I came back down to my stool at the bar Kieran would be just finishing the pour. He stopped etching a shamrock in the head when he realised I wasn't a tourist.

The team and I installed Basketball courts. Handball courts. Volleyball courts and Table Tennis surfaces. It was a huge job. Once the Games were underway I and a smaller team stayed on to deal with any issues that might crop up.

We had tickets to the opening ceremony. Alison came over for the weekend. It was amazing.

It was held in Croke Park, the main stadium for Gaelic Sport in Dublin. The event consisted of the usual parade of countries, but was followed by on stage entertainment. The Games were founded in the US by Eunice Kennedy Shriver - JFK's sister, in 1962. The Kennedy family know people. Muhammad Ali was there, Arnold Schwarzenegger was there. Pierce Brosnan was there. The entertainment line-up included the Corrs and over 100 dancers performing Riverdance. The highlight was a two number gig played by U2. Halfway through 'One', Bono walked into the shadows behind the drums and re-appeared with Nelson Mandela on his arm. Memorable is the right word I think.

The Games hit all the emotional buttons. Seeing these severely disadvantaged men women and children fighting hard to achieve, left a mark that's still with me. They were fiercely competitive, but once the whistle blew and the game ended, then so did the rivalry. Hugs, laughter, cheers and tears ended the battle. I particularly remember one of the young table tennis competitors. Every time he won a point he did a lap of honour around the table, arms raised. The audience stood, applauded, and cheered; Every single time. His competitor soon clocked who was getting more attention and started to do the same. The crowd happily gave him the same rousing support. It was a long game.

The event had been an incredible experience. But after spending the best part of a month in a Dublin hotel room I was very glad to get back to Appleby, to get back home.

We had a heatwave summer that year. Weekends were spent out back on the deck. Beer in hand, BBQ on the go, relaxing to the sound of the water trickling from the big clay urn I'd fitted over the fish pond.

Life was indeed good again.

ANOTHER TSUNAMI

Two Thousand-Four started off much the same. Early in the year, we went to see Shania Twain at the NEC.

She sang one of our favourite tracks.'You're Still The One'

> *Looks like we made it*
> *Look how far we've come my baby*
> *We mighta took the long way*
> *We knew we'd get there someday*
> *......*
> *You're still the one I run to*
> *The one that I belong to*
> *You're still the one I want for life*

It felt like those words had been written for us.

Another year passed.

On Boxing Day a massive earthquake in the Indian Ocean sent tsunami waves hurtling landwards. The coastal areas of Indonesia and Thailand were devastated. A quarter of a million people lost their lives. It happened on the opposite side of the planet to us. I couldn't have known that another more personal tsunami was about to strike much nearer home.

My workload at Gerflor kept increasing. We'd started a training scheme for sports flooring installation contractors. It meant I had to spend more time away from home running courses all around the country. It also meant me spending more time at the factory in France. I was pushing hard. I was passionate about getting the job done right. Often times this meant fighting our corner. The UK trade operated differently to Europe. I knew what was needed. The French didn't. Things got heated now and again.

In June a small delegation from head office said that they'd like to come along to one of my training courses, to see what I was doing. I didn't mind. I thought it might help them understand. On the second day of the course, we took a break to go outside and tune the car radio into an important announcement: the chosen location for the 2012 Olympic Games.

It was between London and Paris. The French were supremely, even arrogantly, confident. As the voice came over the airways "The Olympic Games of 2012 will be held in ….." Their faces were a picture of smugness. As the announcer's voice said "London" their disbelief could not have been greater. I was excited. Gerflor was an approved supplier to the Games. My team had the Special Olympics and Commonwealth Games under our belts. I knew I could handle this ultimate challenge. I should have known they wouldn't let me.

Truth be told I was letting work occupy all my time and effort.

When I was at home Ally often seemed a little remote, preoccupied. I knew her job was high pressure too, she often worked late as I did. I figured that was it.

By this time Jamie was a teenager. He was a handful. Ally quite often lost it with him. There was screaming and shouting. I already described how I handled bad-tempered situations on site. How I could calm things down. To my shame, I never used those talents at home. Instead, I'd join in. I couldn't cope with in my face defiance from a young boy. I never used physical violence,but I used my voice violently. I started to wish Jamie had stayed with his Dad. I'm not proud of that.

I was too close to the rock face to see the cracks, but they were there and growing wider.

In 2005 the tsunami hit, and my world came tumbling down again.

Alison came home one night with tears in her eyes. She told me she'd been seeing someone else. She told me she was sorry. That she'd destroyed everything.

Maybe I'd known. I certainly knew something was wrong. But once again I zigged instead of zagged. Most guys would have screamed at her, lashed out, demanded to know who she'd been with, gone and killed him.

I hugged her tight, kissed her forehead, told her it was OK. We'd work it out, we'd be alright, I still loved her.

It wasn't OK though.

We kept going for a few weeks. Then one Friday night as I waited for Ally to get in after dropping Jamie with his Dad, the phone rang. She wasn't coming home. She was spending the weekend with this other guy.

I begged her to come home, begged her not to do it. Told her I couldn't live without her.

None of it made a difference. It was over.

That weekend and the following weeks are once again, for the most part, erased memories. I do remember thinking that I couldn't spend the weekend alone in the house. I spent half a day packing stuff into my car. For no reason I can think of I decided to disappear. I knew everyone would immediately think I'd gone south to Cornwall, so I went north. I thought I'd go to Scotland, sleep in the car. I just wanted to disappear.

I got as far as Yorkshire before I couldn't drive anymore. I sat in the car at Sedgefield services sobbing for an hour before falling asleep. When I woke it was cold and dark. I felt completely drained. What was I doing? Where did I think I was going? What was the point?

I took the next off-ramp and turned south again. I went back home to Appleby. Only now it didn't feel like home anymore.

PART II
AWAKENING

THE BUILDING YEARS

The desire to build a boat is the desire of youth, unwilling yet to accept the idea of a final resting-place. It is for that reason, perhaps, that, when it comes, the desire to build a boat is one of those that cannot be resisted. It begins as a little cloud on a serene horizon. It ends by covering the whole sky, so that you can think of nothing else. You must build to regain your freedom.

— ARTHUR RANSOME "RACUNDRA'S FIRST CRUISE"

2006 - MY OLD FRIEND THE BLUES

Just when every ray of hope was gone
I should have known you'd come along
I can't believe I ever doubted you
My old friend the blues

— STEVE EARLE

So there it is. That's how in January 2006 I came to be in that rented flat staring at the ceiling.

Alone again.

Broken again.

It didn't feel like it at that moment, but there was a significant difference this time. I was better prepared. I'd been there before. I'd learned a few things. But my weapons were rusty, they'd not been needed for years, so for a while I forgot they were there.

Once again Depression got me cornered and started beating the shit out of me. And I let it.

Perhaps subconsciously I was punishing myself. On the face of it, I was blameless. Alison had cheated on me. Plain and simple.

But these things are never plain and simple. I'd failed to give her what she needed. I was the cause.

I still hung on to hope that things could go back to the way they'd been. Eight months previously Alison had bought us tickets to see legendary Bluesmen BB King and Gary Moore in Birmingham. The concert was in April. I asked Ally to come with me. She said yes.

An hour and a half of the best blues music in the world. Played by two of the best blues musicians in the world. It was always going to be an emotional experience.

Maybe I hoped Mr Moore and BB could say the things I couldn't.

> *I think I'll just fall to pieces*
> *If I don't find something else to do*
> *This sadness never ceases*
> *Woman, I'm still in love with you*
> *My head, it keeps on reeling*
> *It's got me in a crazy spin*
> *Oh, Darling, darling, darling, darling*
> *Is this the end?*
> *Still in love with you*

I caught Ally's eye as I mimed the lyrics. I got the answer to my question.

BB came on stage later and sang 'The Thrill Is Gone'; for her it obviously had.

Once again I felt like a worthless piece of crap who'd failed at everything I'd ever done. There was no fight left in me. At least that's what I thought.

But I kept going. Those dark days in the caravan and my attempt to end it all had built a barrier that could never be crossed again. I used the dark thoughts that came so frequently as the enemy. I'd given in to them once before, and the memory of how I'd felt afterwards had been carved into my brain. That memory was keeping me alive.

I remembered the words of that Scottish welder, Syd Banks. Thoughts weren't going to kill me. They were only thoughts. I just had to wait for them to pass. I read a lot, looking for answers. Trying to understand why this shit kept happening to me. Telling myself that I was a good person, that I didn't deserve this.

Gradually I came to realise it was all about choice. Whatever had happened, whatever thoughts and emotions these events threw up, it was down to me to choose how I dealt with them.

You can't choose to think differently. Thought can't be controlled. But every time a thought arises you have a choice. Every single time. You can choose whether to hold onto it or let it pass.

That simple conscious action makes a huge difference. Because if you hold onto a thought you give it power. It grows, it generates feelings, it becomes your reality. But if you're alert to them you can choose not to do that. You can recognise it's only a thought and that it's just passing by. You can try to ignore it. I said it's simple but it's not easy. I know.

Have you ever been into one of those Sushi places? The ones where you sit at a counter with an endless conveyor belt of dishes trundling round it? That conveyor is your brain, and the dishes are your thoughts. Oh, and you're chained to the counter. There's no walking away from those thoughts. There are guys behind the counter. One is a master sushi chef. He trained for years, his dishes are beautiful, fresh, delicious and healthy. The other is an unenthusiastic amateur. He's using bad fish, it looks foul, it tastes foul and it could kill you. Those dishes, those thoughts, get mixed up at random on that conveyor. They keep trundling round and round forever. You can let them pass or you can choose one and eat. You know which is good and which is bad. Which ones are you going to let go? Which ones are you going to grab hold of?

Slowly I began to realise that for the past two decades I'd never once taken charge and steered a course. I'd let others decide and just gone along for the ride. Twice they'd jumped ship and left me alone to be swept over the waterfall. Perhaps it was time to grab the wheel.

But I was a way off doing that just yet.

I just felt numb a lot of the time. I'd been hurt and I was emotional. To keep things under control I had to numb those negative emotions. There's a problem with that though. You can't selectively numb emotions. If you numb one, you numb them all. No pain means no pleasure, no happiness.

It was a good short-term tactic though. It stabilised me, I switched off, at least out of work hours. None of this ever affected my work, I was kind of a Jekyll and Hyde character at the office. Everyone thought that I was OK. I even convinced a few that I had a new girlfriend. It was a defence. I didn't want anyone to know how lonely and scared I was. So in the hours of daylight, I wore a mask, I seemed fine. But when darkness fell so did the mask. I'd switch off and withdraw from the world. Food was an inconvenient necessity, bed and mindless TV dominated my time.

Winter in the UK isn't exactly conducive to shaking off Depression. I'm sure I've suffered from SAD syndrome all my life, and that just added to my misery. Gradually though winter loosened its grip. The days got longer, the sunshine started to return physically and metaphorically. Time is a healer they say, and it was certainly helping.

I decided to try and shake myself out of my stupor a bit. I bought a mountain bike, I started riding when I got back from work. On weekends I packed a lunch and cycled entire days. Countryside, fresh air, exercise. All great healers. I'd read that St Johns Wort was a natural medicine that helped Depression, so I started taking it.

The darkness still lurked though and I feared for the future. Everything seemed pointless. I no longer had a house to work on, I had no idea what I wanted to do or where I wanted to be. I was just existing, just surviving, just comfortably numb.

As the summer passed I started to think about life more. I was healed enough to at least be able to consider that I could be alive for a few years yet. Given the evidence so far it wasn't difficult to conclude that a 'normal' life didn't seem the right path for me.

I'd given it a damn good shot. Since settling down after losing 'Mor Gwas' I'd married, had a daughter, divorced. Found love again, then lost it. Lived in 5 different houses none of which I'd owned. I'd got no savings, no car. Everything I owned would fit in a couple of suitcases and a few boxes. I was approaching 50 years of age, and what had I got to show from all that conformity? When it came down to it there was only one significant reward for 25 years of doing what everyone else was doing. That was Nicole, my beautiful daughter. I'd always be there for her, but now she was a young woman making her own way in the world. She didn't need me around.

Then one night I decided to go through a box of books I'd bought from Appleby. It'd remained unopened in the corner of the room since I'd moved in. I cut the tape and opened the flap. There sitting on top was a ring bound A4 booklet. On the cover, a sketched drawing of a naked girl stretched out on the netting of a sailing catamaran. She was watching dolphins playing around the bow. It was the Wharram Design Book, and my heart leapt at the sight of it.

Before Nicole was born Paula and I had briefly considered building a Wharram and going sailing. Actually, that's probably not right. I'd sent off for the book, I'd shown it to Paula, we'd leafed through it together by the fire and I'd dreamed. Then it had been forgotten. Now here it was again. Like a message from the Gods.

I thought back to those days on 'Mor Gwas'. Just 18 ft of fibreglass and the most basic of living. Yet the happiest days of my life had been aboard that little boat. Something else struck me as well. That had been the last time I'd really taken charge of my life. I'd made a decision, taken action and reaped the reward. OK, ultimately I'd lost, but there was a huge difference. I'd lost because I'd pushed too far, I'd lost because of what I'd done, not what others had done.

I knew instantly that I'd found my escape. That thin little ring bound book had the same effect on my Depression as a crucifix on a vampire. It screamed, curled up and disappeared into ashes.

One of the many self-help books I'd been reading was by Tony Robbins. I remembered a quote from it. He said, "Your life changes the moment you make a new, congruent, and committed decision". Up until that point those words had been hollow to me. I hadn't believed it could be that easy. Now I could see clearly that he was right. I'd made my decision and it was going to change my life. I was going to build a Wharram catamaran and get back to the sea.

I don't know how many times I read and re-read that book. I knew every design inside out, I was like a kid in a candy store trying to decide which one I wanted. I spent hours online watching videos, reading blogs and trying to find out as much as I could.

I guess now is a good time to talk a little about James Wharram, his boats and his philosophy. As you'll see, there's more than just the boat to consider. Join the Wharram community and you're not only talking sailing, you're talking lifestyle.

James Wharram is a pioneer. Considered by many to be the father of modern 'multihull' sailing craft. In the 1950s he designed and built a 26ft plywood catamaran named 'Tangaroa'. This catamaran was like nothing anyone had ever seen before. Basically, it was two enclosed flat-bottomed canoes connected by beams and decked. It was held together with rope. In 1955 he set sail from Falmouth bound for the West Indies. He didn't go alone. He took two German girls with him, Ruth & Jutte. Jutte was pregnant by the time they'd crossed the pond. Even today folks would raise eyebrows, back in 1955 they did far more.

You can see an old Pathé News video of 'Tangaroa' HERE .

Or search YouTube for '£200 Boat Prepares To Cross The Atlantic'

It's worth it for the music and commentary alone.

James was, and still is, an opinionated and stubborn man. This first incredible voyage was not made for pleasure. It was made to prove a point.

In 1947 a Norwegian by the name of Thor Heyerdahl had sailed a balsa raft called 'Kon-Tiki' over 4,000 miles from South America into the Pacific.

He wanted to prove that people from that continent could have migrated by sea and populated the Polynesian Islands. His expedition had succeeded, just. After 101 days Kon-Tiki was wrecked on a reef. Heyerdahl and his crew survived, but it had hardly been a controlled voyage.

Jim Wharram was adamant that the Polynesians were far more likely to have crossed the Pacific in the opposite direction.

They had been building strong sea-worthy craft for thousands of years. More than that, their navigational skills were legendary.

'Tangaroa' was built to prove just how capable these Polynesian catamarans had been.

He proved his point. It was a hard passage but all three of them, well four technically, reached the Caribbean.

His boat was in a sorry state though and he'd learned a lot. He decided to build another improved design on a beach in Trinidad. While there he met up with legendary French sailor Bernard Moitessier.

Moitessier came to fame during the Golden Globe race in 1968. The Golden Globe was the first ever race around the world for single-handed sailors. Robin Knox-Johnston eventually won in 'Suhali'. But only because Moitessier, who had a substantial lead, decided to retire from the race.

After rounding the Horn and heading up the Atlantic on the 'home stretch', he decided he didn't want or need all the bullshit glory that seemed likely. He changed course and continued sailing back around the planet and into the Pacific again.

It's hardly surprising that he and James hit it off and Bernard helped James get her built. After months of work the 40ft 'Rongo' was ready to sail and in August 1959 Jim and his crew headed into the North Atlantic for the return journey.

It was an epic voyage. They survived hurricane force winds and it took seven weeks, but 'Rongo' became the first multihull to make a West to East Atlantic crossing. James wrote about these first voyages in his book 'Two girls Two catamarans'. It's a good read.

In 1973 Jim teamed up with Dutch woman Hanneke Boon. Together they started producing new boat designs for enthusiasts to build themselves.

The culmination of his vision came with the construction of the 63ft 'Spirit of Gaia' in which he and Hanneke made a circumnavigation in 1994/1998.

He's now been building and sailing for some 60 years. That design book contains everything from a 17ft beach cat to a 63ft expedition boat. All share the same Polynesian ancestry.

Philosophy plays a big part in Wharram Designs. In Jim's words; "the sea tells you how to design. It's about achieving 'oneness' with the ocean". He is of the opinion that "within urban man and woman is an inbuilt deep-seated instinct to be on the sea". I can relate to that.

The designs come out of being on the ocean, living on the ocean. Strong, simple, capable. He describes his larger designs as 'Nomad shelter homes'. I liked the idea of having my own 'Nomad shelter home'.

By late summer my decision was concrete. I was transformed, energised. I had a purpose. Perhaps it was desperation that drove me ,but drive me it did. This was no fantasy or daydream, my feet were firmly planted on the ground, and I knew that I was taking on a monumental challenge.

I realised that this wasn't just about escape either. The loss of 'Mor Gwas' still weighed heavy on me despite the passing of so much time. I was haunted by what might have been had things worked out differently. I'd be haunted until I succeeded. The ghost had to be exorcised.

2006 - PROVIDENCE

After much consideration and hours spent pouring over study plans, I'd decided which Wharram I was going to build. It would be a Tiki 38. 38 ft length, 22 ft beam, 3.5 tons. Big enough to live aboard comfortably. Designed to cross oceans safely. Small enough to sail single-handed and small enough that I could build her on my own. She seemed the perfect boat. This time I was going to do it right.

There were a couple of major obstacles to overcome first.

Money was an obvious one. The months of hermit-like existence I'd been living had meant I wasn't spending much. So I had a few quid in the bank that would allow me to buy the full building plans and the first batch of materials. After that, it'd be down to living cheaply and saving what I could.

But there was another important consideration. I'd walked away from the house in Appleby with nothing, and with no expectation of anything. Alison and I weren't married, the mortgage had been in her name. Legally I wasn't entitled to anything. But Ally had promised to pay me my share. Despite her betrayal I still trusted her. My heart told me she'd do the right thing. There were no guarantees of course, but whether she did or whether she didn't I knew I'd find a way.

The second big obstacle was finding somewhere to build. Wharram's have been built everywhere from fields to beaches, garages to polytunnels. For me, the starting point had to be geographic.

The job at Gerflor was the only permanence, so wherever I built it would have to be within commuting distance of my office in Warwick. I got a map and drew a couple of circles at 25-mile and 50-mile radius and started the search. I spent evenings driving and cycling around highways and byways. I was open to anything.

I needed a sizeable space of 12m(39ft) x 8m(26ft) with a minimum roof height of 3.6m(12ft). But it could be land for a polytunnel, an industrial unit, a barn, a shed. It didn't matter to me. Before long though it became obvious that industrial units were out. I simply couldn't afford one. I'd thought that maybe a rundown empty barn might be had cheap.

But this was Warwickshire in the heartlands of England. The property boom of the 80's had seen plots of land and old barns selling overnight. There didn't seem to be a single empty barn in the County. They'd all become desirable country residences. It was the same with the land. I was beginning to get disheartened.

There's a wonderful publication in the UK called Exchange and Mart. I don't know if it's still going. It was like eBay in the form of a thick tabloid newspaper. I'd taken out a small ad in the wanted column asking for a barn or shed that could be rented.

One evening my mobile rang. It was a guy by the name of Richard Prescott and he said he'd got an empty barn that might be available for rent. I tried not to sound too excited as I arranged to go and see it. It was even harder to control my excitement when he gave me the address. The place was less than 5 miles from Gerflor's offices in Warwick.

The following evening I cycled round to Manor Farm and met Richard. A big no-nonsense guy with a friendly smile and a loud laugh. He thought I wanted to build a canal barge, he laughed even louder when I told him it was a sea-going catamaran.

That may have had something to do with the fact that Manor Farm lies only a few miles from a place called Meriden. Meriden has a claim to fame. It has a stone cross in the centre of the village. That cross marks the point in the UK at which you are farthest from the sea in any direction. My ocean crossing boat was going to be built right in the heart of England.

The barn wasn't perfect. Open at each end, the roof and gutters leaking. But it was the right size, the right location and the right price. Richard seemed a guy worth knowing. We agreed on a price and shook hands on the deal.

I drove away ecstatic.

I'd committed and The Universe had given me my first reward.

The words of that last sentence weren't written flippantly.

There's a quote often attributed to the German writer Goethe. But that, in fact, came from the Scottish mountaineer W.H. Murray. It goes like this:

> Until one is committed there is hesitancy, the chance to draw back, always ineffectiveness. Concerning all acts of initiative or creation, there is one elementary truth. That the moment one definitely commits oneself, then Providence moves too. All sorts of things occur to help one that would otherwise never have occurred. A whole stream of events issues from the decision. Raising in ones' favour all manner of incidents and meetings and material assistance which no man would have believed would have come his way. Whatever you think you can do or believe you can do, begin it. Action has magic, grace, and power in it."

I'd discovered the truth in those words long before I discovered the quote. It's become something I consider before making major decisions in my life, and it's something many overlook completely.

It doesn't matter what your beliefs are. Murray attributes the effect to 'Providence'. But feel free to substitute 'God', 'The Universe', 'Allah', or any other deity of your choice. You can just call it 'Luck' if you want. It doesn't matter. It'll happen just the same.

I choose to call it 'The Universe'.

We're conditioned to plan things out, aren't we? To think things through, make pros and cons lists, arrive at decisions based on facts.

But there's a huge problem with that. If you're thinking big and you stick to what you know, you'll soon reach a point where you become stuck. The facts will stop you dead.

Not enough money, not enough time, not enough something. Your brain wants to keep you safe and well within your comfort zone. Unless you can show it that the way forward is clearly mapped. That every eventuality has been identified and planned for, it'll tell you it's not on, it'll say No.

Big things have never been achieved by people who let their heads have the final say.

You have to follow your heart and trust Murray's 'Providence'. You have to commit, get off your arse and start.

Then the magic can happen.

> All sorts of things occur to help one......
> All manner of incidents and meetings and material
>   assistance......
> Which no man would have believed would have
>   come his way..........

Still sceptical? Well, stick with me. You'll see many more examples in this book.

Finding that barn so near to my office, meeting Mr Prescott. That was just the start. You'll be amazed at what follows.

2006 - IT BEGINS

*S*eptember 2006 was both exciting and frustrating.

Having found a build site my next challenge was to find some new rented accommodation nearby. The flat I was in was OK, but just a little too far away.

Besides, I felt like I needed a fresh start. The place held too many bad memories.

Geographically the search was easier. I knew where I was working. I now knew where I was going to be building the boat, and I knew I wanted to be as close to both as possible.

Once again 'The Universe' helped me out. I found a quirky little terraced cottage in the village of Rowington. It was just a couple of miles from Manor Farm and 15 minutes from the office.

The place had been up for rent for a while, probably because it was tiny. But I knew it was perfect as soon as I saw it.

It was in the grounds of a beautiful Tudor manor house called Shakespeare Hall. I subsequently found out that the name wasn't accidental. The house had once been owned by an uncle of

William Shakespeare, Stratford Upon Avon being nearby. Legend has it that Will spent some time at the hall. And may even have written 'Much Ado About Nothing' whilst staying there.

The cottage was the middle one of three, built into what had once been animal sheds. No2, the one I was looking at, had actually been a bullpen. The original wrought iron and timber stall gate had been left in place as a somewhat impractical kitchen door. Other than that, there was one bedroom a bathroom and a small sitting room. Out back there was a small patio looking out over the landscaped gardens and the duck pond. I didn't hesitate and said I'd take it. All that remained was to wait for the legals to do their business.

With a place to live and a place to build the next thing on the list was the boat. I jumped onto the Wharram website and ordered my build plans. It was scary pressing that buy button. The plans cost £1200. It all but cleared my bank account. But the words of W.H.Murray were still fresh in my ears and that made it easier. I'd committed and I was being rewarded.

Colleagues at work picked up on the fact that something was going on. I was a different person, they could tell. It was amusing to watch their faces when I told them what I was planning. Everyone said how amazing it was. Everyone was supportive. But sometimes the positive words coming from their mouths didn't match the look on their faces.

October was an exciting month. I drove down to Cornwall for the weekend. My Mom and Dad had moved to a place just down the road from the Wharram offices in Devoran. It was great to see them and I was able to pick up my plans. Sadly, James, Hanneke and Ruth were away, so after a quick chat with Liz in the office I drove away with a big black folder. On the cover a label 'Tiki 38 Build Plans Number 107'.

I'd chosen a name as well. My new boat would be called 'Gleda' (*Pronounced GLAYDA*).

I'd considered calling her 'Mor Gwas II'. But I couldn't get comfortable with the idea. 'Mor Gwas' had gone a long time before. There could never be another. This boat was going to be something completely different. She needed a completely different name.

I'd wanted something short. There are occasions when you have to spell the boat name out loud on VHF radio. Not to mention painting the name on the hull. I wanted something English. The boat was to be built in the heart of England after all. And of course, the name had to be female.

Then one day whilst scrolling through a list of Old English girls names I saw it; 'Gleda'. Meaning *'To make happy', 'Glowing, Glad One, Gladden*. The origin is believed to be part Anglo Saxon and Icelandic Norse brought by the Vikings. The alternative Icelandic meaning is *'One who is happy'*. I knew straight away this was it.

Back at Mom and Dads, the contents of my plans folder were soon spread out across the lounge floor.

There were five large scaled planning sheets covering the hull structural details, hull panels and deck. One sail plan & rigging plan, and two smaller ply cutting plans. Also a large A3 Building plan book full of detailed sketches and text showing every stage of construction. Plus an A4 book with useful general information about cutting timber and using epoxy. Lastly a lot of data and an order form for the West Epoxy System.

I was immediately impressed with the information and guidance to small details. Things like wet hanging locker drains, storage and toilet/shower options. There were other details you'd be unlikely to see on any other boat but a Wharram. Like a fire-pit and an opening deck hatch for lifting buckets of water in harbour, using as a toilet at sea and as a place to be seasick.

As soon as I got back up country I got the call telling me the cottage paperwork was all sorted. By the end of October, I'd moved in. Even with few possessions and only myself to think about it was still a bit stressful. I was pleased to get in though. The Indian summer we'd been enjoying had gone, the weather had turned and the clocks had gone back. Wind, rain, chilly temperatures and short days. I didn't care, I'd now got a purpose. I threw myself into it.

There was something else. It seemed I wasn't alone in dreaming of building a boat. While waiting for stuff to be sorted out I'd had time on my hands. I decided to start a blog. I knew I wanted to keep a journal of the project and I figured a website was the easiest way to do it. It was a purely selfish exercise and I had no thought that anyone else would take any interest. To my amazement though I started getting comments and messages of support from all over the world.

I had no-one close by who really understood what I was doing, but online it was different. By the end of October, I had a list of 20 or so 'friends' from the US, Canada, New Zealand, France, Australia and UK

I hadn't even started building and already I felt part of something.

Richard up at Manor Farm had asked for a few weeks to clear the barn and to do a few repairs to the roof and gutters. It was frustrating. I was itching to get started, but it gave me time to study the materials list and start looking for suppliers.

The Tiki 38, as with all Wharram's boats, is of very simple construction. Basically, it is a plywood and softwood frame covered in more plywood. All this timber is glued and treated with epoxy for durability. The exterior surfaces of the hulls and superstructure are sheathed with glass fibre and epoxy.

Here's an idea of some of what's needed:

- 90 sheets of plywood 1.22 m x 2.44 m (4 ft x 8 ft) of varying thicknesses
- 675 metres (2,220 ft) of Douglas Fir or Pine of varying sizes
- 450 kg (992 lb) of Epoxy Resin
- 100 kg (220 lb) of Epoxy Hardener
- 10 kg (22 lb) of various fillers
- 100 m (328 ft) of Glass Cloth
- Paint (a lot of paint)

On top of that come the consumables. The list is endless and includes nails, screws, abrasives, rollers, gloves, brushes, solvents etc.

This was all new to me. I completely underestimated the complexity of sourcing, pricing and procuring all these materials.

Take the epoxy resin as an example.

I found five suitable brands available in the UK

- West
- System Three
- UK Epoxy Resins
- SP Systems
- Sicomin

Pricing comparisons were a nightmare. Epoxy came in different pack sizes, some in litres, others in kilograms. Because they all had different densities conversions could be misleading. This was where I first discovered the value of specialist forums like 'The

Multihull'. I was able to get some great advice about usage and allergy issues.

The timber wasn't straightforward either. I learnt that suppliers of clear grade Douglas Fir were few and far between. And that I needed different suppliers for good Marine Grade Ply.

There was one issue I kept paramount. Whatever I ordered it had to be top quality. There were to be no shortcuts or compromises.

November had flown past and I was desperate to start. On December 2nd I finally got access to the barn and started turning it into a place of work.

First job was to lay a lofting/building floor. Lofting is essentially the process of drawing out the designer's line drawings at full size, on the floor. That needs a smooth clean and level surface. Creating smooth level floors was what I did as a day job. It didn't take too long to get 3 m(10 ft) x 12 m(40 ft) of 18 mm tongued and grooved chipboard down.

It was off season at the local camping and outdoor store. I bought a 3 m x 3 m frame tent to act as office and canteen, and a 3 m x 3 m gazebo to give me a clean area to store and mix epoxy.

I'd also acquired a steel lockable storage container for tools.

After a few work sessions making the barn as homely as I could I was finally beginning to reach the point at which I could start work. I thought back. Four months before, I'd been lost and depressed with no idea where I was headed. Now I had a new home, a barn and a huge project about to start. I'd spent £3000 on the plans, materials and tools so far. Yep, I'd committed alright, and boy did it feel good.

The weather in December was horrible. Two big storms, freezing temperatures, torrential rain and fog. It didn't matter.

I'd ordered up the first lot of materials and while waiting for delivery I started with the lofting out. It was fun. First stage was to draw out the backbone/keel sections with the sternpost and skeg. For the first time, I was able to get a feel for how big a Tiki 38 actually was. It was scary and exciting at the same time.

Materials started arriving. Enough 9 mm plywood to build the lower hulls, enough 18 mm plywood to make the keels and skegs. Hardboard for making templates.

The Douglas Fir for stringers and supports arrived. Beautiful wood, clear grade, no knots and a lovely smell.

I had decided to use Sicomin epoxy resin from Matrix Composites in Bristol.

Given my complete ignorance of epoxy systems, I had taken advice from other builders. Matrix/Sicomin came highly recommended. I'd had several long discussions with a guy from the company with the wonderful name of Wiz Deas. He was building his own boat and I was impressed with his knowledge. He helped me not only with advice but worked out quantities for me, and gave me a good price.

The day after I ordered, a small pallet was delivered to the barn. It held a blue keg holding 33 kg of epoxy resin and two white drums containing Cotton Fibre, Glass Bubbles and Silica. Also a starter kit of brushes, rollers, mixing sticks, hand cleaner, acetone etc. Finally some fast hardener for the resin. Glass bi-axial tape, and a roll of something called Peel Ply. It didn't look much for £600.

It was beginning to dawn on me how much I had to learn.

Wiz had told me that working with epoxy in near-freezing temperatures was difficult. On his advice, I built a warmer for the resin and hardener. I fitted a 100 watt light bulb into a wooden tea chest and made a tin foil flap as a door. I knocked together a wooden rack to fit the 33 kg keg and it worked perfectly.

On December 12th, 2006 I cut out the first two pieces of my boat. The skegs. I wondered how long it would be before I'd cut out the last pieces.

Soon the lofting was finished. And I started cutting plywood for the backbones and adding all the little Douglas Fir floor supports and strengtheners. It was enjoyable work. I was taking it slow. Measure twice, cut once as they say. It felt good to be working with my hands again. Creating something.

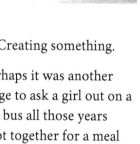

There was another reason to feel good. Perhaps it was another sign of my recovery, but I got up the courage to ask a girl out on a date. It was the same girl I'd compared to a bus all those years before. She said yes, and on 21st Dec we got together for a meal and a drink at the Tom O'The Wood pub just down the lane from my new place. It was a cold night with thick fog. I had to drive down to meet her at the main road so that she could follow me to the pub. She'd never have found it otherwise. We had a good night, we got on, it was nice. I don't think either of us had any idea what we'd started.

I took a short break for Christmas in Cornwall with family, but was back before New Year to carry on. It was the end of a momentous year. It had started with me mired in Depression, lost, lonely and without purpose. All that had gone. Now I was happy, excited and driven. I'd come a long way. I couldn't wait to get cracking into 2007.

2007 YEAR ONE (629HRS) - WORKING THE PLAN

*F*rom this point on I'm going to include many of the blog posts and journal entries I wrote during the build. They'll be shown in italics.

I did think about rewriting them. But they convey my thoughts and emotions at those particular points in time better than any rewritten words could ever do. There's a downside to that. I do repeat myself sometimes, and the writing standard isn't great. But as I said, they tell it as it was.

So for the main, I'll restrict new writing to filling in the blanks and things that only became clear with the benefit of hindsight. This and each of the following chapters will cover a year. The hours in brackets will show how much time was spent working on 'Gleda' during that year.

January threw up a few weather obstacles. For most of the time, the temperatures were in low single figures. I started glueing all the sections of backbone together, learning about epoxy as I went. Wiz had already told me that you can't mix epoxy when it's cold. In low temperatures, the resin becomes thick and viscous, like treacle. The tea-chest warmer I'd built worked well but it wasn't enough. So I enclosed the gazebo epoxy area in thick polythene to make it into a tent, and purchased an infrared heater. I now had a 'warm' area to mix and work in.

The epoxy in a Wharram build is used in many different ways.

Firstly it's used neat for coating i.e. Just resin and hardener mixed together, sometimes thinned. Every sheet of plywood was coated at least twice to give added protection to the timber.

Top quality marine ply should be completely impervious to water, but I boil tested every batch to make sure. Coats of epoxy give added insurance, particularly when below the waterline.

The second way of using epoxy is to mix it with wood fibre to make adhesive. Every joint on the boat, even those with mechanical fixings are glued.

The third mix comprised epoxy with silica and glass micro balloons. This thickens the mix to the point where it stays on the mixing stick like thick treacle. This is used for 'filleting'. Basically, this is forming triangular gussets along the edges of joints to add strength. There are miles of fillets in a Tiki 38 build.

There are two methods of mixing epoxy; by weight or by volume. I opted for weight and to be cautious I mixed in small quantities. I used electronic scales, small round plastic containers like those used for takeaway food, and mixed it using big lollipop sticks. It worked well, a little slow, but easy to control and it ensured a good mix. I used this method right through the build.

January 18th was a notable weather day. Near 100mph winds were recorded, 7 people lost their lives and at the height of the storm, I drove to the barn fearing the worst. I had to negotiate tree debris and branches to get there. I expected the place to have no roof. The barn was something like 100 years old. It had been re-roofed but the timbers and brick end walls were original. I was relieved to find that although the power had tripped out and sections of the roof skylights were lifting in the wind, the place was still standing. I didn't get any work done that night.

It turned out the storm had been the strongest for 17 years. A few days later temperatures plummeted below zero and we had snow. It was frustrating. I was fired up with enthusiasm but I knew I was playing a long game. If I'd had a fully weatherproof, heated workspace I could have cracked on. But I hadn't. There was no point bleating.

That evening I took my girlfriend Gail to see a movie. It was called 'Deep Water' and told the story of the 1968 Golden Globe race around the world. The first for single-handed sailors. This was the race I mentioned earlier. The one Bernard Moitessier had retired from to keep sailing. The film focused on the tragedy of Donald Crowhurst and his plywood trimaran 'Teignmouth Electron'. He and his boat fell apart. It's believed he committed suicide by jumping overboard. He was never found. Gail was just getting her head around the fact that I was building a plywood boat and going sailing. I could probably have chosen a better film to take her to.

February; A few of my blog posts.

February 1, 2007 - Stepping Up The Pace

My long weekend started today and I put in a solid 6 hours. I sanded down the work I did earlier in the week and then flipped both backbones over so that I could start on the other sides. It was no easy task on my own. I was a little fearful of straining or breaking one of the joints. I was pleasantly surprised though how strong the backbones are, even with only half the fittings and strengthening in place. After a good sweep up I screwed and epoxied all the remaining skeg and keel doublers and all the plywood butt straps. Tomorrow I plan to get both hull side flanges and the last four stem and stern glassed joints done. I am thinking about leaving the coating until I have the backbones upright, I think it will be quicker as I will be able to get to both sides at once. I'll see how it goes. I will need to change the workshop layout to give me more room, make some temporary supports, and also get some help to lift the backbones into position. The weather has been freaky again today, 12-13°C and I was working in a T-shirt, this time last week we had snow! Suits me fine though!

February 5, 2007 - Miserable Day

Today has just been a write-off. I had a migraine last night and felt down and weary this morning. Despite that I was determined to crack on, I got to the barn and spent an hour sanding. The weather has turned again, only 2°C and wet. Really miserable after the beautiful weekend. Too cold for epoxy and frankly too cold for me. I was getting so annoyed sanding because when wearing a dust mask my glasses kept steaming up! After a cup of tea, I started thinking about lifting the backbones upright. The next two hours were then wasted pissing about with bits of wood and levers. Only to realise that there is no way the backbones are going to stand without some bulkheads to support them, and some manpower to lift them into position. I was just being stubborn and stupid to think otherwise. I ended up pissed off, cold and annoyed and called it a day. Lessons learned! I am now away until Friday on a business trip to Scotland so nothing will get done until the weekend. Time to reflect and plan I think.

February 11, 2007 - A Lost Week

Weather and work have conspired together to prevent any progress at all this week. We have experienced the heaviest snowfall for a good few years on Thursday and Friday, and now a thaw has set in we have flooding. Ironically I was in snow-free Scotland when the worst occurred, and it was Saturday before I was able to get to the barn to check things. It was as wet as it has ever been. Snow had blown in and then melted, leaving pools of water in places that have never been wet before, even in *the torrential rains we have experienced. Thawing snow seems to find its way into places that rain doesn't. There was no damage to the backbones but the lofting floor is wet and so are the covered pallets of timber. Applying epoxy to damp cold timber is not a good idea so there really is little I can do. I need things to dry out and warm up a bit. I'm trying not to get stressed but having just pulled my work hours/days average ahead I am now losing again. Roll on spring!*

The first part of the month was tough. I had a bad cold, my job was pulling me away for days at a time, the weather seemed to be fighting me. It was something I'd just have to get used to. I was beginning to realise that the success of a project of this scale depends more on slow steady movement than intense sprints. Despite the setbacks, I reached a landmark by the end of the month.

February 26, 2007 - Can You Tell What It Is Yet?

It appears that 'Gleda' is beginning to take some shape! After fitting the temporary legs to the bulkheads I slotted them back onto the backbone. Then, whilst looking at it sitting on the trestles, I thought, 'I should be able to tip it off using the legs as support, and over into position'. It worked perfectly! No ropes from the ceiling, no extra manpower, just me! I was so pleased I cracked on and did the other hull as well. I'm really happy to have reached this landmark today. It's my 50th Birthday tomorrow, and I can now celebrate safe in the knowledge that my dream of sailing my own Wharram is getting closer!

Now is probably a good time to explain this stage of the build process. I'd started with the construction of the thick plywood 'backbone' of the hulls. These 'backbones' also form the keels of the finished boat. Once built, all the lower hull bulkheads are cut. These form the shape of the lower hulls and slot onto the backbone. The landmark I'd achieved by the end of February was to have these bulkheads in place, and each lower hull skeleton supported upside down. This made it far easier to fit the long Douglas Fir stringers and eventually sheath the skeleton in plywood epoxy and glass fibre. The exterior of both lower hulls is finished before turning the right way up.

March saw the first signs of a change in the weather and a change in my mindset.

March 14, 2007 - 100 Today!

Today is the 100th day since I started building and I have clocked 124 hours actual work, far more than that at the build site, and yet more on related jobs. Is this enough? Am I progressing fast enough? Frankly, I don't know. I do know that I'm comfortable with the current balance between full-time job, boat building, relaxation and other essential tasks. I have a decent break coming up at Easter and should be able to boost things along, the weather is improving and things will get easier. I am still only at the start of a very long journey, and I am happy that as long as I keep moving in the right direction when I can, I will eventually reach the end. There will be times when I must go slowly and times when I can go fast, but even if I have to crawl I will get there! I am having a rough time at work just now and 'Gleda' is the thing that keeps me going. Oh, how I long for the day when she will set me free. Free from the stifling oppression of this work culture trap where the rewards for years of hard work and loyalty are threats and insults. How could I have been so stupid to think that my efforts would be recognised and rewarded in proportion? I will never again waste my precious time and energy on people who couldn't care less.

My words about work in this post give the first hint that another major challenge was looming.

With the bulkheads and stringers in place, I could for the first time see the shape and size of the hulls for real. I spent time studying the plans and getting clear about where things were going to be. Suddenly these random pieces of timber began to turn into something resembling a boat. I could see where the galley would be, the main cabin, the heads compartment. I got a big black marker and wrote these names on the floor. I began to feel her coming alive.

April followed a similar pattern to the months before. Part of the month would be great. My mood would be good, the weather would be kind, I'd get loads done. Then the pendulum would swing and productivity drop.

I put in some big days. One eight hour day, 3 kg(7 lb) of epoxy mixed and applied with a 3" brush. On another eight hours doing nothing but sanding. Temperatures that month varied between 5°C (41°F) and 23°C (73°F).

I'd used most of my Christmas bonus from work to pay for another batch of 9 mm and 15 mm plywood. It had been on long delivery and I was pleased when it arrived, but when I shifted the 15 mm sheets that were stacked on top of the pallet my heart sank.

I knew straight away the stuff wasn't up to standard. It was about half the weight of previous batches, only three-ply, thinner (nearer 8 mm than 9 mm) and I found some voids and even a crack in one of the faces. It may have been stamped up as BS 1088 but it wasn't right.

First thing on Monday morning I was on the phone with the supplier. Initially, they said they'd checked their own stock and could see no problem. I emailed photos of the issues and they said they'd get back to me. I left them in no doubt that I wasn't accepting the crap they'd sent me.

The following day I finally got to speak to someone at the supplier who knew what they were talking about. Although reluctant to admit fault, he did agree that the sheets I had received seemed to be "at the lower end of the acceptable parameters". It was obvious he couldn't say more, and there was no point arguing. He agreed the batch could be returned for a full credit.

This was helpful, but left me with a problem. He said that all their remaining stock was from the same batch. The only alternative he could offer me was super expensive (£42 per sheet) Lloyds approved Sapele, or a high-quality Birch WBP. Neither was an option for me. Their next large shipment of Far Eastern Marine was due at the docks in 2-3 weeks. So I told him I'd wait and see if this new shipment reverted back to the quality I'd had before. I had enough ply in stock to clad one lower hull, and I knew I could use the time to see if I could find another supplier just in case.

It's kind of obvious that if you're building a boat out of plywood it's crucial to build it out of decent plywood. Wharram is flexible on materials. The designs are built all over the world. Sources of supply and available materials change with geography. Each individual builder has to make choices based on budget and personal quality standards. Would I have liked to build 'Gleda' from Lloyds approved Sapele hardwood at £42 a sheet? (and remember this was 2007)? Maybe. But even that choice isn't simply financial. Hardwood ply would be a lot heavier, there are nearly 100 sheets in the boat. It may be too heavy. I'd compromised with Far Eastern. It was reasonably available, reasonably priced and reasonably light. I checked every sheet visually for defects, and like I said before I'd boil tested samples from every batch to make sure it wouldn't delaminate.

I was now ready to clad the lower hull skeletons. And turn these strange looking flimsy pieces of ply and timber into something resembling big canoes. I had to get it right.

As May Day arrived I was facing my first really challenging part of the build.

May 1, 2007 - First Real Challenge

Up to now I have been surprised how easy the build has been. Yes, I've had a few problems, and I've had to stop and think a bit, but at no time have I felt really challenged. That's changed! The dry fitting of these lower hull side panels is causing me grief. It's ironic that I have just rejected a batch of 9 mm ply because it was too thin and light! This bit of the job would be so much easier if my ply wasn't thick and heavy! I have been using blocks, pieces of wood, clamps and screws to try and hold things in place whilst still allowing small adjustments. I am working on the individual pieces. I want to ensure that they fit correctly before I start taping them together into even bigger heavier panels. I'm trying not to think of handling these and getting them fixed with the epoxy.

The lower hulls of a Tiki 38 are beautiful to look at, graceful curves tapering to points at the bow and the stern. But this beauty can only come from torture. The plywood is tortured into shape, the builder is tortured getting it there.

It took most of May to get the port hull cladding finished. I'd finished the port hull and now I was ready to start the starboard, But there was a problem. The replacement batch of plywood still hadn't arrived. I chased and chased then I got a call. They told me they couldn't resupply the same spec.

It probably didn't help that I got the phone call just as I was checking into a grim hotel up north after a tough day on site. Yes, I had a problem, but keeping things in perspective when you're building alone can be difficult. This is where my friends online showed what they could do.

I'd posted from the heart as usual.

June 14, 2007 - Major Problem

I have a major problem. After weeks of assurances and waiting, my timber supplier now says they cannot re-supply me with the same spec 9 mm plywood as I have used for the port hull. I have foolishly trusted that they would sort things out and I am angry with myself for letting the situation drag on. I now have to try and find another supplier who can match the ply I have already used. I am really worried that if I can't find one I will have to face the choice of having mismatched hulls, or of scrapping my port hull and starting again. I can't believe I have let this happen! At best I am going to lose a lot of precious time, at worst I could lose months of work and hundreds of pounds. Right now I feel gutted.

Within hours I was getting comments back. Advice, thoughts, ideas, and they brought me back to reality.

A week later I'd found another supplier and there was a pallet of plywood sat in the barn, identical to the first batch I'd bought.

I was feeling tired. Work had been crazy, as had the weather. June in the UK that year saw torrential rain, flooding and strong winds. I needed to get away for a while. Gail and I packed the car and headed to the South of France for 10 days.

I came back refreshed and got stuck into the starboard hull.

There's one benefit to building catamaran hulls. You get to do everything twice and you learn. The second time is always easier than the first. I calculated that work on the port hull that took me 36 hours took just 21 hours on the starboard one. Not only that but it was probably done a little better.

There are folks who've built Wharram's without the benefit of having a building space that allows them to bring up both hulls together. Having to finish one hull in its entirety and then going right back to the beginning again. I can't imagine that. I was determined that the two sides of 'Gleda' would grow up together before being joined.

It was now July, and what should have been the height of summer. I've lived in the UK most of my life. I should have known better.

Although temperatures were higher and we had the occasional proper summers day, for the majority of the time it was windy and wet. The summer of 2007 went down as the summer that never was. Much of the country suffered serious flooding. Having already worked in the barn through one winter I was beginning to realise that I needed to try and make it a little more comfortable.

The biggest issue was the wind. The barn I had was one of three attached to each other and orientated east-west. The huge open ends of the two barns to the north of mine did nothing to shield me from winds coming from the open fields beyond. Cold winds, winds that sometimes whistled through the rusted iron slats of the old feeding pens. I spent a day zip tying heavy tarps along the pens to at least give me a bit of shelter.

The second and biggest job was to put up a heavy PVC canopy right over the workspace. The roof leaked in more than a few places and whenever it rained the hulls got dripped on. The wind also dislodged dust and crap which fell onto the hulls. I had epoxy coating and painting to do and I couldn't have that.

It took me a full weekend to get 15 m x 11 m of polythene stretched across from one wall to another and slung from the roof. Hard and slightly dangerous work when on your own up a tall ladder. Once it was in place I fitted some more fluorescent strip lights underneath. It was a non-productive few days as far as the boat was concerned. But I knew it would pay dividends as the project progressed.

August was a good month and I pushed on almost every evening and weekend, doing as much as I could while the weather was kindest. Ironically I spent the few hot dry days we had that year kitted up in hooded overalls, goggles and dust mask, sanding. No suntan for me. There was a lot to do. After both lower hulls had been completely covered in plywood the real work began, All the joints between sheets had to be glassed over. The joints between the plywood cladding and the keel had to be filleted and faired ie. Filled with epoxy and rounded. The skegs had to be shaped and rebated holes made for the rudders to hang from. The list went on. All this had to be completed before the next major stage. That of completely covering the hulls in fibreglass.

I was enjoying my labours though. For the first time, it felt like I was working on an actual boat. I may only have had two big canoes to look at, but they were beautifully shaped and an impressive size.

August 13, 2007 - Building Therapy

After a hard day of 8 hours driving on congested motorways and 2 hours on site. I got home feeling really stressed and in two minds whether to go to the barn or not. I decided that maybe some boat building would be good therapy and so it was. I got in the groove, focused on the job in hand, and completely forgot about my day.

I was pushing hard at the barn and at work. I needed to.

September 2, 2007 - Still Glassing

This is another job where the sheer scale of the task facing me starts to hit home. Today I have glass reinforced the full length of both hulls from stem to stern including the leading edges of the skegs. In doing so I used: 36 m (117 ft) of 150 mm (6") wide bi-axial glass tape, 42 m (136 ft) of masking tape and just over 3 kg (7 lb) of mixed epoxy. I would estimate that have used about the same again in the glass work I have already done. I was overly optimistic that I would finish today but I am getting close. I reckon on a couple more nights glassing then another mega sand and clean up, and I will be ready to start sheathing.

September 15, 2007 - Tired Restart

As predicted the demands of the past few weeks left me with no time for 'Gleda'. Hopefully, things will ease a bit now. But I was working

till the early hours of this morning in London
and got to the barn having had only a few hours of poor quality sleep.
What better job to start back with then than sanding! I'm not saying I
slept whilst doing it but it isn't the most stimulating type of work.
Actually, I did sleep whilst at the barn, I sat down with a cuppa and the
next thing I knew I woke with a start having nodded off and tipped the
cup of tea down my leg! I must have an early night tonight and catch
up some.

September saw me making another big investment in my long-term future. I decided to have my eyes lasered. I'd been short-sighted and had worn glasses since primary school. I needed glasses and that was that, there was nothing I could do about it. Even when you've worn glasses all your life they can still be a pain in the ass. I'd spent the past weeks wearing a dust mask and goggles because of all the sanding I'd been doing. The goggles didn't fit very well over my glasses, dust got in my eyes, my glasses got steamed up. On the rare occasions when it was hot and I was sweating, they'd slip down my nose and I'd have to keep pushing them up. In winter whenever I'd come through the door from cold to hot they'd steam up. All in all, I was getting totally fed up with them. Thinking ahead to going sailing I knew being spectacle-less would be a joy, not worrying about rain and spray, swimming and snorkelling. I'd just got a bonus for a big project I'd been working on. This would be money well spent.

The big day came and I drove the 30 minutes into town to the clinic. I went on my own. Gail doesn't do anything to do with hospitals and medical procedures. It was finished in less than two hours. No pain, just a little stress. The staff and surgeon were great, very reassuring. But when your head is strapped tight to a table and a giant machine swung over your face it's natural to get anxious. That anxiety isn't helped by the rather unpleasant burning smell reaching your nostrils as the laser does its work.

After half an hours rest and a checkup, I was free to go. I couldn't believe it. I could see. OK it was a slightly watery world I was looking at, but the improvement was miraculous. I'd told Gail I'd stay in a hotel overnight; I didn't. I got in the car and drove home.

As it turned out having this laser surgery was one of the best investments I ever made. Apart from the life-changing benefits of not wearing glasses, I got the surgery almost free. I'd paid a small deposit with the full amount to be invoiced afterwards. That invoice never arrived, and despite having a couple of checkups in the months after, they never chased. I figured I was due some good fortune.

I'd been told to rest for a few days, but boredom set in pretty quickly, and the following day I was back at the barn finishing the epoxy coating of the hulls. I'd got a big challenge next on my list and I'd taken a full week off work to get it done.

It was time to get these lower hulls covered in fibreglass.

October 6, 2007 - Double Celebration!

I have two reasons to celebrate today. First I have passed the 500-hour mark and second I have finished sheathing the hulls. The work I did yesterday has turned out fine despite my difficulties, and today everything went smoothly. Sheathing the hulls (not counting the first epoxy coat) has taken 24 hours work. It's used approximately 11 kg (23 lb) of mixed epoxy resin, and 34 sqm (366 sqft) of glass twill and PeelPly. Pretty intense but incredibly rewarding. I intend to rest tomorrow!

By the end of the month, I'd got the hulls sheathed and had started applying fairing compound. This is a very fine epoxy filler that, as the name suggests, fills in all the imperfections and fairs the surface ready for paint.

I'd already decided 'Gleda' would have a 'workboat' finish. Mirror-like gloss was never an option. It was to be another long job. Applying filler with a trowel and then sanding it back with a longboard. Re-apply filler and repeat. Once both hulls were faired everything needed washing down so that I could apply the first of two primer paint coats.

All this in an autumn that was particularly cold and wet.

I pushed hard during the last three months of the year. I wanted to get the lower hulls externally finished and turned before Christmas.

I succeeded, just.

On 4th December I reached an important milestone.

December 4, 2007 - 1st Build Anniversary!

It seems incredible, but it is now a full year since I started building. I've averaged just over one and a half hours work per day. I missed my target of getting the lower hulls completed and turned. Looking back I'm pleased with what I have achieved nonetheless, I've learnt a hell of a lot and proved to myself that I can make 'Gleda' a reality. My enthusiasm is undiminished and I am determined to get to my hull turning target before 2007 is done. Strictly speaking though I am treating December 12th as 'Gleda's' official birthday, because that is the day when I cut the first actual pieces of wood. Looking ahead I know that I must make more effort to increase productive building time. If I were to continue at the current rate, and assuming a 3500hr total, I would be looking at a 6-year build. I can't live with that.

December 12, 2007 - Happy Birthday Gleda!

Today was an appropriate day to reach a highly visible milestone. A year ago I had two pieces of plywood and I said 'Gleda' Lives! Now I have two beautiful white hulls. More than that I feel like I have a boat, there may be a huge amount of work left to do, but I know

that these hulls will carry me and my dreams wherever I want to go. She's real. She's strong. She's beautiful. She grows day by day, week by week, month by month and now year by year. Getting closer and closer to being at one with the wind and the waves, sailing to distant shores. 'Gleda' really lives now!

I closed the year out with 629 hours of building time on the clock, and headed down to Cornwall for Christmas in a cottage with Gail. I was a happy man.

Perhaps I should have been paying more attention to the world outside. During 2007 the seeds were sown for the worst global financial crisis since the Great Depression. In September the Northern Rock Bank had to be bailed out by the UK government. It was the first British bank in 150 years to fail due to a run. I'd never heard of Subprime mortgages, Fannie Mae, Freddie Mac or Lehman Brothers. There was no way of knowing it then. But the aftershocks of these seismic events were going to be felt very close to home.

2008 YEAR TWO (715HRS) - THE MYTH OF SECURITY

*J*anuary 7, 2008 - *New Year, New Start*

Well, here I am again, back to work and back to 'Gleda'. A most enjoyable break has left me wound down and lethargic. I confess that keen though I was to get back to building it came hard tonight. It's still dark and it's still freezing, and I have got used to sitting in front of a log fire with some nice company and a nice bottle (or 2) of wine of an evening!

Nothing constructive achieved tonight. Just swept out the leaves, reminded myself where everything was, and did some token key sanding down in the stern section. My next job is to make all the hefty epoxy fillets down in the keel/backbone joints, so it's back to mixing epoxy again. I need to start building some momentum again and crack on!!

The hull sheathing stage had used a lot of epoxy. I cracked open my third 33 kg drum. Given that the average weight I mixed at a time is 200 grams, that equates to some 330 little pots mixed since I started the build.

January 21st - History repeated. It happened in 1987 and it happened again. There was a global crash in share prices. £77 billion was wiped off the value of the City's blue-chip stocks in the biggest one-day points fall in London's history. This meant nothing to me of course. This time I didn't have a mortgage to worry about. It may as well have been happening on another planet. I couldn't see any way this would change my life.

January 30, 2008 - Music Hero

No work on 'Gleda' last night because the evening was spent in the company of Mr Steve Earle and his wife Alison Moorer. OK, there were quite a few other people there as well, but I didn't mind sharing! What can I say? Two and a half hours of raw, mainly acoustic stuff straight from the heart.

I'm not one for having heroes but Steve's music has been hitting the spot with me for many years now. He has been described as a rebel and a maverick. But I just see him as a supremely talented guy about the same age as me. Someone who ploughs his own furrow and doesn't tolerate bullshit. In the latter two, I like to think we have some similarities. He is a survivor, on his seventh marriage, past alcohol and drugs problems, and a spell in prison. He's still standing and he ain't 'laying his hammer down' just yet.

I think this quote sort of sums up his character.

> *"I make an embarrassing amount of money for doing something I love -*
> *- especially for a borderline Marxist. I like to tour in a bus, but if you*
> *think I couldn't hitchhike with one guitar and play a show and get the*
> *money, you'd be sadly mistaken. Don't ever f!!!!g bet against me."*

January and February saw me starting work inside the lower hulls. The bilges had to be filled with epoxy. The floors cut and fitted, and the cabin layouts sorted.

February 21, 2008 - Idling

For some reason I seem to be struggling to be productive at the moment.

Time at the build seems to be spent with head and hands 'hopping' from one place to another, without really achieving anything. I need to get a grip, work out an ordered task list and then crack on and follow it.

I think part of the reason is some dithering about the cabin layouts. Comments about the en-suite shower and toilet re-awakened some niggly doubts about the layouts.

If I was just going to live aboard in tropical climes I would have no hesitation in doing away with the en-suite facilities. But it is highly likely that I will be living aboard in the UK For a few years at least. And I know from previous experience that the larger en-suite option will make life a lot more comfortable. The issues about smells and dampness are solvable. The right ventilation and provision for a decent solid door between the two areas will sort those out.

Then again, will I regret not enduring a bit of discomfort for a few years when I take off to the sun indefinitely? Or maybe I will decide to explore north for a while. See what I mean? I'm going to poll opinions on the Multihull Forum and ponder some more.

Meanwhile, I'll concentrate on other jobs that need doing first anyway. Eg. proper fixing of the hull-side stringers and more filleting. But I will make a final decision before next week.

To some, the difficulty of this decision might seem puzzling. Some would say you don't need anything. Use the deck hatch or the 'bucket and chuck it' system. Others wouldn't hesitate to fit the ensuite and a separate guest facility. One of the great things about Wharram designs is that when it comes to cabin layout there is a lot of flexibility. In fact, the Wharram Design book uses the term flexi-space. They encourage builders not to add too much in the way of permanent seating, cupboards and shelves. But rather to keep as much space as possible open and to use portable storage that can be moved around as necessary.

For me though, 'Gleda' was to become a permanent home for

years to come. Gail and I were getting along well enough that I wanted to consider the possibility of cruising as a couple. I wanted 'Gleda' to be comfortable.

In the end, I opted not to have the 'en suite'. Having now lived permanently aboard for a few years it was, on balance the right decision. That said having outside facilities is - pardon the pun - a pain in the ass sometimes. Particularly when the weather is cold and wet.

Perhaps the biggest issue is that in poor conditions at sea the heads compartment becomes unusable. It's in the forward part of the starboard hull. Not only is that a potentially dangerous place to be in a seaway, but also you don't want to be opening up a big hatch and risking a flooded compartment.

On the rare occasions where either is a problem temporary solutions are available i.e. pee in a bottle. But a small Portaloo in the main cabin is a far better standby. As for showers, we never take them below deck. The pod has drainage in the floor and can be screened off for privacy and warmth. Our shower is a pump up garden sprayer. Hot water comes from the kettle.

Simple, reliable and flexible. The watchwords of any Wharram build.

April 23, 2008 - Masts Ordered!

I must be crazy! I just wired several thousand dollars to Canada to pay for two 10.5 m masts and one 6 m stern beam. Getting ahead of myself or what?

Ok on the face of it it seems like madness but I think it's a good move. Martin Hivon another Tiki 38 builder in Quebec, Canada, had done a lot of work. He'd researched availability and cost for the correct marine grade mast material. 6061 T6, 140 mm OD, 4 mm wall thickness aluminium tubing in long lengths to avoid sleeving. He managed to find a supplier. But the price was very high if ordering only enough for one boat.

So in true enterprising spirit, he posted on the Wharram Forum. And, after much correspondence and work, got together a group of 4 who can all benefit from a bulk order. Even with international shipping, the cost is way lower than we could achieve as individuals.

The gang of 4 are Martin, myself, Jacques Pierret in the States, and Daniel Ganz in Switzerland. What a great example of the international Wharram community! Many thanks to Martin for the time and effort he has put into this, wouldn't it be great if we could get all four boats together someday!

As far as my build goes it's still slow going with nothing exciting to report. A couple of hours filling and sanding is all I've managed the last few days.

April 30, 2008 - Still Ready To Work!

After the welcome sunshine of the weekend, we have reverted to the seemingly endless cold wet and dull weather that is so wearing. I had planned to start epoxy coating the 12 mm plywood sheets that will be used for the main cabin bulkheads tonight, but the weather put paid to that. I have laid out 8 full sheets on the barn floor and plan to coat them in a 'production line' way as soon as things dry up a bit. This may be a little monotonous but it will allow me to speed up the progress when I start drawing them out and cutting them.

May 10, 2008 - Sunshine Day!

Today has been one of those landmark days when the project seems to take a huge step forward. It's all an illusion of course, and bears no real relation to the work put in already and the enormous amount still left to do. Nonetheless, the huge psychological boost is real, and I can't tell you how good it feels to see for the first time the shape and size of the hulls. I simply couldn't resist offering up the bulkheads. Putting in a few screws to see how they sat, and then I thought why not try them all! Here I am sat on the main double berth looking aft through to the small single and feeling pretty chuffed. To help with the good feelings the weather is still unseasonably warm and sunny, so I cut short the day for beer and barbecue by way of a celebration....... She's coming along!

May 25, 2008 - She's Growing On Me!

A cold, wet, dark, miserable day weather-wise but I'm pleased with the progress I've made. I gave the toilet and shower components their second coat of epoxy. Then moved onto marking and cutting out the remaining upper bulkheads and the beam trough sides. As before these needed careful work to draw them out correctly, so I took my time. I also coated up another full sheet of 12 mm ply for the second set of beam trough doublers. The doubler at bulkhead 1 has a measurement which the plans say needs checking with the actual hull, and is measured in relation to the stringers.

So I decided to have a play and temporarily wire in a few stringers to the bulkheads to help me see things more clearly. It was fun to do, and suddenly the beautiful shape of the full height bow section started to appear. A nice way to brighten a miserable day!

Those blog posts give no hint at what was going on behind the scenes. I'd been working at Gerflor for years. When I started the build I figured I'd be there when the boat was finished. All that changed in the first half of 2008. At the

time much of what was happening within the company seemed unprompted and mysterious. Gerflor was a French-owned multi-national. The global financial crisis affected everything it did. None of that mattered to us then. All we saw was long-serving loyal employees being treated unfairly. Things came to a head in June.

June 16, 2008 - Off Plan

I have taken a big leap into the unknown today. I have resigned from a well-paid job that I have been in for 13 years. Four weeks from today I will be unemployed. This blog is not the place to give details, all I will say is that I had to decide which was more important, a pay cheque at the end of the month or my integrity and responsibility to others. I chose the latter. By doing so I have put many things at risk, not least the project. I have no safety net, I have to keep my balance and get to the other side. Ah well, stepping out of my comfort zone is something I need to practice before sailing beyond the horizon!

Looking back, 2008 really was a watershed year. For the first time in a long long time, I took control and made decisions that were right for me. All through my relationship with Alison and the subsequent breakdown, there had been one stabilising factor. My work at Gerflor. I was well paid. For the most part, I enjoyed the work, and I had a great crowd of colleagues. Some of them came as close to friends as I've ever really had. I'd met Gail at Gerflor and she'd become far more.

There were other things that kept me there. I felt valued, I felt I was part of something and that I was contributing. It brought out one of my strongest traits, loyalty.

All that changed in 2008. At the time I couldn't write about it. Now I can.

The first signs of trouble had come at my annual review. Gerflor was French owned and that summer I'd spent a few days in Lyon looking at a new sports floor system the company had developed. It was innovative, but I could see some major problems should it be introduced into the UK market.

I was under the impression I was there to give my feedback, so I gave it. I made some suggestions about how changes could be made to improve, and headed back. It'd been a strange trip.

Usually, our French hosts looked after us well. This trip had been the opposite.

I should have been picked up from the airport but they 'forgot', and I had to take a taxi. The hotel was poor and I was left alone there for three nights. I couldn't put my finger on it, but I felt like I was being shunned. I never found out why.

Anyway, when the annual review came round, my boss told me that I wasn't getting a pay rise this time. Every previous year I'd been given something above inflation. I worked bloody hard ,and those raises were hard earned. To me, it'd been a tough year and I'd expected the same. It was a shock.

I asked why. The answer came back ,'because of your negative attitude'. I thought it was a joke, the boss had said the words without conviction, then the penny dropped. He was following instructions. The word had come down from elsewhere. From France. He as good as admitted it.

I walked out of that office feeling like I was now working for a completely different company. I realised my life was being affected by nameless shadows who knew nothing about me and cared less. For the first time since starting work there, I felt my time was numbered.

The next shock came when all the UK employees were told that some significant changes were to be made in pension arrangements. Historically the company had run what's called a final salary pension scheme.

This type of scheme makes pension payments calculated according to the length of service and salary at the time of retirement. They'd actually stopped offering it to new employees a few years before, but now they wanted to stop it for those of us still receiving it. Not only that, but we were told that there was a significant deficit in the fund. This was a big deal.

It was a good scheme and a significant part of our reward package. What the company offered as a replacement was unacceptable to us. For months there were meetings and negotiations, but ultimately we were left with only two choices. Sign a new contract of employment, or become unemployed. It seemed a pretty shabby way to treat their most loyal employees.

In those few months, years of loyalty, mutual trust and goodwill were destroyed. What made it worse was that we felt betrayed by one of our own. It seemed to us that the then UK MD, who'd claimed to be fighting hard for us, had in fact been some kind of double agent. In the end, it appeared that he'd made sure his own nest was well-feathered before turning us out into the cold. When the deed was done he 'resigned', and ran off to feather another nest.

It all left a very bad taste in the mouth. In my naivety, I thought a contract of employment was just that, a contract. What I hadn't realised was that when the employer decided they didn't like what it said anymore, they could just tear it up and write a new one. All within the law.

The new MD seemed to have been lined up ready. Within days of his arrival, he was making his presence known. He didn't know the flooring industry, he didn't know us. He didn't seem to want to. It wasn't long before he turned his attention to me and my team. I say team, but there were only three of us. Myself as Technical Manager, a Technical advisor, and an Administrator. We worked well together, we worked hard and got the job done, I couldn't see much he could change.

I was wrong. My assumptions were based on the fact that the work we did was valuable and important. He thought otherwise.

In his words, we were "a department that doesn't contribute to revenue". In his world, anyone that didn't actively sell stuff was an overhead, a burden on the rest, something to be got rid of.

It was bullshit. If one of our products was installed incorrectly or failed subsequently, the company was pursued for costs. It was my job to avoid that happening. Proactive prevention through training and information. Mitigation and avoidance by investigation, conclusion and rectification. I represented the company on Standards committees and trade organisations to keep us ahead of the game. I ensured that we understood the legal and ethical requirements of our marketplace.

To him, that was all worthless. He said I was to make my assistant redundant. That I was to cease any activity outside the company. And look for other ways of reducing the costs of running the department.

I was passionate about what we did, and I wasn't about to sacrifice my values for this arsehole. He knew I wasn't happy, but he thought I'd just do what most others would have done, and put myself first.

The look on his face when I handed him my resignation letter next day was well worth the pain I'd had writing it. He'd tried to bully me, but he hadn't expected me to go.

I wasn't the last. It's all been downhill for the company since then. I couldn't care less.

Eighteen months before, I would have clung to that job by my fingernails if necessary. I'd have done anything, put up with anything. But I'd changed. I'd changed because of my decision to build 'Gleda'. I'd changed because of the decision to change my life.

A few of my closest friends thought I'd been reckless to resign as I did. That I should at least have waited until I found another job. Sure that's probably right, in the 'normal' world.

But in my head, I wasn't living in the 'normal' world anymore. I'd already demonstrated that by my actions. Did I resign because of it? Yes, partly I think that's true.

To some extent, I had an advantage. I get that. I did what I did without having to worry about anyone else. Many of my colleagues would have said they didn't have the 'luxury' of choice. A mortgage, a wife, kids in school. They needed the security of that paycheque. They couldn't afford to make rash choices like that.

It's a strange phenomenon, and one I've come across many times when folks have questioned the life we live now. They feel secure. They have a good job and a nice house, they take holidays, they're living life right.

They talk about owning their own home and yet few of them do. They're years away from that, and until that mortgage is paid off they're really just renting from the bank. It happened to Paula and I in 1991, and it could happen again, to anyone. If you can't pay that monthly mortgage the bank will take the place off you. You'll be homeless. And how do you pay the mortgage? With a monthly pay cheque from that steady job. But all it takes to change that is the stroke of a pen. A pen held by someone you've never met, someone who doesn't know you exist, and doesn't care anyway. Maybe your car comes with the job, that goes too. How much have you got in your savings account? How long would that last if you tried to continue your current lifestyle without an income? Are you one pay cheque away from you and your family being broke and homeless?

Crazy talk? Maybe. Likely to happen? Probably not. But it doesn't change the reality. If you live like that you've delegated your happiness and quality of life, along with the well being of your loved ones. You have no control over what they might do. Is that security?

There's an old saying about having all your eggs in one basket. Living like this takes it further. You're not even holding that precious basket yourself.

Ultimately it's about comfort zones. Over millennia the human species has evolved. But part of our brain still lives in caves. It's scared of the sabre-toothed tigers roaming about outside. It wants to keep us safe, so it tells us to stay put. So we do just that, we make ourselves comfortable. What we don't know is that just over the hills there's a land without tigers where we can live in the sunshine. We'll never find it. Because we won't take a risk.

Leaving my 'Gerflor' cave was a big deal for me. But I hadn't yet escaped my caveman thinking. I figured I would soon be out there with the tigers. I needed to find another cave fast.

I had to work a months notice, and I spent a lot of time getting the word out that I was looking for a new job. My years in the industry gave me a head start. I knew people and they knew me. It only took a few weeks to get an offer from a construction adhesives company called Mapei. I accepted.

My last day at Gerflor was emotional. Thirteen years is a long time, and I was leaving some good people. They bought me a bulkhead compass for the boat. It's been fitted in the pod since day one. It reminds me of good times when I'm on the night watch.

All this meant I'd done no boat building for nearly three weeks. It was mid-July before I started getting back into gear.

I started a new month with a new job and renewed enthusiasm. There were some differences this time though. Yes, the job I'd taken had some appeal, but there was really only one reason I'd taken it. It was for the pay cheque.

Secondly, I was expanding my world outside of work and locale.

July 30, 2008 - Powerful Connections

I always hoped that one of the things 'Gleda' could give me would be new friends from far-flung places. People with a common interest and similar values to mine. What I didn't expect was that I would start making these friends long before 'Gleda' was even on the water.

I have written many times of my surprise and gratitude for all people who have made contact with me since I started the project. Giving words of advice and encouragement when I needed them most, and helping me towards my goal when I felt the pressure of building alone. Although I have never met or spoken to most of these people, nor indeed even written at length, the connections we have made are powerful nonetheless.

This has been demonstrated by one person in particular. This individual went further than words and promised to send me a gift that they felt would bring me luck.

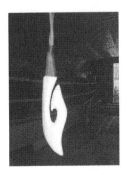

That gift arrived yesterday and words cannot express my gratitude. It is a 'Hei Matau' pendant. Carved in bone using traditional methods by a Maori artist in New Zealand called Stanley Nathan. A 'Hei Matau' is a very stylised fish hook bone carving that symbolises prosperity, abundance, fertility and strength.

They are also seen as good luck charms, particularly for those travelling over water. They would most certainly have been worn by the navigators of the original Polynesian Vessels. This gift has now become one of my most treasured possessions. By wearing it I feel another powerful connection. A connection to the sea, to the traditions of the past, and to the people whose spirit is guiding me towards my dream.

August saw me working on the beam troughs. As the name suggests these are the recesses where the crossbeams holding the two hulls together are located. It took me 60 hours of work to get them finished. A lot of that time was spent getting them lined up correctly. Any small error made here can cause big problems later on when the beams are dropped in.

With that job out of the way, I was able to move on to another project milestone. That of adding the upper bulkheads and hull sides. As had been the case before, the boat suddenly seemed to move forward quickly. Suddenly I could clearly see my progress.

August 19, 2008 - Home Maker

Something really strange is happening, all I'm doing is adding a few more sheets of plywood to the many that I've already put in place. Just another step on the long long road to a completed boat but. More than any other stage so far, the effect of fixing these sheets is out of all proportion to the effort involved. For the first time, I really feel like I am creating living space, enclosed, real, and beautiful. 'Gleda' will be my home for many years to come and only now, for the first time, can I really see what that means.

I fitted another two panels tonight and enclosed the main cabin sections aft of the double berth. I was able to sit where I envisage the chart table will be, and look down the cabin into the berth. It's just plywood, softwood and epoxy. But they are coming together to create something much greater than mere building materials. Now I am really starting to feel that 'Gleda' is coming alive. That soon she will be able to give me shelter, safety and comfort, to give me the place of my own that I so desperately want. Nothing can stop me now.

summer had been another washout. It'd been a stressful year from the start. At the end of the month, Gail and I escaped to Portugal for some R&R.

September 7, 2008 - SunDowner

Hi all, I'm back from the sunshine and straight into the torrential rain and gloom of the UK's washout summer. In the Algarve there had been no rain since May, temperatures were in the high 20°Cs and it was almost always sunny. Here, there has been several inches of rain in the last 24 hrs, it's about 15°C and the sun is nowhere to be seen! I'd forgotten what it was like to live outdoors, and if I needed any reminder of why I want to sail away I got it big time! The holiday was fantastic, a great mix of relaxation, exploring, good food and drink and general good times.

Highlights for me were seeing a pod of pilot whales from the awe-inspiring Cape St Vincent. And snorkelling for the first time since having my eyes lasered. Cape St Vincent marks the south west corner of Europe. Turn east around that corner and there lie the Straits of Gibraltar and The Mediterranean.

As Gail and I stood on the towering cliffs looking out to sea, I turned to her and said: "we'll be out there soon babe, sailing 'Gleda' to the sun". I spoke with absolute certainty in my mind. Gail nodded, her doubts well hidden. Who could blame her for having them? I'm nearly two years into the project and nowhere near the end.

Whilst the holiday acted as a great incentive to get cracking again, I confess that returning to the cold wet and gloomy barn was challenging. The rain had got into the electrics. I had to spend some time with WD40 and screwdriver drying plugs and sockets before I could get the circuit breaker to stay on. Rainwater had leaked onto some of my Douglas Fir stock and into the port hull forward section. No damage done though.

As you may recall I spent a lot of time some weeks ago getting the hulls at the right distance apart, and level to each other. I realised though that

I simply hadn't got enough working room down the outside of the port hull. The leaking gutters would continue to dump water on me and the work area if I left things as they were.

So I decided to move the hull about 4 feet further away from the wall, before I got started on the port hull upper hull sides. It was a pain in the ass but I'm glad I did it as it made things much easier, and I was able to crack on and get 6 panels dry fitted this weekend. I know that the next few weeks could prove a bit testing as the nights start to draw in and the weather continues to be bad. Another autumn and winter is approaching fast so I'd better get used to it!

September 10, 2008 - Two Left

I'm keen to keep some progress going after my holiday, not least because I am away in Scotland next weekend and will lose yet more time. I'd really like to get all the upper hull side panels cut and dry fitted before I go. I managed another couple of hours today and got the last bow panel finished. I just have the two stern panels on the port hull to do and I will have a complete set of panels cut and ready for final fitting and glueing.

I'm beginning to get concerned that my work rate is not as high as it needs to be if this build is going to be completed in a reasonable time. This year I've managed to bump up my average from 1.5 to 1.75 hours per day, but I really ought to be hitting at least 2.

I had it in mind that by the end of this year I would have the decks on. But looking at the huge amount of preparation, filleting, sanding and interior fit-out work needed before then. That target is looking ambitious, to say the least. I am also going to need some more expensive timber soon, and finances are not great right now. I see some challenging months ahead.

When I wrote that last line I didn't realise how true the words were. The rest of September was a struggle. A bout of the flu, work demands, poor weather. I was struggling again.

September 23, 2008 - Building Blues

This feels like one of the harder periods of the build. My energy levels seem low. The work is not particularly interesting. There are no visual changes. The nights are getting darker and chillier, and I will be doing the same thing for some weeks to come.

It's OK though, because this is like putting money in the bank (not that I can remember what that's like!). I know that no matter how hard it is to get out and do something, all I have to do is just that. Every hour I put in brings me an hour closer to finishing, an hour closer to the new phase in my life I've planned for so long. I've failed in the past because of a weak spirit, that's not going to happen again. Building is the same as sailing, you can't get the heaven without taking the hell. Another two hours closer tonight, another panel glued.

October came round and with it another setback. The job at Mapei hadn't been going well. It was beginning to dawn on me that maybe I'd just been recruited so that they could bleed me for my contacts and knowledge. My immediate boss had a poor reputation. A mouthy salesman promoted above his abilities. He'd have been out of his depth in a car park puddle. From where I was sitting he didn't have any apparent management skills and I wasn't happy.

At Gerflor, for the most part, I'd been my own boss. Here I was just a small cog in a very big machine. I'd been brought in as 'Business Development Manager' but I had nothing to manage, and no clear objectives. Every time I requested a meeting to put forward ideas or discuss options the reply came back they were too busy. I had no office, no desk and worked from home a lot.

Maybe I was too focused on the build, but I missed all the warning signs. On October 8th I got a call to meet my manager at a pub down the road. It was a short meeting. He gave me some bullshit story about 're-structuring', and told me they were letting me go. He said I could go on immediate gardening leave and that I could keep the car until the end of the month. I was shocked and angry, it felt personal. Bastards.

Mapei was another multi-national. Italian owned this time.

At the time I got booted the financial world was in turmoil. Lehman Brothers in the US had gone under in September. In the UK the Bradford & Bingley building society had to be rescued.

October of 2008 saw more unprecedented events. The UK government had to rescue 3 of the countries largest banks. Royal Bank of Scotland (RBS), Lloyds TSB and HBOS. The main Icelandic banks nearly collapsed. It seemed shocking to most ordinary folks. These seemingly rock-solid institutions had apparently been built on foundations of sand.

If, like me, your understanding of world financial markets is somewhat sketchy. I'd make a recommendation. Find a copy of 'The Big Short' movie from 2015. This award-winning film tells the inside story of this 2007-2008 financial crisis. But it does it in an entertaining and easy to understand way.

It's fascinating and scary. Watch it and then re-read what I wrote above about the myth of security. You might find yourself thinking a little differently afterwards. I know I did.

October 13, 2008 - Escapism

I threw myself into the build today with a solid eight-hour shift. The weather has turned unseasonably warm, and yesterdays day of rest was spent enjoying the gorgeous sunshine. Although more overcast today the temperature was up in the high teens with little wind, and it was dry. Ideal working conditions really. I drove home from my girlfriend's place this morning feeling a bit low. It was Monday morning and I should have been heading into a new week of paid employment. Instead of which I was heading into the unknown.

The boat is my escape right now. Whatever may happen over the next few months it seems logical to take advantage of the situation. For the next few weeks at least I can pretend that I'm just on holiday and free to put some hours into the total. I have enough materials on site to keep me going for a while without spending any money. Over the next few days, I'll look at the finances and work out a timetable of actions I may need to take. I figure I can keep things together for a couple of months. But after that, unless I start bringing in some cash, things will start falling apart pretty quickly.

The maths are easy really. I have no assets except a part built Tiki 38 and some bits and pieces I can e-bay, but on the plus side, no debts either. If I really tighten up the budget I must surely be able to scrape enough together for the rent and bills. I'm even wondering if I can tarp over one of the hulls and move on board, only kidding? Escapism is OK but I can't bury my head in the sand. Tomorrow I start firing off some e-mails, making some calls, and getting my CV out.

Anyone know of any vacancies for a technical/sales guy in contract floor coverings with some boat building experience?

I was angry about the way I'd been treated. It felt like a repeat of what had happened at Gerflor, only this time I'd not had any control. Throwing myself into boatbuilding took my mind off it. Eight hour days of hard physical work left me aching and tired, but it distracted me from the reality of my situation. I'd reached out to my professional network. I'd got sympathy and a few promising leads, but I knew the clock was ticking.

Speaking of clocks, British summer Time ended, the clocks went back. It snowed.

November was a quiet month as far as 'Gleda' was concerned, but in other areas, it was a different story. Something else had changed as well. Over to the blog posts.

November 3, 2008 - Making Work

Mindset is everything right now. In past years pressures such as the ones I'm experiencing at the moment would have caused me to break down. Those days are gone. All these problems are but minor irritations. If I couldn't cope with these, then there'd be no point continuing. I will face bigger ones when I start sailing 'Gleda' over the horizon. Thanks again for the supportive comments but don't worry, all will be well!

November 14, 2008 - Priority Task

Having neglected 'Gleda' for a week, I set out through the rain to spend some time at the barn. I started working on the starboard side aft deck stringers, cutting the last of the bulkhead notches and preparing them for glueing. I finished off by giving what will be the undersides of the stringers a coat of epoxy. Although I made some progress my mind really wasn't on the job. Rather I was thinking ahead a few weeks to what my situation will be if I haven't started bringing some money in.

To be honest I've started getting angry with myself. I've let things slip away from me, and I can feel myself reverting back to my pre-'Gleda' days of Depression and self-pity. I'm not letting that happen again! I've realised that I can no longer carry on with my head in the boat building sand. I must dedicate all my time and effort to getting myself out of this situation, safeguarding the project, and securing a future.

I'm sorry to say therefore that posts to this blog will be sporadic for the foreseeable future (although that's not long!). Normal service will be resumed as soon as possible.

November 20, 2008 - Inching Forward

Hi to all, thanks for bearing with me during these challenging days. My particular thanks go to Gail for caring and sharing, as well as David, Nonthawat, Brian, Martin, Ben, Daniel and John the Kiwi! for the fantastic messages of support. I've said it before and I'll keep saying it, I can't tell you how much of a boost these messages give me when I'm down.

I've been working hard in many ways to get myself sorted. This blog is not the place for details. But my efforts haven't been wasted. And although I wouldn't go so far as to say that there is a light at the end of the tunnel, I think I'm getting an occasional hint of fresh air!

I also want to make something clear. There is absolutely no way that I will ever give up on 'Gleda'. Building a boat has become the stereotypical 'they never get finished' project. And we all know of cases where this is true, but like bad news, they get talked about more than the success stories.

I've drawn huge inspiration from Dave Vinnicombe (Dragon), and Beat Rettenmund (Aluna). Both have slogged for years before me, and then launched their Tiki 38's in the time I've been building.

They have shown the way and overcome huge obstacles to reach their goals. I will do the same, some say that the longer the build goes on the harder it gets to stay motivated. I've found the opposite to be true. It's hard to be fired up by flat sheets of ply and bits of timber. But when they start to come together into something recognisable as a boat, the enthusiasm grows. Stopping becomes unthinkable. If you have enough motivation to find a building site and get started, you will finish!

By the end of November, things were looking better.

November 25, 2008 - A Brighter Day

I went to the barn today for the first time in 10 days. It was quite an exciting bike ride due to ice and slush in the lanes. I had to concentrate to stay upright and the rear wheel span out a couple of times on the climbs! The sun was shining though and it felt good to breathe in the cold crisp air.

All was well in the barn, although the place was full of windblown dry leaves. 'Gleda' was as I'd left her and I hope I'm forgiven for neglecting her.

I've not wasted my time whilst I've been away. I'm beginning to feel that

I've ridden out the storm, and that I'm starting to sail towards the sun again. So what have I done?

Well, #1. I've got another job. It's in my chosen field. It's a decent package, I get a vehicle, and although it's a national role the head office is fairly local, so I don't have to move me or the boat. I start on 8th December.

#2. I've started a long-term personal project to bring in some extra income. It's a project that will hopefully build something that can be continued whilst sailing. #3. I've had a major de-clutter at home. Ditching the crap, sending anything useable to the charity shop, putting any valuable but redundant stuff on eBay. The combined effect of these actions is renewed energy and optimism for the future.

I may well look back at this year and say "you know what"? "That was the year when things really began to come good". I still have a way to go but I'm going to give it my all.

December 14, 2008 - **Two Years In**

There is so much going on at the moment, that I almost missed the fact that 12th December marked two years since I cut the first pieces of 'Gleda'. I'm painfully aware that the pace of construction has slowed almost to a halt. It's something I intend to rectify as soon as I can. There are many things demanding my attention right now. And I need to get my time organised and prioritised to get back on track. I think I'll have to cut back on sleep!

It'd been another momentous year but I'd survived. Winter 2008/2007 turned out to be the coldest in the UK for a decade. I didn't care. Now more than ever I was determined to escape. I was sick of the bullshit, sick of being a pawn on someone else's chessboard, sick of the system. I'd taken this new job on the clear understanding that it was simply a means to an end. I looked forward to making 2009 a year of real progress.

2009 YEAR THREE (213HRS) - TAKING CONTROL

$\mathcal{A}$t the beginning of January, I was back to the boat. An entire month had slipped past without any progress. I'd needed the break though, and returned ready to crack on. The weather wasn't helping.

January 5, 2009 - Icy Icy Icy

After what has been the coldest December for a decade, January is continuing the same. The forecast for tonight is minus 6°C or 8°C. Not world class but getting extreme for us soft Brits. This is the first time in years that we've had continued low temperatures day and night. I'd forgotten how hard it makes things. The lanes up to the barn are treacherous with sheet ice, and I saw some interesting tyre tracks leading off road! These years of mild winters mean that there are many drivers on the road, or should I say off it, who have never driven in these conditions and have no idea how to.

I spent a couple of hours tonight sanding and prepping the port aft compartment ready for filleting and glueing. The cables on my power tools had all gone stiff with the cold, and kept getting tangled up. This week will be one of re-adjustment. Getting back into the weekday routines of daily work and evening building whilst also finding time for basics like eating and sleeping. Oh, how I will enjoy remembering these days when lounging on deck in the tropical sun!

Us Brits have a reputation for talking about the weather, and I'm aware that I'm upholding that reputation here. It's strange in some ways because generally, the UK climate is pretty benign. That's why any temperatures below freezing tend to generate sensational newspaper headlines. Such as, 'Britain locked in Arctic blast'. Or, after a few inches of snowfall, my absolute favourite, 'Snowmageddon!'. We forget that on many parts of our planet they experience proper cold and feet of snow. Fellow builder Martin Hivon in Canada reminded me of that when he replied to one of my cold weather blog posts.

Hi Neil,

As far as miserable weather is concerned, I hate to brag, but we are now sitting at minus 37° in temperature and the wind makes it feel like minus 50°. I will not miss this place once I am done with my boat.

January turned out to be a bad one as far as boatbuilding went. What work I did was slow and monotonous. I mentioned earlier that there are miles of epoxy fillets in a Tiki 38, and that's what I was working on.

The new job meant I was back to my old routine of early starts and late finishes. With miles on the road between, and for sure, the freezing temperatures weren't helping.

The highlight of the month was undoubtedly a trip to Paris to celebrate my daughter Nicole's 21st birthday. It was bitterly cold but the sun shone and it was great to share time with her. Paula was there with her new husband. I returned full of a father's pride, but tinged with sadness for what might have been had Paula and I not parted. But, as they say in France 'C'est la vie'.

Back to the weather again, sorry.

February 8, 2009 - Snow Drift

It's official. We are now in the midst of the worst winter weather for decades.

There has been snow on the ground for over a week, and temperatures haven't got much above freezing for weeks now. We had another few inches of snow tonight and severe weather warnings from the Met Office have become the norm.

Any kind of work in an unheated barn exposed to the weather at two ends is unrealistic and, even if attempted, would likely lead to poor quality. I'd really wanted to get cracking again, but I have to be patient. I realise now that I was spoilt during my previous two winters, with work hardly being interrupted at all.

This year is different, and there is no point complaining. I feel lazy, lethargic, and unable to relax properly for the constant nagging in my head that I am letting things slip. I know it's unavoidable, but somehow it doesn't help. I can only hope that in a few weeks time things will look very different.

I had nothing to complain about really. It was around this time I discovered that my friend Creed O'Hanlon, (he who'd sent me the Hei Matau gift), had his dreams shattered. Soon after his Tiki 38 'Ahmad Bin Majid' was on the water he started to discover deficiencies and defects. They concerned him so much that he refused to take delivery of the boat.

The boat had been constructed by an outfit in Thailand. Creed had done his research, the yard had built other Wharram boats. He wanted a boat built professionally. He had the money. He placed an order.

I'd been a little envious at first but the envy didn't last. Even before Creed had his problems it'd made me think.

Firstly to my mind, Wharram boats were never designed for professional building. I'd been asked many times 'why are you doing all the work yourself?' My answer had usually been, "because I couldn't afford a boat like this any other way". To some extent that was true, but it wasn't the main reason.

For me, a self-built Wharram is far more than just a boat. The blood, sweat, tears, and sheer bloody-mindedness needed to complete the project are absorbed into the boat and make her part of the builder. Knowing every single nook and cranny. Every imperfection. Every joint. Everything there is to know, means that the builder and boat are forever linked, and that no one else can ever truly 'own' her. This for me is a huge part of the Wharram magic.

February 24, 2009 - Timber!

After a slight logistical hiccup that was sorted with a few phone calls, my timber order got offloaded this morning. Just over 200 metres (656 feet) of lovely clear grade Douglas Fir planed to 3 different sizes. Plus 18 sheets of 4 mm and 6 sheets of 9 mm marine plywood.

As I said last night, this should be enough to complete the hulls and deck pod. I'd had a long tiring physical day at work. By the time I'd sorted and safely stored all this timber, I wasn't really fit for anything else except a meal and some sleep!

One thing is for sure though, I find that these occasional big purchases really bring new motivation and focus to the project. It's not just the scary financial outlay, but a real desire to turn this beautiful wood into something even more beautiful. It reminds me what a crazy thing I'm doing here. Turning bits of wood into something that will be a home, a refuge, a means of global transport and an object of beauty. Well, that's the plan anyway!

March 11, 2009 - The Cycle

It's an inescapable fact, as true to boat building as it is in so many other things. It is impossible to get the reward without putting in the effort.

I get a real kick from making really visible things happen on the boat. Most recently it was getting these small stern deck sections fitted. A small step, but one that had a greater significance for me, as it was the first time I'd enclosed space aboard.

Now I have to pay the price and work towards the next 'kick'. My work for the next week at least will consist of sanding and shaping the exterior of these new decks. Then filleting and painting the undersides, working in my newly created cramped space. It's doubly hard to get motivated and out the door for an evening work session when the work involved is not particularly interesting.

It has to be done though, and I know that the 'kicks' will just keep coming.

April 22, 2009 - One Of Those Nights

Only yesterday, during a conversation about the build, a colleague asked me if I would prefer to have more help with the building or would I rather continue working alone.

My answer was that if I was starting from scratch I would love to have someone to share the pleasure and pain. But, having now come so far on my own, it would be difficult to accept such a change. I'd be fearful of losing complete control. And I didn't want to dilute the ultimate satisfaction of seeing things through to the end and knowing that I'd done it all myself.

Yet there are times when the sheer frustration of not being able to do something alone comes boiling up. Tonight was one of those times. As planned I decided to start on the tumblehome panels.

There are no dimensions given for these in the plans. JWD feel that they are better fitted if measurements are taken from the boat. Neither are there detailed instructions on the best method for fitting them. Although the ply pieces are not particularly large. They are 2.44 m (8 ft) long, and need to be held in place high on the hull sides to enable any marking out to be done. They have to be bent in 3 planes, and there is nowhere for them to locate until they are fixed.

Holding them in place requires pressure on the outside. Marking them requires drawing on the inside. Trying to do this alone whilst standing on step ladders is impossible.

I tried temporary screws, clamps, scrap pieces of ply as retainers, you name it. I cut one piece of ply completely wrong, and slipped off the ladders grazing my wrist and twisting an ankle.

The air was blue and nothing was working. I did eventually get one piece very roughly in place but I'm not happy with it. I know glass tape and epoxy will make good many a poor fit, but I also have standards that I won't compromise.

May 10, 2009 - Not Good

I'm getting stressed. I'm simply not getting enough build time in.

It's mainly due to the hours and demands of my full-time job and the knock-on effect of fatigue associated with long working hours. If I gave up my little remaining rest and relaxation it would damage my personal life, and ultimately result in burn out. What's the solution?

Well, I can't see one at the moment. It's a catch 22, I need to put the hours in to get the money needed to continue living and building the boat. I have some ideas that could make things easier but they are long-term and also demand time. I feel stretched thin, trying to do it all and not making much headway with any of it.

So what do I do? I don't see any choice but to throttle back on the boat and to invest more time in changing the situation. If I continue as I am it will take another 4 or 5 years to finish 'Gleda' and I can't live with that.

This means that I will have to sacrifice my evening sessions at the barn.

As it is I usually only manage one or two hours anyway. And if I've pre-made the decision, then I won't beat myself up about it when I get home late. I'll just sit at my desk and work on Plan B. If I do this for a few months then I'll have lost about 48 hours of build time. But I should be able to some light at the end of the tunnel.

It's a shame that they are valuable summer hours. But the timing is out of my hands, it's just something I have to do to safeguard the project as a whole.

Given that I had all these thoughts buzzing around my head you can imagine how much I wanted to make today's eight-hour building session productive. You can equally imagine therefore how annoyed I was that at the end of it I was further back than when I started! In a nutshell, I've made a balls up of the tumblehomes.

I was far too keen to get them fitted and trimmed, and it wasn't very long after starting to make what I thought were final adjustments that I realised it. As I've mentioned before, there are no dimensions given for these panels in the plans, and the drawings have scant detail. I'd quite happily done what I've previously done when cutting panels ie. dropped on a long batten and 'faired' it by eye.

I missed something critical though. The tops of these tumble home panels have to be level fore and aft. And level athwartships, so that the pre-fabricated curved sandwich deck panels drop on nicely. Because I had followed the hull lines I reckon 8 out of my 12 panels will have to be re-made. A huge waste of time and a pricey waste of ply.

I would advise anyone following in my footsteps to use hardboard templates! Anyway, after discovering my error I spent hours measuring and using the water and laser levels to get what was needed clear in my head. I'm still not sure I have it nailed, but I'll get there.

I suppose I've been lucky to get this far in without any serious mistakes, and at least I spotted it before it affected anything else. Like I said at the beginning, stressed.

In that blog post, I referred to a 'Plan B'. It was the first hint I'd given that my mindset was changing. When I started the build the plan had been simple. I'd continue in my well paid full-time job with all the boat work coming on evenings and weekends. Initially, it had seemed to be working, but now I felt differently. Bit by bit it was beginning to dawn on me that not only was I building a boat, I was building a different way of life. I'd thought the life change would happen only when the boat was finished. Now I realised it would have to happen sooner.

I pasted a new inspirational quote above my computer.

> If you're willing to do for a year what others won't, you can do for a lifetime what others CAN'T.

For the rest of that summer work on 'Gleda' all but stopped as I explored possible ways of escaping the 9-5. One option stood out. An internet-based business of some sort. It ticked all the boxes. Work from anywhere with an internet connection. No fixed work hours. Generate income while you sleep.

I was about to go down a rabbit hole.

My tiny cottage at Shakespeare Hall had a kind of loft space above the bedroom. It was an open platform really, built around the roof beams. The only access was a loft ladder in the hallway, but as the space was open to one side I managed to get a desk and chair up there and set up an office. Every evening after eating I'd climb the ladder and go to work, often until the early hours.

I had a lot to learn. It felt strange not to be heading out to the barn. But I knew I was doing the right thing. I may not have been working on 'Gleda' but I was working on the 'Gleda' Project. It was just as important, maybe more.

By the time September rolled around I was ready to test the 'Universe' again. I committed.

September 18, 2009 - Making It Happen

I've waited a long time to write this post. For nearly three years now I've been trying to sustain progress on the project. Whilst at the same time, balancing the demands of full time employment, family, friends and a 'normal' life.

For the most part I think I've managed fairly well. But, as regular readers will know, this last 6 months or so saw things change.

It started with frustration at lack of progress. Then developed into a burning desire to change things. I realised that if 'Gleda' were ever to be finished and, even more importantly, if I was ever going to go sailing seriously. Then I had to achieve two things. I needed more free time and I needed more money. Not much to ask for eh? It would probably be easier to find the Holy Grail! My old self would have said "dream on.... keep buying the Lottery tickets because there's no other way, sunshine".

Well I've changed, I'm no longer prepared to accept that, I'm no longer prepared to be one of the 'unlucky' ones watching with envious eyes those who have it all. I know without a shadow of doubt that I can get to where I want to be, it's just a matter of wanting it badly enough, and I do!

So how do I get more time and more money? Well, time is fairly easy isn't it? Where do most of us spend the bulk of our waking hours? Working for 'The Man', just to have enough money for shelter, sustenance and maybe a bit of pleasure. Now I know that's not true for those who have a vocation and truly love what they do. But I submit that the majority of us would quit tomorrow if we had enough money in the bank. How did we get to a point in our civilisation where it's considered admirable to defer real freedom to enjoy life until the age of 65 or later?

I thank Tim Ferriss for illustrating this point so well in his book The 4-

Hour Work Week. In the book he describes retirement as 'Worst-Case-Scenario Insurance'. ie. becoming physically incapable of working.

He talks about three flaws with the system:

First, that it's based on the assumption that you dislike what you are doing with the best years of your life. That you'll want to stop as soon as you can.

Secondly, he highlights the fact that many pensions won't be large enough to maintain a decent standard of living anyway.

Thirdly, he suggests that to achieve a large pension payout you'd have to be a high flying, workaholic. The kind of person who needs challenges to stay alive. The kind of person who would be bored to death within weeks of retirement. The kind of person who can't stop.

I read Tim's book some time back and it's really thought-provoking. There's some stuff in there that may be difficult to go with. But the basic thrust of his theories, as can be seen from the text above, actually fit perfectly with those of us contemplating a long-term life afloat. I recommend it, without doubt, it was the starting point for where I am now.

Anyway to get back on track, the answer to finding more time was obvious. Give up the day job.

That leaves a bit of a glaring problem, I don't have money in the bank. That led me to start thinking about alternative ways to generate income. Ways that allowed more flexibility, and did not demand my constant attendance or attention.

This is what I have been working on over the past months. And although I have yet to earn a penny, I now know what I need to do. More than that I know without doubt that it will work (more on that later). All that was required was for me to take committed action and make it happen.

So, last week, I gave one months notice to quit the secure, well-paid day job! I can tell you that it was one of the hardest decisions I've ever had to make. My self-belief is high, but a decision like that is contrary to every rule in society's book.

If people doubted my sanity when I announced I was building a boat, they now have no doubts that I should be sectioned immediately. Strangely, once the deed was done, my overwhelming feeling was one of relief. At last I was free to be honest and open about my plans and to focus on achieving them.

An hour later however, there was an unexpected twist. My employer, who to their credit, claimed understanding and acceptance of my reasons for resignation, suggested that a compromise could be reached. The end result is that I have signed a new six months rolling contract to work part-time three days a week. To be honest, it was a bit of a no-brainer, and works well for both parties.

So there we have it. A new chapter commences. I have shifted the balance towards my final goal, and I am free to make the best use of my time, and free to be more open about my plans.

There are some scary times ahead and I'm under no illusions that it will be easy, but as I said, my mind is set and I will get there. If you've read this far, you have my thanks for your interest. Over the next few weeks, I will be working towards the change and I can promise many interesting things ahead for those that choose to follow me.

Remember my chapter about Providence back in Part 2? Here it was at work again. There's no way I could have expected that offer of part-time employment to appear. Providence rewarded me with the best solution.

The rest of the year slipped by with hardly a tap of work on 'Gleda'. I started my 3 day week on 1st November. Up to that point I'd had a company van but now I was going to be without wheels on my off days. I needed to buy a car and it needed to be cheap.

Gail's brother put me onto an old Peugeot 406 diesel estate and I acquired it for the princely sum of £100. It belonged to a dog-owning smoker and the interior was trashed. It took hours of cleaning to get it habitable. But it ran, and the brakes worked now and again, so it did the job.

It took a while to adjust to my new routine. I worked my paid job on Tuesdays, Wednesdays and Thursdays, which meant I got 4-day weekends at each end. The years of evening work on 'Gleda' had taught me something about self-discipline. On 'my' days I'd set an alarm, grab a coffee and climb the loft ladder to my office. I worked hard, immersing myself in the world of affiliate marketing, blogging, and SEO. I set up websites, bought domains, took courses. By December I was getting clearer about the direction I wanted to go, and set an ambitious plan for 2010.

1. To become self-sufficient financially.
2. To create more build time and more flexibility to work when it suits me.
3. To significantly advance the build with a view to getting 'Gleda' on the water in summer 2011.

Clear goals, clear intent. Would they be enough?

2010 YEAR FOUR (246HRS) - DOING IT FOR MYSELF

$\mathcal{I}$ started 2010 energised and committed, but it wasn't easy.

I'd made some difficult decisions and I was paying the price. My salary had gone down substantially. I now had to run a car and pay for fuel. I spent a lot of time on my own. On my paid work days it was just me in the van driving. On 'my' days, it was me in the loft sat in front of the computer.

On days when things didn't go well it was easy for the doubts to crowd in, and I got scared. But I'd forgotten something. I'd committed.

Providence once again provided.

In February I got an email from Alison. She'd sold the house in Appleby, she had a cheque to the value of my share waiting for me. It'd been nearly four years since we'd parted. She'd been sending me occasional small payments as and when she could afford it. But this was different. This was to be the last. It wasn't a huge amount but it was fair. She'd put much more into the place than I had, and she'd got Jamie to look after.

I drove up to see her a few nights later. It was tough. I'd driven that same route so many times, happy to be heading home. Junction 11 of the M42 motorway. It doesn't sound like somewhere with emotional ties does it? But for me, it was and still is. The villages of Austrey, Appleby Magna and Overseal. The Church where Paula and I got married. Homes where I'd once been happy. So many memories. All within a stone's throw of that motorway junction.

It was tough for another reason as well. I knew this would probably be the last time I saw Alison. She'd deceived me once but now she'd been true to her word. That money was going to make a big difference to me. I should have driven away feeling elated. I didn't.

With my immediate financial worries over I was able to make some changes.

My first move was a sensible one. I paid off my credit card debt. Monthly minimum payments had been part of my life for decades. It felt good to rid myself of the shackles and cut up the card.

My second move wasn't so sensible, but I reckoned I deserved a treat. My £100 Peugeot had proven good value for money. But now the radiator was leaking and frankly, the novelty of driving a shed around had long since worn off. So I bought an old Land Rover.

I'd loved the SWB Series III I'd had when I was with Paula, and had always hankered after a Defender. Within a few weeks, I had one. Big wheels, chunky tyres, snorkel, bull bar, roof rack. And fitted with an upgraded Discovery engine. I loved it.

I'd done some math and worked out that I now had enough of a cushion to take another risk. I could quit working for Instarmac completely.

After my months of experimenting and learning, I'd started a little business called 'Website Voodoo'. I now knew enough about building websites, keyword research and search engine optimisation to offer it as a service to small businesses.

Working for myself, free to work my own hours, more free time to work on 'Gleda'. No more charging around the country dealing with all that crap. It was an easy decision to make.

So in March, I gave notice. They were a good crowd. I'd not been there long, but they gave me a nice send-off, a cake and a gift.

During April I adjusted to my new found freedom. I revamped the 'Gleda' Project website. Cleared out the barn ready to work again and checked my stocks of epoxy and timber. I also gave the Landy its first proper run on a trip down to the Beaulieu Boat Jumble on the South Coast. Best buy being six portlights for the hull sides.

April 28, 2010 - Properly Back

It's been ten months to the day since I clocked up my last work on the boat, I find it hard to comprehend. If anyone had told me at the start of this project that I'd make no progress on the boat for ten months I'd have ridiculed them. But it's happened and now it's history. It's been a tough ten months but I've pushed through. And now I'm back stronger than before and raring to get things moving.

My first major job was constructing the curved sandwich decks for the cabin tops. It got me back into practice mixing epoxy. Each of the four curved sections required 16 x 200 g batches of various combinations of epoxy, silicell and micro balloons.

I was relishing the flexibility of my new working lifestyle. On days when I found myself struggling to be productive at my desk, I was able to switch off and head up to the barn to work with my hands instead of my head. Other days I did the opposite.

I guess I've always been a Jack of all trades. There are other descriptions; a Renaissance Man, Polymath, Multipotentialite.

I'm proud of that. Jacks (and Jills) of all trades get bad press. Folks forget the full rhyme goes like this:

"Jack of all trades, master of none, though ofttimes better than master of one!"

I believe that being multi-skilled, innovative, knowledge-seeking, exploratory, and multi-purposeful is a good thing.

The "Dean of science fiction writers" Robert A. Heinlein once said:

> "A human being should be able to change a diaper, plan an invasion, butcher a hog, conn a ship, design a building, write a sonnet, balance accounts, build a wall, set a bone, comfort the dying, take orders, give orders, cooperate, act alone, solve equations, analyse a new problem, pitch manure, program a computer, cook a tasty meal, fight efficiently, die gallantly. Specialisation is for insects."

I agree.

June 20, 2010 - More Tiki 38's On The Water!

Hi all, I'm back after a super relaxing break in Portugal, and now I must pay the price! So much work to do over the next few months I don't know where to start! It's been all go elsewhere in the Tiki 38 world over the past few weeks.

Martin Hivon now has 'Al Raso' on the water, and there are some great photos on his website. Also, in the past couple of days, Jacques Pierret has launched 'Pilgrim'. Jacques has worked for 5 years with a small budget to get 'Pilgrim' built, and I feel a close affinity with him. These guys have set a fine example of what is possible and I'm proud to follow in their footsteps. Another notable event is the departure of 'Aluna' from Hawaii, bound for the Polynesian Islands, fair winds to Beat and Beatrix.

June and July saw my focus switch more towards my new business. Having seen how blogging could attract an audience and eventually be monetised I set up a new website called 'DreamToSail.com' and set to work. This was to be the first of many such ventures, none of which proved successful. It was a lesson I'd learn the hard way. You have to fail many times before success comes along.

July 1, 2010 - Hectic Hot & Happy

The last two weeks have been two of the most intense weeks I've experienced in a long time. But at the same time, they've been incredibly satisfying. Because the intensity has been entirely self-driven and that's something I've rarely experienced.

I was determined to regain ground after our fantastic holiday in Portugal, and so I've been entirely focused on my business. As always I have pangs of conscience that I'm not making progress with the build. But then, as always, I remind myself that I'm still working on the project, and without the business, there will be no boat. That said I'm coming round to the idea that I should schedule a minimum of build time in every week and stick to it. Not only will I feel easier about building progress, but the enforced change will probably make me more productive at my desk.

Despite these niggles though I am happier than at any time since I started the project, and confident about the future. Today I started construction of the second large section of the main cabin roof. I also spent a bit of time playing with the fit of the completed one over the starboard main cabin. Pleasingly it dropped into place really well. It was immensely satisfying to see how well the curved deck section married up to the curved top of the main bulkhead I fitted so many months ago.

July 29, 2010 - Time & Tumblehomes

It's happened again. A little over two weeks just disappeared without a tap done on the boat. I can look back and say it was unavoidable. We went down to Cornwall for a few days, I was busy working on my business etc. And it's all true. But the reality is that it keeps happening, and if it keeps happening then my launch date will keep getting pushed further and further away. I'm not going to let that happen.

To be honest this time management issue affects everything. I have 5 important areas of my life I need to keep making progress with, and 'Gleda' is just one of them. So I've made some changes and from now on I've scheduled at least 2 full days a week on 'Gleda', with some extra flexible time available as well. This means I should be able to make some steady progress from here on in

I'll let my blog posts tell the story of the rest of 2010

August 3, 2010 - Half Tumblehomes Down

A six-hour session today. I cracked on with final fit and glueing of the tumblehomes on the starboard hull. All went relatively painlessly apart from one. It got away from me as I was offering it up and in trying to catch it I got epoxy mix on my arm, neck and forehead. I don't recommend this as acetone isn't the ideal thing to wash with!

August 5, 2010 - Worn Out

I put in a 7 hour day today and feel like I made some really good progress. But I'm worn out tonight, as is my belt sander, which finally gave up the ghost today after many many hours of use. It's an indication of the scale of work involved with a project like this that you wear out decent power tools before it's finished

August 13, 2010 - Tumblehome Saga Ending

Unbelievably it's been over a year since I started construction of the tumblehomes. Talk about dragging a job out!

Today though I re-cut and re-fitted the ones on the port hull and they are now ready to glue. It was all relatively painless and if I'd known then what I know now I wouldn't have wasted so much time. But there's no point moaning, they're nearly done now and I can move on to more exciting things.

Despite being on my own today I managed to manhandle the completed cabin deck section down onto the floor so that I could sand it and get the first coat of epoxy on.

If I can keep this pace up I should have both deck sections glued in place next week and I can make a start on the raised doghouse sides.

August 21, 2010 - Building Workout

The weather has been lousy today, very heavy cloud and regular heavy rain. The temperature was high though and very humid with it. I put in a seven-hour session and I think I'm going to pay for it later! Seven hours of climbing up and down step ladders, clambering around, in and on the hulls. Handling heavy power tools and general lifting. It's definitely a good workout.

August 23, 2010 - Annoying Little Mistake

Notwithstanding my planned day of rest on Sunday I did nip up to the barn. I had the intention of whipping out the 40 or so temporary screws I'd used to hold the two half round cabin roof/tumblehome strips in place. A 5-minute job that, I thought, wrong!

I soon discovered that the small screws I'd used were quite soft and as soon as I tried to remove them they just rounded out. A stupid little mistake that's cost me two hours today. I did manage to get about half of them out using a perfectly fitting pozidrive and a lot of pressure. But the others required a bit of clearance chiselling around the head and then a vice grip wrench to twist them out.

Just one of those annoying things that knock you back occasionally, but they're out now and I shan't make the same mistake on the other two edges!

September 8, 2010 - A Measured Approach

I'm very pleased to say that my business venture is beginning to gain some momentum. But as a consequence build time is being squeezed yet again. I've learned not to get too stressed though as I now consider my business activities to be as much a part of the project as the actual building. This is a concept that's taken some time to get to grips with after so many years of treating work as a hindrance! I'm finalising plans to bring the two things together on the web as well. I've had a couple of false starts with 'Affiliate Afloat' and 'Dream To Sail'. But I'm going to make it third time lucky.

September 29, 2010 - Closed In

There's a phrase that cropped up in my Internet Marketing activities recently - 'Celebrate Small Victories'. Well, today I'm celebrating the small victory of having gotten the starboard hull enclosed. I can now officially do things like 'go down below','sit in the companionway, and 'go up on deck'. Blimey, I've almost got a boat!

October 7, 2010 - Milestone Reached

After a good nights sleep I was feeling a bit better today so I pushed on and did what I'd planned to do, and got the final cabin side cut and glued in place. It's been a long time coming but I now have two hulls structurally complete.

Now I'm not about to get carried away just yet. Make no mistake there is still a huge amount of work to do. That's before I even start thinking about beams, deck, deck pod etc. There are miles of filleting to do. Not to mention glass reinforcing all the joints. And then the monumental task of sheathing, fairing and painting. After that, hatch work, portlights, ventilation, rubbing strakes.

Nonetheless, I'm still marking today as a significant milestone. Starting with a couple of pieces of 18 mm plywood in an empty barn two months *shy of four years ago, I've created something (well two things actually)! of substance. Three dimensional, strong and, to my eyes at least, beautiful.*

Whilst being under no illusions about what's left to do I feel incredibly optimistic and excited about the remaining time I have left. It's going to be a long run home but I really feel like I'm over the hardest time. I have my target and nothing is going to stop me reaching it, nothing!

I have my boat and she will be on the water in just over 18 months time.

I shot a video to celebrate this milestone. You can see it on YouTube HERE if your device is connected. Or search YouTube for 'Gleda Update Oct 2010'

October 17, 2010 - Dog Pile Day

A three-hour session today and I've accomplished next to nothing.

I started with plans to get the glass taping finished on the forward section of the starboard hull, but I ended up going backwards. I really should have known better than to try and glass into a sharp internal and external corner at the same time. (that's what shape the lower part of the hull side stringer to hull joint is).

But I tried anyway. And spent a ridiculous amount of time stippling, rolling with my new metal glassing roller, pushing with a rubber squeegee. Only to see the glass bubble up away from the edge almost instantly. I decided to wait a little while until the resin had gone tackier, thinking it would grab better. So while I waited I went and made a cuppa and drank it in the nice sunshine coming in at the opposite end of the barn from where I was working.

When I went back to try again the whole strip of wetted out tape had fallen off and was crumpled on the floor amongst the sawdust and leaves.

Suffice it to say that my anger management skill was sorely tested. Some days things just don't go right. It's easy to start imagining there's someone out to get you. I also banged my knee and got my hand covered in wet resin when my glove split!

Now whilst I'll fight tooth and nail if I have to, there comes a point where tactical retreat is the best option. So I just mixed up some filled resin. Made a small fillet underneath the stringer to take away the sharp angle, something I should have done before I started. Then left to do something more constructive.

I'm annoyed because build time is precious right now. And next week already looks really busy for me. So I know I'm not going to get much done. But there's no point making a meal out of it, we all have days like this and tomorrow's a new day.

I didn't know it at the time but that was to be the last blog post I made that year.

Autumn was already closing in. My paid and unpaid work was piling up. Something had to give and it was work on 'Gleda' that suffered.

In hindsight, I wasted a lot of time and money in 2010. The previous year it had been matters outside my control that had hindered the build. In 2010 I had no such hindrances. My time was my own, money wasn't an issue. I should have focused 100% on 'Gleda'.

But I was in completely new territory and I wasn't equipped to deal with it. I wasn't equipped to deal with money in the bank and I wasn't equipped to deal with time on my hands. I let myself get distracted by shiny new things, and fooled myself into thinking I was investing in the future. I worked hard, but I worked stupid.

It took me years to realise that just because something feels like 'work', it doesn't mean that you're being productive.

It's so easy to spend hours, days, weeks, years, doing things that bring you nothing of worth.

It's clear to me now.

My work on 'Gleda' was undoubtedly worth my time. My 'work' away from 'Gleda' was not.

The last two months of 2010 flew past. I was pleased not to be working in the barn during December. It went down as the coldest in the UK since the 1600s.

The Landy came into its own getting us through the snow down to Cornwall so that Gail and I could take a Christmas and New Year break. Then 2011 arrived. And it arrived like a hurricane.

2011 YEAR FIVE (46HRS) - A PHILOSOPHICAL APPROACH

*R*emember that the chapter headings show the number of hours actually spent working on 'Gleda' that year? Well, that piddly little number above shows clearly that 2011 was a bad year for the build. There was a lot going on.

The January weather in 2011 was typical for a UK winter. Temperatures just above freezing, bitter wind, heavy cloud and steady rain or sleet.

Work at the barn was plodding along, slowly. But life was about to stop it completely.

January 6, 2011 - Where Did The Day Go?

I'd planned to carry on with my cleanup today but instead had one of those days where events conspired to keep me chained to the desk.

This is not a habit I intend to get into again. I was sorely tempted to be bloody-minded, stick to my plan and go anyway. But the sensible thing was to stay put, keep grafting and thereby get ahead of the game so that I can put some extra time in tomorrow without stressing.

There's no doubt that just sitting down and doing your work is immensely rewarding, and that's exactly what I did today.

I've recently re-read a brilliant book by Steven Pressfield called 'The War of Art'. I'd highly recommend it to anyone, who like me, suffers from procrastination and resistance to doing what most needs doing. I have a quote from the book stuck to the wall next to my computer monitor and it goes like this:

> Never forget. This very moment. We can change our lives. There never was a moment, and never will be, when we are without the power to alter our destiny. This second, we can turn the tables on Resistance. This second, we can sit down and do our work

I was a sucker for stuff like this. When I was feeling down I could spend hours seeking motivation, solace, solutions.

My blog posts for early January reflect that.

January 8th, 2011 - Think Less Feel More

Although I don't have a television I do like to watch the occasional selected program via the Internet when I feel like being entertained.

Last night I watched the first in a new series on the BBC in which the adventurer Bruce Parry is exploring the Arctic. In this episode, he visited remote tribes in the Sakha region of Siberia within the Arctic Circle.

He arrived during the summer Solstice. Hoping to experience the intense spiritual link these people have with nature and in particular the Sun. Apparently, this is the part of the world where the word 'Shaman' originated.

He met one by the name of Kulan who invited him to join everyone at the Welcoming of The Sun ceremony to herald the sunrise on the first day of summer (3.30 am that far north).

All the townsfolk stood with their arms outstretched towards the Sun. As the Shaman played a Vargan Mouth Harp, an instrument like a Jews Harp but far more expressive.

It was fascinating to watch and Bruce was obviously very taken with the Shaman and his outlook on life. When it was time for Bruce to leave, he asked Kulan if he had any words of advice to help him on his travels. He received this reply:

> *"Try to think less and feel more. Try to ignore the endless barrage of information. Try and experience the here and now. Just as you and I are sitting here together we can feel the wind. We feel alive, we can feel our heartbeat, nature is all around us and it is summer".*

Wow! What incredibly wise words. Even more so coming from a guy living in a small village in a sparsely populated Siberia. Endless barrage of information? He has no idea!

His words really struck home with me though. Because one of the things I decided to change whilst undergoing my digital cleanse in Cornwall was to restrict my intake of information.

I've stopped watching the news. Cut right back on the blogs I read, I've eliminated aimless web surfing completely, and I'm reading random stuff far less. To be fair this wasn't entirely my own idea.

Whilst away I re-read Tim Ferriss's Four Hour Work Week in which he talks about the 'low information diet, freeing up more time and space for the important stuff.

Anyway, the point I wanted to make here is that those Shamanic words of wisdom sum up perfectly one of my goals for 2011. And whilst it's a real challenge right now I can imagine that feeling the wind, feeling alive, experiencing nature all around will be far easier on the deck of a Tiki 38 out on the ocean, and yes, it will be summer.

And another

January 11th, 2011 - Free Writing

No time spent at the barn today as I needed to spend time at my desk. Being without my Landy has necessitated the rearrangement of some meetings and changed the priorities on projects. So basically my planned week has gone tits up.

I have one meeting in the morning (the client is picking me up). And then when I get back I'm going to the barn come hell or high water. I'm not letting excuses get in the way of build time this year come what may.

I did take some time out today to think about the 'Gleda' Project as a whole. And to try and analyse why I've found it so hard to keep on track both with the build and with creating my business.

I'm using a technique I discovered last year called 'Free writing'. Basically, you set a timer and just dump your thoughts onto paper or keyboard. You do this without stopping or editing. No grammar or spelling correction as you go. And if you come to a point where your thoughts stop momentarily. And you can't think what to write, you keep scrawling or typing even if it's complete gobbledegook. The idea is that by doing this your brain is sent a clear message that you're serious about this writing. And it had better start working!

I have to say I was sceptical when I first tried it. But it really does work, and it's surprising what you find out about yourself by doing it.

Oh, and I forgot another very important aspect of the process. When your timer goes off (I use 30-minute blocks). You save the file, shut the notebook, put the writing out of sight or whatever, and forget about it for at least 24 hours. When you come back and re-read it later you'll be seeing it with fresh eyes. It's amazing what a difference that makes.

If you are writing creatively you can then edit and correct as you wish. If you've just dumped your thoughts you can throw it in the bin. It's up to you. Either way, the result is a far better piece of writing and/or clearer thoughts.

I've fallen off the wagon many times since I wrote those posts. But I still restrict my passive consumption of media, and I still free write. They are good habits to adopt.

Back then I needed all the help I could get on the motivation front. My Landy blew its transfer gearbox and I was back cycling to and from the barn whatever the weather. There was no point moaning. I even started getting some masochistic pleasure from it. Freewheeling down a steep lane more akin to a fast flowing stream than a hard surfaced road. At 25mph everything below my waist got pressure washed.

All in all, I was feeling optimistic and happy. I was productive in the barn, productive in my home office and productive at my paid job.

I was learning and improving.

One of the experiments I tried was changing to a stand-up desk at home. I'd read about the benefits and it seemed crazy enough to try.

So I decided to knock up a sort of 'coffee table' affair. It was 12" high and sat on top of my desk bringing the work surface up to the optimal height for my towering 5' 6". I also made a mini version 6" high which brought my Apple Cinema screen up to eye level. I'd read that there's a subconscious connection between sitting and 'relaxing'. Which makes it all too easy to slouch, lose concentration and become drowsy when sitting. Standing breaks that connection. Do a bit of research and you'll discover some famous and productive people used a stand-up desk. It really does work.

I was settling into a new way of work in more ways than one. Everything seemed to be settling down. But surprise surprise, it wasn't to last.

January 23, 2011 - Cutting Free of The Puppeteers

Yesterday I had two reminders of how easily we can fall victim to the myth of security. First, my girlfriend Gail received a call from her landlady. She told her that the house she'd been renting for nearly eight years was to be sold. Gail was upset, she always knew that it might happen someday. But she put it to the back of her mind and carried on day to day, living her life and taking the roof over her head for granted.

Now she had suddenly been told that the place in which she felt safe and secure, 'her home', was to be taken away. To be fair her landlady had wanted to tell Gail face to face and she is not rushing things through. Nonetheless the change has to be made and Gail has now been forced to think about making a fresh start elsewhere.

It will take a few days for the shock to fade. But I know she is strong and will soon see this as a fantastic opportunity. One that fits perfectly with other changes she has been working towards for some months now. I'll help her all I can.

The second reminder came earlier in the day. Gail was telling me about how the husband of one of her friends was having a tough time at work. He'd been told by his boss 'they wanted him out'. To add insult to injury he was also left in no doubt that they wanted to avoid paying redundancy. They simply intended to make his life hell until he quit.

It's shameful but sadly not unusual. Up until that point, the individual concerned had been working away 9-5 never really imagining such a thing could happen to him.

Now, whilst I'm living in a rental property at the moment. I've been planning a way out for some time now. I like the place. It serves its purpose. But not a day goes by when I don't remind myself that it's not mine, I'm a tenant, someone else has control.

Of the many changes I've gone through this past couple of years the most important one relates to this issue of control. It was actions by others that resulted in me being alone and depressed six years ago. It was actions by others that got me angry enough to start thinking of alternatives. And it was actions by others that forced me into making decisions I was avoiding.

Looking back I now realise that despite fooling myself otherwise up until 2 years ago, my life was being controlled by others. By individuals and institutions with the power to make significant changes to my life. At the drop of a hat and without care or consequence. I now find it unbelievable that I allowed it to happen, and yet it's the norm for most people. We're brought up to accept that there will always be a 'they' who can tell us what to do and when to do it. Why do we think that's acceptable? Is it fear? It's far easier to blame someone else when dealt a poor hand, far easier to be a victim. The hard road is to take responsibility, refuse to accept delegation of our lives and make our own decisions.

For me personally, something fundamental has changed. After the best part of half a century of taking the route of least resistance I know that I'll never do it again. Even if I make a complete hash of things, I'll be living under a hedge before I'd go back to a 'job'. But that's not going to happen. Because although I don't have any particular talent or ability. I now have something far more important. Something that eluded me for years, I'm in complete control of my life. To quote my favourite songwriter Steve Earle:

"Right or wrong, win or lose, it's all up to you"

January 26, 2011 - Life's Like a Box of Chocolates

I was obviously tempting fate yesterday when I said I was determined to get some build time in every day. My girlfriend Gail, who had been ill for a couple of days with what we thought was a stomach bug, was taken to hospital with suspected appendicitis. In fact, I'm writing this in the hospital waiting room waiting for her to come out of surgery (UPDATE - one very inflamed appendix removed)

These events combined with essential business tasks mean I've done nothing today. I'm not stressing about it though, because these things will happen now and again and I need to be here for Gail. It's only the entirely self-imposed procrastination and failure to organise that I'm desperate to avoid.

January 27, 2011 - How's It looking?

Well, January has almost run its course and so I thought now was a good time to review how the New Year has gone so far. Here are the main points in no particular order:

1. *The weather has been cold, dark and miserable*
2. *The Land Rover blew its gearbox and cost me £600*
3. *Then it needed a service and an MOT and some brake pads so I had to lay out another £400*
4. *While the Landy was off the road I had to cycle miles in the cold and rain because the garage didn't have a courtesy car*
5. *My business accounts for last year show a considerable loss*
6. *Several 'hot' prospects for business have gone distinctly 'cold'*
7. *My girlfriend had an emergency operation for appendicitis and will be off work for weeks*
8. *My girlfriend was also given notice to vacate the house she'd been living in for 8 years*
9. *I'm going to have to move to a bigger more expensive house so that she has somewhere to live*
10. *I haven't been able to spend as much time on 'Gleda' as I wanted*
11. *I can't afford the epoxy supplies I need for the next stage of the build*
12. *I nearly sliced the top of my thumb off today*

13. *Money is going out far quicker than it's coming in*
14. *I'm working harder than I've ever done in my life*

Get the gist? I think I have every right to feel aggrieved. I came back from a fantastic Christmas break in Cornwall, all fired up to make 2011 my best year ever. Now look what's happened. The Gods have conspired to throw all this crap at me. I should have expected it, nothing ever goes right, it always happens to me, what's the point? I might as well just give up now, I'm never going to succeed in anything anyway.

STOP!

OK. that's probably how I would have felt a few years ago. But here's how I actually feel.

1. *It's January in the UK what else is it going to be? We're past the solstice and summer's coming.*
2. *I now have a faster, more economic Landy because I took the opportunity to upgrade to a Discovery gearbox with better ratios*
3. *The Landy is running sweet and is set for the rest of the year*
4. *I'm fitter for all that cycling and screaming through big puddles with the wind in my face was fun!*
5. *Most of the loss is what the company owes me!*
6. *They've been replaced with hotter ones*
7. *The problem was diagnosed quickly and she's recovering well*
8. *The time is right to move on and start afresh*
9. *It's the cottage next door, sunnier patio, room for guests to stay and we get to live together :)*
10. *Still done well though, and progress is being made*
11. *But if I absolutely need them I have a credit card*
12. *I didn't slice it all the way through*
13. *I'm working hard on a plan to reverse that big time!*
14. *And it's great because I'm working for me!*

Strange isn't it? What brings about the shift in a persons mind that allows them to see the positive rather than the negative?

I don't think anyone on the outside can do it. In fact the more a negatively minded individual gets told to 'cheer up'. Or in the words of Eric Idle, 'Look on the bright side of life' the more they are likely to do the opposite.

No, I think it has to come from the inside. Some gradual realisation that playing the victim, blaming everything and everyone for your misfortunes will ultimately destroy you. I thank the Universe that I've made that shift, it took years to happen but I believe it's now irreversible.

Whatever life throws at me now I can't be knocked down, well maybe I can, but I'll damn well just get up again. I will succeed, 2011 will be a great year, just you wait and see. For those that can't ever see that positive shift coming. I can only offer myself as proof of the possibility, I'm not special. I'm not gifted. I'm just a guy who hung in there until the sun came out again.

So do the same, hang on, survive. Do something, and I guarantee that good things will just start appearing. And once that happens you're never going to look back. Trust me I'm a boatbuilder!

Back then I was changing. I'm writing these words seven years later. I can confirm it was a permanent change

January 29, 2011 - Under Pressure

I said a few days ago that I'd been tempting fate with my determination to make some progress with 'Gleda' every day. Well, boy, did fate respond!

There have been two significant events this week that have brought about new demands on my time. Both necessitated 'Gleda' being put on hold for a couple of weeks at least.

Firstly finding somewhere for Gail and I to live. It looked like we were in

for a difficult hunt. Rental property in this area is in high demand, and it's in short supply. We have some severe financial limitations hindering the options. As luck would have it though, the larger two bedroomed cottage next to mine had been vacated a couple of weeks ago. And, with some prompt action by me, and an accommodating landlord, I've been able to secure the rental by the skin of my teeth. It's a great relief. And we're both really looking forward to moving in together and starting afresh. It's another example of how something that at first appeared unwanted and negative, has, in fact, pushed us into making changes that will make life a bit easier. And I'm sure it will make us both happier. So over the next few weeks I'll be moving all my stuff next door, and wading through all the paperwork to change address and utilities etc. Then once that's sorted, making a start on Gail's place.

Which leads to the second time suck!. Gail is recovering well from her operation and hopefully will be out of the hospital in a few days. But her recuperation will take 4-6 weeks. During which time she'll be unable to drive and certainly won't be able to lift anything! She'll be staying with her mother for the first few weeks at least, and that means a longer drive for me to go visit. It also means that she's going to need a lot of help to sort out, pack and move her stuff, and there's a lot of it! Let's just say that a major de-clutter was well overdue!

Added to these two little tasks is the ever more urgent need to increase my income. My business is beginning to grow, but I need to do more, particularly now that my day to day expenses are increasing. I'm working hard on two sides of my business at the moment. Website Voodoo is the 'public' face of my company. I'm providing Internet Marketing Services to small and medium businesses, with particular emphasis on Keyword/Market Research, Google Places and SEO. My primary lead generation vehicle is Business Networking. It's effective but time-consuming. As is the work that results from it. But it is my best income generator at the moment and will continue to be so for the next year at least.

Behind the scenes, I am also starting to build up my website and domain trading business Webmark Trading. This will be my long-term asset builder and income source, and it's the area of online business I most enjoy. It's absolutely essential that I dedicate enough time to this to keep it moving forward, as my aim is to start winding down Website Voodoo in 12-18 months so that I can replace time-consuming income generation with this lower demand higher reward business. Then I can start moving closer to the lifestyle laid out in the 4 Hour Work Week I've dreamed about for so long!

As regular readers will have spotted I've made a concerted effort to write something on this blog every day, and I will continue to do so. I've found that trying to separate different parts of my life into different blogs simply didn't work. The 'Gleda' Project is my life, and as I've said many times before, it's not about building a boat. It's about creating a better life.

It just so happens that for me building 'Gleda' has been the key to making huge changes. Changes that have made me happier, healthier and more excited about the future than I've ever been. Because of that, I feel that all my experiences outside of the build are vital to the understanding of who I am and why I'm doing what I'm doing. I truly hope that those that have followed me thus far will agree. And to those that are simply interested in building boats, I apologise.

But I will continue to write from my heart. And although a lot of it will be of little interest to others. I truly hope that some of it might amuse, educate and inspire. Either way, I'll keep it coming.

January 31, 2011 - Hidden Strength & Gratitude.

The events of this last week have been unwanted without a doubt. But as I've written before, what a difference the right attitude can make to the impact these inevitable events have on our lives. I wanted to explore a bit more and try to understand what it is that's going on here.

The way we treat these events is not just a case of forcing the mind to think and act positively. But rather nearer to something waking up inside us that we didn't really know was there. Something that was hidden inside with the capacity to boost our mental and physical abilities.

I suppose it's not unlike the stories you hear about ordinary folks lifting a car off its wheels to free a trapped child or something. It's a trigger that instantly removes all negativity and previously entrenched beliefs. It makes anything possible.

For nearly a week now I've been working at a pace that I simply couldn't have sustained before. Why is that?

Well, there are deadlines to be met for sure but aren't there always? I need to earn a living, I need to pack everything ready for moving house on Sunday, I have a hundred things on my task list. Some of these things are exceptional, but even when there was important work to be done before, I still managed to procrastinate. So what's different?

Why is it that although I'm tired, I don't stop to think about it? I just plough on with the next thing on the list. If I sit down for a minute and start to drift, I instantly snap out of it, start moving again and get working.

Previously I'd probably have nodded off. Personally, I think being forced to face up to the fact that being able to work hard, eat well, and make choices can't be taken for granted. As I've seen this week things can be turned upside down in just a few days, and it could happen to any of us at any time. That thought instils a greater sense of urgency to the work, a greater desire not to waste precious time, a greater need to 'ship'.

I'm not suggesting we should dwell on the fact. That would be damaging. But equally, it's something that should perhaps be remembered first thing in the morning or last thing at night. Because we can then give thanks that we are free to choose, free to work, able to make things happen. I'm certainly going to make sure I never forget it, because then I can't fail to try and make the most of every day.

February 2, 2011 - Worried, Angry & Powerless

I'm going to get into some personal stuff here as I've given fair warning I would. This is my personal blog and my writing has to be a true reflection of my feelings or it becomes worthless. When things happen in my life I feel the need to write about them. And for over four years now this has been my chosen depository for documenting my life as I work towards my dream.

On that basis I make no apology for writing like this, please feel free to click away now.

As some of you will know my partner Gail had an emergency Appendectomy a week ago. She initially recovered well, but after a couple of days some complications with her bowel appeared. She's been fighting a bit of an uphill battle ever since. We're told it's nothing unusual. We're told there's nothing really amiss. We're told it's just a matter of waiting.

But the worry doesn't go away. So for the past 7 days I've spent a couple of hours each evening visiting the hospital and trying to support Gail as much as possible. But here's the thing. I've been forced to face up to feelings of absolute powerlessness. And something dawned on me this evening. For the past year I've been working at creating an environment where I have a far greater level of choice and control than I've ever had in my life. Despite all the failures, setbacks and financial worries, I've been high on that feeling of control. Of being master of my own destiny, free to choose which path I follow and how I lead my life.

I think that's why I've found this week so hard, because there's nothing I can do that really helps someone I love. I have no choice but to trust that people I've never met are going to do the best job they possibly can. To give Gail the care and attention she needs to make her better.

Now I am in no doubt that there are some good people involved in her care. And I now know some of their faces at least. But the more I visit the more I see signs of a lack of attention to details.

Every night Gail tells me of some little incident where something has been overlooked. Or she had been left to fend for herself. It just adds to the worry. She's fighting a psychological battle to stay positive. But the longer she stays in that ward the harder that battle gets.

Trouble is, I'm just a simple guy with no medical knowledge. I struggle to see how Gail is going to get better when for 7 days she hasn't eaten anything. Hasn't had any decent sleep. Hasn't seen daylight. Has no fresh air. Endures multiple repeated intrusive procedures each day. And, as someone particularly sensitive to personal hygiene and bodily functions, has to be helped by strangers to do these things, and on at least one occasion it seems, begrudgingly.

As if all the above weren't enough she has to suffer acute embarrassment and a lack of respect and understanding. AND THERE'S NOT A DAMN THING I CAN DO ABOUT IT! As the post title says, worried, angry and above all powerless. It's hard to take but it's nothing compared to the suffering of my girl.

To those with loved ones in ill health I send my sympathy. To those lucky enough to be free of such worries, be grateful.

February 5, 2011 - Like Sand Through The Fingers

For Sale: Tiki 31 plans -- unused.

Unused set of plans for the Tiki 31. I bought these at least 15 years ago but never built my dream boat, and now, due to my failing health, I know I never will........

I saw this on the Wharram builders and friends forum today. It struck me as incredibly sad, and led me to start thinking about why it is that most people with a dream never take action and start moving towards it.

I've noticed that a high percentage of members on the WBF site have entered the words 'I want a Wharram' in their profile. I often wonder why more of them don't quickly change into 'I'm building a ....' or, 'I've bought a.....'. The very fact that they have taken the trouble to find the forum and join in, would seem to indicate more than a passing interest. And we all like to passively consume content about things that interest us. But those words 'I want a Wharram' show that they have more than that. Yet it seems only a few actually do something about it.

I'm not being critical, I spent some 20 years kind of thinking about building my own Wharram, but never doing anything about it. It's a common story. So what is it that finally triggers the action and continued commitment needed to start moving forward?

For me, it was a traumatic relationship breakup followed by a period of Depression. It was as simple as waking up one day and thinking, 'Sod this, I've had enough of moping around feeling sorry for myself'. 'What's stopping me building that bloody boat I've been thinking about for so long'?

The strange thing is that at that point in my life I was mentally weak, and poorly equipped to tackle the not insignificant problems. Little details like finding the money, a place to build, the time etc. It's easy to come up with reasons you can't do something, isn't it? There's never a right time. Too young, too old, too busy, no money, the list is endless. It has to be a leap of faith. The one thing that sticks in my mind is finding the barn I'm building in.

I told the story of my search earlier. I kept drawing a blank. It would have been easy to say, 'this is hopeless'. But I didn't. I just kept believing, then out of the blue my phone rang. I recite this story again as an example of the sort of thing that can stop a dream in its tracks. If I'd been 'sensible'. Done thorough research. Talked to lots of people. Made a list of pros and cons. I would have concluded beyond doubt that I didn't stand a chance of finding anywhere in the area at a price I could afford.

This I think is the reason most people never get started on stuff. They spend too long thinking it through. Planning and researching, considering all the potential problems. It's a fine thing to do but it holds a hidden danger. If the project you're thinking about is a big one, your brain simply can't cope with all the possibilities. It's too scary, there are too many unknowns, so it does what the human brain has done for thousands of years, it induces fear. It may be conscious or subconscious, but either way the result is the same, we run away, we find reasons we can't do it, we are paralysed.

Don't end up like our friend who waited 15 years for the right time ,only to find that it had passed him by. The right time is now!

February 11, 2011 - Positivity Or Delusion?

It's probably not the best time to be writing this, as I've just finished a large Chicken Madras with Peshwari Nan and a pint of real ale. But what the heck, this blog is all about me dumping my thoughts, whatever physical or emotional state I'm in. Regular readers must be real gluttons for punishment!

Anyway, here's what's running around my head tonight. Over the past two or three years I've transformed myself. From a pretty depressed pessimist, with zero self-confidence, into an independent confident 'entrepreneur'. (OK that's a bit of a stretch but kind of true). Now I'd like to say that this transformation was carefully planned and perfectly executed. But it wasn't.

As I mentioned in one of my posts a while back, I just woke up one day and thought ,'sod this for a game of soldiers, I need to change things'. It's been a long and expensive road, and yet I have little to show for it apart from my new found confidence and a certain knowledge that I can never go back.

On paper right now things look a bit bleak. The first month and a half of this year have been draining financially and emotionally. My business is not bringing in enough income. And the enforced (albeit welcome) move to a bigger rental property have increased outgoings. So am I depressed? Am I losing sleep wondering how we're going to pay the bills, and how I'm ever going to finish 'Gleda'? Well no, I'm not.

So here's the question I asked in the title of this post, positivity or delusion?

Now I'm guessing that some of you reading this will think it's the latter. But I'd have to disagree. Because everything I've learned over the past few years tells me that there's absolutely no reason why I can't make it. I'm (reasonably) intelligent, I have the tools, I have the knowledge, it's just a matter of applying them. I say 'just', but actually, that's the biggy, that's the thing that stops most people from achieving their goals. We're conditioned to look for excuses, reasons why we can't just knuckle down and do the work. I've battled with those demons for too long, and up to now, it didn't matter because I could get away with it. Not now though, my back's to the wall, and there's only one thing to do, crack on and make things happen.

As for delusion. Well, the only people who will really think I'm delusional will be those that haven't made it themselves, who let the excuses block the way. They don't want to see anyone else succeed because it'll force them to face up to the truth. So they'll say anything to try and knock me off track. Well they can try but I'm not listening, I've said it already, 2011 is my year, just you see.

March 7, 2011 - News Of Sunshine

Well, here's a turn up for the books. Not only am I writing something for my blog, but I'm doing it sat outside in a T-shirt. Enjoying the gorgeous warm sunshine and, double shock, I'm still at home in the UK! At the risk of being ridiculed for being a typical Brit, always rattling on about the weather. I have to say that the last couple of weeks have been diabolical. Without so much as a hint of sunshine, dull, damp and generally depressing. So I have no feelings of guilt whatsoever. Sitting out here for half an hour and tapping away on the keyboard so as to avoid the accusation of being completely lazy.

Yet again I find myself having to apologise for the lack of blog posts over the past weeks. In my defence, I've been busier than an extremely busy person at a busyness competition. So what's been happening I hear you ask.

Well, firstly I'm very pleased to say that Gail has recovered from her illness, she is back driving and will be back to work next Friday.

Secondly, we have finally got everything moved out of both our rental properties. And we are officially under the same roof and pretty much sorted out. Thirdly my business is picking up due to some concentrated effort on my part. I'm going through a bit of a re-branding exercise and fine-tuning of my services at the moment, and I'll tell you more when that's all done.

This week I'm working hard to catch up with a backlog of client work. And to get everything back under control, so that next week, unbelievable though it might seem. I can get back to a routine that allows me to do some boatbuilding.

It's a real shame I've lost over a month of work on 'Gleda'. But it was completely unavoidable. And I think that in the long run, the changes that have resulted from my messed up February will ultimately be beneficial to the project as a whole. Now all that nonsense is out of the way though, I need to get cracking again and catch up.

As shown by the fact that I'm sitting outside in the sunshine the year is moving on already. The first quarter will be gone in just a few short weeks and I need to maximise my productivity during the spring and summer months. On that vein, I'd better quit rambling now. Pull myself away from this garden chair, and get working at my desk (which by the way is still a stand up one. It works brilliantly for me and I'll never go back to sitting down to work again) it makes sitting in this garden chair even more enjoyable though.

OK, I'm going now, catch you next time!

The rest of March and April passed quickly. Work on 'Gleda' ground to a halt once again. My focus switched to business.

'Website Voodoo'. Client work and early morning networking meetings dominated my time. Not much distracted me. There were a couple of things though.

Over the Easter weekend, Gail and I broke a Guinness World Record. To be fair it wasn't just us. There were several hundred others involved. It happened at a Land Rover charity event called 'Convoy For Heroes' held at the Jaguar Land Rover proving ground at Gaydon, just down the road. The event aimed to break the record for the longest ever convoy of Land Rover vehicles.

It took place to raise money for a charity called 'Help For Heroes' that assisted British servicemen and women injured in combat. It was a huge success and fantastic fun. With flags flying we were one of 348 Land Rovers. Led off by the most famous Landy of all - HUE 166 (affectionally known as HUEY), the very first production vehicle made in 1948. It was an unforgettable experience.

Another unforgettable event comes to mind.

I remember sitting in the lobby of the Kenilworth Holiday Inn one morning early in March pitching a client. Over his shoulder, the television was on. It was impossible to ignore what was being shown. Just off the shores of Japan, a magnitude 9.0 earthquake had triggered a tsunami that reached up to 40 m (133 ft) in height. It hit the coast and rolled up to 10 km (6 miles) inland, pushing all before it. Helicopters were filming it. The broadcast was live. There we were discussing a business website, while on the other side of the world people were losing everything. More than 18,000 people lost their lives. The client seemed unaffected. I made my excuses and left.

Note the date on the blog post below. Nearly two months went past without any more work being done on the boat. I had to make a tough call.

May 2, 2011, - News From The Trenches

Hey there, remember me? I'm the guy building a catamaran.

Except I haven't lifted a saw since the end of January. And I'm the one who used to write stuff here regularly but hasn't written anything for nearly two months.

Truth be told I've been putting the writing off. I could have, should have, written this some weeks ago. But I guess the thought of committing to print what was in my head scared me too much. I needed some time but now, I'm ready.

You see I've made a big decision. I had too, it was the elephant in the room and there was no avoiding it. My long-planned launch date of May 1st, 2012 simply wasn't going to happen, and accepting the fact changed things. Those that have followed this blog over the past four years or so will know that it's called 'The Gleda Project' for a reason. It's never been about building a boat. It wasn't even about going sailing, it was about finding a better life.

This project has affected every single part of who I am and what I do. When I started building four years and four months ago I had no thought that I would start my own business, cut loose from the 9-5 before the boat was even finished. But that's what happened and it seemed natural, it seemed obvious and it felt right.

It's the same with the decision I made a few weeks back. So what have I decided? I've decided to stop the build......for 12 months.

Why? Well, there are many reasons but time and money are at the top of the list.

I've survived my first year in business but only just. I'm a long way away from covering the bills. Even further away from generating enough income to buy the materials I need to finish 'Gleda' and go sailing. I am working all hours on my business, and it's essential that I do. Without the business the project fails and that's simply not going to happen.

I came to realise that trying to divide my time between the business and the boat just wasn't working. Neither of them were getting the attention they needed and it was stressing me out. To carry on down that path was leading to the risk of double failure.

So a choice had to be made, and actually, there could only be one winner because without the business, without the income, the other won't happen. Why a year? Well, I needed to create some defined space. A realistic period of time to get where I need to be, and a year seemed right. It fits with that quotation I've had pinned by my desk for quite a while now, but up to now haven't actioned, it says:

If you're willing to do for a year what others won't, you can do for a lifetime what others CAN'T

So the clock is reset, the launch is now 1st May 2013. It is as it is, and the next twelve months are going to set me up for life. I hope you'll stick around for the ride.

Six months passed in a new routine of networking meetings, website building, client meetings and more.

While I was grinding away, Jacques Pierret and his crew sailed his Tiki 38 'Pilgrim' across the Atlantic from New Jersey to Marseilles. I was beginning to doubt 'Gleda' would ever see salt water.

November 13, 2011 - Out Of The Mists

You could be forgiven dear reader for thinking that the 'Gleda' Project had gone the way of so many grand ideas. Neglected and forgotten. Lying crushed beneath the relentless pressure of living a conventional life. Another pipe dream, ethereal, intangible, without substance.

But no, the 'Gleda' Project is not a pipe dream, it's physical, real, and very much alive. The 'Gleda' project is me, it's my life, and will remain so whilst I have breath in my body.

I could claim that this apparent neglect was all part of the plan. Just as I said back in May when I told you that I'd made the hard decision to take a year away from the build to focus on my business. Still part of the project of course. But nonetheless, an action that could be considered as the thin end of the wedge. One that would ultimately lead to the end of my dream.

So what has been my reward for these months of inactivity? Well, not what I had hoped for, but looking back I realise now that my aim was off. Financially I'm still living hand to mouth. There have been times when I was just a few days away from being in real difficulties. But I've scraped through. And I'm very optimistic about the next few months and next year in general. But as things stand today, from a financial point of view, my time away has been wasted.

But there's more to it than that. These past months have taught me some valuable lessons. They've given me space to step back a bit. Get to know myself better, to become clearer on the direction I need to go. And now I feel ready to get back into the race and really kick on. If there is anybody out there still paying me an occasional visit, I thank you for your patience.

I promise that your faith will be rewarded with regular and, I hope, interesting posts from this day forth. I look forward to sharing my onward journey.

Before I go I must pay homage to Beat and Beatriz on the Tiki 38 'Aluna'. Beat has been posting beautifully written articles whenever they get access to an internet connection, as they cruise around the Polynesian Islands. For me these occasional postings can be likened to glorious bursts of sunshine breaking through the clouds of a dull day. I leave you with a passage from his latest offering.

> *Before nightfall we were back on Aluna's spacious deck staring at yet another blood-red sunset. Soon the sparkling stars sprinkled their twinkles across the firmament. Staring down at us seafaring earthlings*

from their trillion and one little lighted homes in the mysterious depths
of space. Soothing sweet slumber awaited us under a light bed sheet.
Ruffled slightly by the tropical breeze. Within the plywood-lined womb
of our streamlined ocean-ploughing vessel

Now tell me that doesn't constitute inspiration.

2011 was a bad year for the build, but a hugely important one for me personally. My last blog post of the year shows how much I'd grown.

November 28, 2011 - Impossible Dream?

The end of the year fast approaches. As my thoughts turn to 2012 I'm working harder than ever at getting myself in a position to really move forward with the build.

Looking back on the two years since I quit my full-time job on the corporate hamster wheel, I can take some satisfaction in the fact that I've survived, just.

But at the same time I'm nowhere near where I want to be in terms of income and lifestyle. I knew it would be tough, but I underestimated how tough.

There have been many times when I started to think I'd made a terrible mistake. One that was going to mean 'Gleda' would never be finished. That I'd never achieve my goal of freedom to live life as I please.

But thankfully those times have been few and far between, and now more than ever I'm absolutely convinced that I made the right choice. Apart from which I'm probably unemployable now!

Over the past two years I've learned many lessons and made many mistakes. I'm still learning, but these mistakes have left me far better placed to move forward and create the life I want.

My biggest mistake was to focus entirely on my 'business' and failing to recognise that I was just re-creating a 'job'.

All those years of conditioning left me blind to the fact that I needed to get away from having a life separated into 'work'. i.e the stuff I 'had' to do to earn an income. And 'play'. i.e All the things I do for pleasure and because I want to. To realise in-fact that the only way to be really successful is to merge the two, and in effect get paid to play.

That's where the title of this blog post comes in, because that's an impossible dream right? Well I don't think so, it's taken a while to sink in but now I can see clearly that the world has changed.

When I entered the world of work in the late 60's there really were far fewer opportunities. Our paths were dictated to a great extent by outside factors beyond our control. Our family background, place of birth, education etc.

Today all that has changed. The power of the internet means that we can all educate ourselves on any subject we wish. More importantly, communicate with large numbers of people without social or geographic boundaries. It's unprecedented. It's a Revolution as historic as the Agricultural and Industrial Revolutions that have gone before. We really can be who we want to be, we really can do what we want to do, we just need to shake off the shackles of traditional work practice and start again. I need to find a way to harness these opportunities. For now I'll leave it to my favourite sage Seth Godin to sum up:

> *"When exactly were you brainwashed into believing that the best way to earn a living is to have a job?" "...Acknowledge to yourself that the factory job is dead. Having a factory job is not a natural state. It wasn't at the heart of being human until very recently. We've been culturally brainwashed" . "You have everything you need to build something far bigger than yourself"*

2012 YEAR SIX (456HRS) - A NEW WAY OF WORKING

*J*anuary 7, 2012 - *Twenty Twelve... Wow!*

Well, here we are, the start of another year, the year 2012. Is it just me or does that sound weird? Twenty twelve. It sounds ridiculously futuristic.

Or maybe it's just because this will be my fifty-fifth year on this planet and when I talk about things I've done in the past it now sounds like ancient history. Like over Christmas when I happened to mention that I joined the Navy in 1975, and then realised how long ago that was!

Anyhow here it is another year and, scarily, the beginning of my sixth one building 'Gleda'.

I've always been wary of falling into the trap of 'perpetual building' as many others have done. I've always tried to stay focused on the fact that I was actually a sailor who just so happened to be building a boat. I set out on this journey with a five-year build in mind. Loyal readers may recall that my original launch date was May 1st, 2012.

For reasons documented elsewhere I made the decision to extend that deadline by twelve months in spring last year. My intention was to focus all my time and energy on building a business. One that would finance the completion of the build and cruising funds thereafter. Unfortunately, it hasn't happened. If anything I've gone backwards, and truth be told, at this moment completion and launch of 'Gleda' seem like an impossible dream.

I confess that I've been in a dark place these past months. It'd be easy to succumb to Depression and helplessness, and I have the scars to show how hard I've been fighting. But this New Year has brought new hope. My head is in a much better place, my optimism has returned, and I'll be doing my damnedest to make 2012 the best year of the build yet.

It'll need to be if I'm to reach my target for this time next year. Because by then I want the hulls sheathed and painted. Portlights and hatches installed, and the interiors fitted out well enough that I can live aboard. I also want the beams built, sheathed and painted, so that the boat can be assembled and put on the water if needed.

It's a big ask I know, but if I'm to reach the revised launch date of May 1st, 2013, a year and four months away, it has to happen.

January 21, 2012 - Getting Ready To Work Again

It's been a long time coming but I'm finally moving towards a project re-start. Over the past two weeks, I've been clearing the barn from one end to the other. Getting rid of 4 years worth of accumulated crap. Sorting tools and equipment, making an inventory of my timber and epoxy supplies, and making improvements to the lighting in the barn.

I'd be lying if I said times were good, and the weeks since Christmas have been particularly tough for a number of reasons. But what's important is that I'm working hard and making progress. My next target is to raise sufficient funds to be able to buy my next lot of epoxy by the beginning of February, so that I can get motoring again.

February 12, 2012 - Unexpected Act of Kindness

Shortly after publishing the 'Getting Ready To Work Again' post a few weeks ago I received the following comment. It came from a long time follower of 'Gleda' Eric Dobson. I reproduce it below:

> *Great picture! I don't care if they've been a bit neglected for a while, when I see those hulls ready to receive a dose of love (and epoxy), I see a picture of freedom. Please drop me an email with your PayPal (or preferred method) address. I don't have a lot to spare right now, but it would mean a lot to me to contribute to your epoxy fund. I'd really like to do what I can to help you reach your dreams, while I'm also working to reach my own. Thanks!*

You may imagine my feelings to receive such an offer and, as Eric knows, my initial reaction was to politely decline. But the way that Eric had worded his comments left me feeling that such a refusal would be churlish, and so I wrote a grateful acceptance. Eric's lengthy reply touched me even more, and with his permission, I reproduce some of Eric's words below:

> *I'm so glad my brief comments came across as intended. I just came back from a week in the Dominican Republic. And after seeing the clear blue water and white sand, it was quite easy to imagine 'Gleda' out of the barn and exploring a tropical paradise.*

When I look at that picture, I'm awed by the magnitude of work that has already been accomplished. It's just so incredible to picture... those hulls started from NOTHING and were built, one step at a time, with your own hands. As you said, there are people who can't recognize a dream in progress. But then, there's a small group of us out there who DO see the dreams and the potential. And how it's simply a matter of taking one step at a time until your reality matches your imagination. It's important to me to support such dreams whenever I see them.

After so many years of work, and with so much left still to do, it's easy to lose sight of how far I've come. Easy to fear 'Gleda' will never be finished, easy to lose sight of the dream of sailing. I'm left dumbstruck that someone else, someone so far away. Has been able in just a few sentences, to blow all those doubts away, to remind me what has been achieved and of what is yet to come.

I'm incredibly grateful for the money, but those words are worth far more.

The former has been added to the epoxy fund which is now at a level which will allow me to order fresh supplies this week. The latter will be saved and re-visited every time I get weary and fearful.

Eric you have my eternal gratitude. I very much hope that one day you will be able to join me on 'Gleda' in some tropical paradise. That we may share a drink or two and toast those who turn dreams into reality.

After 18 months of distraction and lack of focus, I had renewed determination at the start of 2012. As mentioned below I even sold my Land Rover, and replaced it with an old Mazda that was a lot cheaper to run. I also sold my hi-spec mountain bike. It was finally beginning to dawn on me that if I was to get this thing done I was going to have to be harder on myself. I had to be all in, I had to commit fully.

February 16, 2012 - Replenished

The combination of a few 'cash in hand' jobs, sale of my beloved Land Rover, and the generosity of others, has allowed me to replenish my stock of epoxy and has put me in a position to get cracking again. The photo shows the materials that arrived today

- 1 x 33 kg Epoxy Resin
- 1 x 9.7 kg Slow Hardener
- 1 x 5 lit Acetone
- 1 x 30 lit Bucket Silica
- 1 x 30 lit Bucket Glass Bubbles
- 1 x 30 lit Bucket Cotton Microfibre

I got very little change from £650 for that lot. But I'm not cutting corners on something as vital to the structural integrity of the boat as this. Now all I need to do is to find some time to put the stuff to good use!

February 23, 2012 - springing Into Action

Shock News! I'm back building a boat!

I can't believe that the work I've done today is the first I've done on the boat for over a year. 25th January 2011 to be precise.

Even more incredible is that what I've done today is pick up a job I originally started on 17th October 2010. A job I gave up on because I couldn't get the glass tape to stay in place!

Ah well, that's all ancient history now. What's important is that I've started again and I will be doing all in my power to ensure that I now keep going until 'Gleda' is launched.

It seemed fortuitous that I'd picked today to re-start as the weather turned out to be amazingly spring like for February. The temperature peaked at 16°C (61°F) which is way above what it should be. Let's hope it's a sign of things to come.

If the weather stays kind it's my plan to continue work on the outside of *the hulls, reinforcing all the structural joints of which there are many. Upper/lower hull, upper hull/deck, beam troughs, deck/cabin tops and more besides. The process involves applying 150 mm (6 in) glass tape to each and every one. I'm using the masking tape method to keep nice neat edges and to be honest, it's fairly straightforward work.*

The joint that caused me the problem back in October 2010 was the one between the upper hull stringer and the hull sides. It's got sharp angles underneath. Which, as I'd discovered, are impossible to get glass tape to stick to.

The building instructions suggest forming an epoxy fillet underneath to smooth the angle. But I decided to speed up the process by ripping down some of my timber stock into triangular fillets that can be glued underneath the stringer. Stronger, better looking and easy to glass over.

I was able to do this because I now have a fully fitted woodworking shop at my disposal, right next door to 'Gleda's' barn. I can't say too much about it right now but it's an exciting development in more ways than one, not least because of the time I'll save cutting timber.

It feels great to be back and I'm excited to be making progress again. I know exactly what I need to do over the next few weeks. I have all the materials I need for some months to come. And I'll be scheduling at least two full days of building every week as we move into spring, so look out for regular updates from now on!

What I hadn't been able to say too much about at the time was that Providence had helped me out again.

Facts had to be faced. I'd spent the best part of 18 months working on my internet business. I'd started from scratch and I'd learned a lot. But despite all the work I'd put in, the reality was that I'd failed to create any sort of viable enterprise.

Blogging, affiliate marketing, domain trading. None had been in any way successful. My website and SEO business 'Website

Voodoo' was generating some income. But at the expense of long hours and a huge investment in dealing with difficult clients.

For many folks with a job for the 'Man', working for yourself sounds like a dream. That's how I'd felt when I quit Instarmac.

I read somewhere that one of the best things about being self-employed is that you get to choose which 18 hours of the day you work.; seven days a week. I'd discovered the truth in that.

The money that Alison had given me 2 years before had gone.

Website Voodoo wasn't bringing in enough to pay the bills, let alone pay me any sort of salary.

On top of that, I had no time to work on 'Gleda'. That's what had been getting me down.

The sale of my Land Rover had given me a bit of a cushion but I was beginning to think that I'd have to go crawling back to the world of employment.

Then one day Richard came round to see me in the barn. Richard, you might remember, was the 'landlord' of my build site.

Manor Farm wasn't a working farm. Richard ran an exhibition design and build company (EDB) out of two big sheds in the yard. I'd done some labouring work for him over the years and he seemed to get involved in all sorts of interesting and exciting projects.

A few months before, I'd help build a giant ramp at the National Indoor Arena in Birmingham. It was part of the track for the World BMX Championships.

Richard told me that he'd just taken on another contract with the British Showjumping Organisation. He was going to be responsible for storage, maintenance, and construction of their complete stock of horse jumps.

To be honest I was fearful that he'd come to tell me that he needed the space, and that I'd got to move 'Gleda' out. That would have been a nightmare. But no, there were two other similar sized barns next door that were going to be cleared out. One would be used for storage. The other was going to be converted to a woodworking shop. He was already on the lookout for a bench saw, a bandsaw, a planer, a lathe etc.

He came to the point. He needed someone to work in it. Jumps would need repairs after every event. New ones would need building. There would be other jobs as well. For some reason, he thought that if I could create a pair of half decent looking boat hulls from a pallet of plywood, then maybe I could cope with building gates and fences. So how did I feel about working two or three days a week for him? Oh, and you can use the woodwork shop yourself anytime you want.

There it was again. A few weeks earlier I'd recommitted with no clear outcome. Once more 'Providence' had rewarded me. I now had:

- Paid work on my own terms.
- Work I'd enjoy doing.
- A workplace right alongside 'Gleda'.
- A fully equipped woodwork shop to use as my own.

Really, you couldn't make it up.

March 2, 2012 - Back In The Swing

I put in a good solid day today and I'm really beginning to enjoy working again. Seeing progress lightens my mood, reminds me what it's all about and leaves me with a warm glow of satisfaction.

My focus for the next few weeks is to get all the hull joints glassed over. By my estimate, that's something in the region of 223 metres (732 feet) of jointing. It all needs to be filled, sanded, masked, epoxied, layed over with 150 mm (6") biaxial glass tape, epoxied again, and finally trimmed.

That's a lot of work, but what keeps me going is that once it's done I can move onto sheathing and then painting!

March 11, 2012 - Cracking Day

I arrived at the barn at 8 this morning expecting to be doing a days work for Richard.

As it turned out that plan changed and I ended up putting in a solid 8 hours on 'Gleda'.

I was pleased, as the last week has been somewhat manic and I was afraid things were slipping again. The weather has been fantastic today, bright sunshine and a very pleasant 16°C. Not at all bad for mid-March.

This served to lighten the mood even more, and I thoroughly enjoyed the work, so much so that the time flew past.

I spent a few hours glassing joints then set to with the sander again and finished prepping all the main joint areas except for the cabin tops. I'm now well placed to really crack on with the glassing without interruption.

The only slight mishap of the day came when I swopped over my epoxy drums. As I was lifting the new 33 kg keg into the epoxy warmer I realised that the tap was open, and that I had neat epoxy running down the leg of my overalls.

Luckily I managed to stem the flow quite quickly and salvage some of the spillage back into a pot. I was more concerned about the cost than the mess!

April 4, 2012 - I'll Be Happy When

I'm a big fan of Seth Godin. He posts something on his blog each and every day and it's always insightful, inspiring and stimulating. I have no idea how he does it.

A few days ago he posted one called 'If your happiness is based on always getting a little more than you've got...'

In it he describes how the 'system' conspires to condition us to always be looking for the next thing, always wanting more, always wanting better. Saying to ourselves "I'll be happy when...."

It made me think about my own situation.

I'm struggling every day to find the time and money to build 'Gleda'. I have a distant goal to see her on the water, to live on her, to sail the oceans. There have been many times when I've thought to myself "I won't be happy until I've finished the build". "I won't be happy until I'm back on the sea". "I won't be happy until I've escaped".

Seth reminded me to think differently. I'm privileged to be doing what I'm doing, to be building a boat, to be planning future adventures.

Yesterday we lost a family member to cancer, he was 10 years old. I'll remember him when I start wishing things were better.

April 11, 2012 - Mixing It Up A Bit

After working for Richard 8 days straight, including through the Easter Weekend, I finally managed to get back to working on 'Gleda' today.

During my time away I'd been thinking a lot about the next stages of the build and how I am going to tackle them. There are three tasks I want to focus on.

1. *Get the port hull joints glass reinforced as per the starboard hull*
2. *Get both hulls sheathed*
3. *Build the cross-beams*

I struggled a bit with the glass-reinforcement on the starboard hull as it's quite repetitive work and there are a lot of joints!

The sheathing will have to be broken down into small sections. I'm doing the job on my own and the amount of epoxy I can mix and work with at any one time is limited. And, even with a mixture of differing hardeners, the temperature needs to be right.

Building the cross-beams is a huge job and technically quite challenging. The work needs to be of a high standard and not rushed. There are many jobs on a Tiki 38 where you can cut corners and still get a workable result, but not the cross-beams.

So what I intend to do over the coming months is work on all three of these tasks as mood, time and weather suit best.

After all, it's a principle I'm finding works well in my income generating activities. So why not apply it to 'Gleda' as well?

Today I've started glass reinforcing the port hull. Working from the stern forward. And I've built a sturdy construction floor on which I can make the cross-beams.

Obviously, it's critical that they are put together on a perfectly flat surface. With no twists or distortions.

So I made up a 6.5 m long 'table' using 3 lengths of 4"x2" and some 1/2" birch ply. Then levelled it using plastic shims, before epoxying it down to the concrete barn floor so it can't move.

Should do the trick.

April 29, 2012 - Lying A-Hull

It's been a heck of a week.

I've now worked seven straight days and will likely work another 3 more before I get a break from paid work.

It's all good, but once again 'Gleda' is being neglected.

I wish I could tell you more about what I've been working on but I'm sworn to secrecy until early August. What I can say though is that it's interesting fun work, connected with a rather large event being held in London this summer!

Anyway, the upshot of all of this is that work on 'Gleda' will probably be sporadic and sparse until the end of June. But this short-term 'pain' will put me in a fantastic position to really kick on from July onwards.

Today had been pencilled in for a possible visit to the Beaulieu Boat Jumble down on the South Coast. But with my workload, we decided last week that it wasn't on.

As things turned out that was a good call as the event was cancelled due to the gale force winds and torrential rain that's blown through us today.

We've had a really unusual North Easterly 5/6 gusting 7/9 which has caused some damage and brought down trees and branches. At the barn today we lost part of the roof (luckily not anywhere near 'Gleda').

I got a taste of working the rigging on a windjammer round the Horn as I worked off a pallet lifted to roof height by the fork truck. Trying to nail down flapping roofing sheets that were in danger of being ripped off. The wind chill and stinging rain made it feel more like January than the end of April.

More fond memories to store away for recollection one balmy evening in some faraway tropical anchorage!

May 6, 2012 - One Year To Go

Eagle-eyed readers may have spotted that today my countdown clock has reached 1 year till launch, and that I've now been building for 5 years and 5 months!

I'm not sure which is scarier!

With so much yet to do having 'Gleda' on the water this time next year is a big ask, but it's one I'm going to fight hard to achieve.

Although I am again at a bit of a standstill with regard to hands-on work I'm still beavering away behind the scenes, and 'Gleda' is part of my daily routine.

This week I've acquired some bargain hatches and an opening portlight from eBay. Plus the extra timber I need for construction of the crossbeams has been ordered. As I've said already 'Gleda' time will be short until the end of next month, but I'll then be in a really great position to accelerate the build significantly.

Look at it this way. I've actually been building for 1,952 hours over a period of 1,978 days. So that's an average of about an hour a day (ignoring the fact that I actually put the build on hold for 8 months last year).

From July onwards I'll be in a position to put in maybe 40 hours per week. So that gives me the potential to put in something in the region of 1600 hours of work over the 10 months to 6th May 2013. JWD suggests that 2200 hours is needed to build a Tiki 38. Everyone who's built one says that's wildly optimistic. If I use the figures above, I've got a total of 3552 hours, which is a pretty decent margin.

Particularly as I now have access to a lot of time-saving woodworking machinery right next door to 'Gleda's' barn.

There is, of course, another aspect that can't be underestimated. And that's the cost of additional materials, fit out items, and expensive equipment like sails, rigging, engines etc.

But with the help of hard smart work and eBay, I'll find a way. So here we are, heading into the home stretch, hang on it's going to be fun!

Although I couldn't say so at the time many would have guessed that the 'secret' project I was working on had something to do with the Olympic Games in London.

Some weeks previously Richard had told me that there'd been a significant addition to his contract with British Showjumping. As part of the deal, we'd be responsible for construction of a number of special jumps to be used at the Showjumping Venue in Greenwich Park.

He showed me a folder of design drawings. The jumps were all themed around places and famous characters from London. Charles Darwin, No 10 Downing Street, Victorian Red Postboxes, The Houses of Parliament, Big Ben. The list went on.

Some of them had a nautical flavour, and that's when Richard came to the point.

He wanted me to take responsibility for two in particular.

The first looked straightforward enough. It was a cutout scene representing a Thames Barge under full sail.

The second was far more of a challenge.

They wanted a 3D replica of the famous Clipper Ship 'Cutty Sark'. It had to be to scale and detailed for TV close-ups.

Richard reckoned that if I could build a real-life sailing vessel, then a model should be a piece of cake.

I thought back to that summer day in 2005 when I'd listened to the announcement that London was going to host the 2012 Games. I remembered how crestfallen my French colleagues were about losing. How excited I'd been at the prospect of working on such a prestigious project. After leaving Gerflor I'd not given the event a thought. Now here I was, involved after all. Installing Sports Floors I'd have believed. Building horse jumps I'd never have guessed in a million years.

It's probably the fact that I'd been involved with these hard deadline events before that gave me the confidence to say yes to Richards request. It's hard to think of work with more 'failure not an option' pressure.

That night I started researching straight away. I'd visited the 'Cutty Sark' but never studied her in any detail. My interest had been sparked though, and I spent many hours trawling the internet and printing off pictures and plans. I even sent off for an old hardback book detailing the building of a small scale model from scratch.

Famous though she is, you may not have heard of her. So here's a bit of history.

'Cutty Sark' is a British sailing ship built in 1869. She was a Tea Clipper designed to race across the globe between China and London. The tea trade was highly competitive and faster ships could demand higher prices for their cargo.

Built of teak on steel frames, she is 280 foot long, 36 foot on the beam and could set 32 sails on her 3 masts. She could carry 1,700 tons of cargo at an average speed of 15 knots.

When the transportation of tea was lost to steamships she switched to the wool trade between Australia and Britain. That too was lost to steamships eventually, and in 1895 she was sold to a Portuguese company.

She spent years transporting various cargos across the Atlantic. In 1916 she was dismasted off the Cape of Good Hope. In 1922 she was sold again and based in Falmouth, she spent years as a sail training ship.

In 1936 she made her last voyage. From Falmouth to London where she was moored on the Thames as a static sail training vessel. By 1950 her working life was over, and by 1954 she was moved into a dry dock at Greenwich. She'd been afloat for 85 years. Since then she's been in the care of the 'Cutty Sark' Trust.

She was almost lost in 2007 when a huge fire engulfed her. But she survived, and is now a beautifully restored museum ship.

There are many things to see if you ever visit London. I'd put 'Cutty Sark' high on the list. Stand on deck, look up at the masts. Try to imagine her screaming along in a gale. Try to imagine climbing those masts, hanging off those yards, clawing at acres of stiff canvas flogging in the wind. Look around the decks. Think about where she's been, what's she's seen.

So my challenge was to do justice to this amazing vessel.

In the end, I used the same Wharram building methods I'd used for 'Gleda'. I made plywood bulkheads and clad them with fibre-glass sheathed plywood. There were a few problems but it worked. Once I had the hulls constructed it was fairly easy. One really fun job was modelling the figurehead. We'd been told that detail was important as the TV cameras would be zooming into features and broadcasting them around the world in HD. Obviously, the 'Cutty Sark' figurehead would attract attention so I put a lot of work into it.

There's a fascinating story behind the figurehead. The ship herself gets her name from the garment worn by a young Scottish witch called Nannie, in the Robert Burns poem Tam O' Shanter written in 1790. In the poem, a drunk farmer called Tam, while riding home one night, happens upon a group of witches and warlocks dancing within the churchyard (or kirkyard) of Kirk Alloway, a derelict church. The devil himself was sat there playing the bagpipes as they danced around. Tam watched them quietly, but after they stopped Tam carelessly applauded the witch Nannie Dee who had caught his eye. He shouted out "Weel done Cutty Sark". Not knowing her name he had addressed her by her dress, a Cutty Sark. Scottish for short shirt or shift. This, of course, betrayed his presence to them and they immediately gave chase.

Tam fled on the back of his horse Maggie (sometimes named Meg) toward the bridge over the nearby river Doon. Folklore had it that witches could not cross running water. Nannie was right behind him and managed to grab and pull off the horses tail just before Tam reached the bridge. This is what's held in the figurehead's outstretched hand. It was close call!

The actual model of Nannie finished up being about 8 inches high. We even cut off a bit of the tail hair from 'Trevor' Richard's horse to put in Nannie's hand.

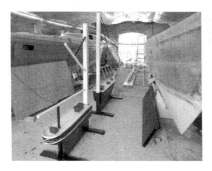

The Thames Barge jump was far easier to make. But I then had to re-discover my long lost art skills to paint the silhouette up into something pretty.

June 28, 2012 - Ghost Boats

After 22 consecutive 10 hour days working on the 'top secret project' I really needed a quick recharge of the batteries. What better way to do it than with a trip to Cornwall to spend some time watching sailing boats. So for the last two days, I've been in Falmouth watching the 'J Class' yachts racing in the bay. For those that don't know, the J's were designed in the 30's for the Americas Cup. They hadn't raced in the UK since 1938 and were visiting Falmouth as part of a series of races timed to coincide with the Olympics. For anyone interested in sailing it was far too good to miss.

I'd never seen anything like these 'J Class' vessels. Until you see these boats on the water it's impossible to grasp just how big they are.

But here are a few stats for starters. Displacement: 143 tons. Overall Length 39.4 m (129 ft). Beam 6.55 m (21 ft). Draught 4.57 m (15 ft). Mast Height 53 m (174 ft). Sail Area 1738 sqm (18,700 sqft).

The other thing that really can't be understood without seeing them under full sail is just how utterly gorgeous these boats are. The lines, the sail shape are perfect, just breathtaking.

My favourite was 'Velsheda'. Built in 1933. Rescued from dereliction in 1996 by the Dutch businessman Ronald de Waal, she looked stunning.

It's impossible to reconcile how such incredible power can be matched with such incredible beauty. There surely cannot be any other vessels afloat that even come close.

Sadly a sea-fog detracted from the spectacle on the last day. Although seeing these vast sails appear slowly out of the fog was an evocative sight in itself.

Once back in the barn I worked another 3-week stint to get the Olympic project finished.

At the end of July, I even got chance to go down to Greenwich Park and see the action close-up. The last show-jump event I'd been to had been in a field in Leicestershire. This event was a tad bigger. I confess to some pride at seeing my handy-work on such prominent display.

If you're interested I found a couple of YouTube videos with some good shots of my jumps.

VIDEO 1 URL for those who can't click:
https://www.youtube.com/watch?v=4AOAhuJ4rU4

Watch at 5:15 and there's a good shot of the Cutty Sark jump.

VIDEO 2 URL for those who can't click:
https://www.youtube.com/watch?v=UemukhxyZFw

Watch at 2:28:00 and you'll see both my jumps.

The project had been fun. It'd put some much-needed money in the bank. But for nearly four months 'Gleda' had been neglected. It was time to crack on again.

In September I got the decks sheathed.

Then Jacques Pierret emailed me. How would I like to come over to Marseilles for a few days and sail with him on 'Pilgrim'?

I've mentioned Jacques a few times before. He was one of my online 'mentors'. He was a few years into his build when I started.

Always ahead of me he never hesitated to help me out when I got stuck. Like 'Gleda' 'Pilgrim' was built in a barn. But his was in New Jersey USA.

He launched her in June 2010. Then sailed her across the Atlantic to Marseilles the following year.

It was an invitation I couldn't refuse.

A couple of weeks later I found myself in L'Estaque, just down the coast from Marseilles sitting on board a Tiki 38 drinking red wine with Jacques and his friends.

Truth be told I'd been a bit apprehensive. This was to be the first time I'd seen a Wharram Tiki 38 in the flesh, let alone the first time I'd sailed on one. What if I didn't like it?

There was never any danger really. She was fantastic and a perfect reflection of Jacques's character. Strong, no bullshit, purposeful and typically French, I loved her.

Jacques was very apologetic when I arrived. He'd got another friend using the spare room in his apartment. It would mean I'd have to sleep aboard 'Pilgrim' if that was OK. It was more than that. It was perfect.

'Pilgrim' was moored in a nice marina with all the facilities. From the deck, I could see across Marseilles Bay. I could relax, spend time aboard while Jacques was at work and explore around. In the evenings we'd get together for an aperitif before eating.

At the weekend we could go sailing. The weather was typically Mediterranean. Either there was no wind or the Mistral whistled through at 30 knots. I wanted to sail but I was rusty. My preference was for a gentle reintroduction.

Ultimately that's what I got. We went out for the day with probably less than 10 knots. It was great. I helmed most of the time. We anchored for lunch and swam around and under the boat. I got to see a Tiki 38 afloat from all angles. It was magic.

That evening as I sat up on the bows talking to Gail on the mobile, she asked me how I felt. I choked up. I could hardly speak. For six years I'd been slogging away trying to make my dream real. Sailing 'Pilgrim' bought the reality of what I was aiming for home to me. All the doubts dropped away in an instant. Jacques had done it. I would do it. I was absolutely on the right course. It was just a matter of time.

That night we all went to a music concert in the next bay to L'Estaque It was like no other music event I'd ever been to.

There was no seating. The audience just sat on the beach and rocks around the little horseshoe bay. The stage was a floating platform anchored a few metres off the waterline. For a backdrop, the glittering lights of Marseilles across the bay.

Actually, there was more than one stage. At one point another appeared, propelled by swimmers hanging onto the sides. On the raft was a white grand piano and a pianist in white top hat and tails. Later on, an opera singer in a flowing white evening dress jumped off her raft and waded ashore. All the while singing into what I presume was a waterproof microphone.

All very bizarre. All very magical.

I returned from the trip re-energised. The show jumps workload had dropped off. I had some money in the bank. It didn't stay there long.

I bought the gas stove. A Nelson Spinlow, with two burners, a grill and a proper oven. There were cheaper alternatives, there always are. But all my decisions were influenced by the fact that once completed, 'Gleda' would be home. Things like the oven were going to be used every day, hopefully for years. I wanted the best I could afford.

The biggest dent to the bank account came from ordering the engines.

In the past, I'd spent time with a romantic notion that perhaps 'Gleda' would be engineless. I liked the idea of pure sailing and developing an enhanced level of seamanship as a result. The time I spent on 'Pilgrim' with Jacques convinced me that it was indeed just a romantic fantasy. And that engines are a necessary evil.

A Tiki 38 is a big boat. There will inevitably be times when close manoeuvring in harbour will be required. Tiki 38's don't tack quickly and easily and take up a lot of space to do it.

Coastal sailing means, of course, bringing the boat close to hard bits of land. A sudden change in wind direction/strength can quickly turn into rapidly approaching disaster. So the decision was made. 'Gleda' would have engines but, they would be used as little as possible.

So two four-stroke 9.8hp Tohatsu extra long shaft outboards arrived. They were the same engines as on 'Pilgrim'. Jacques recommendation gave me all the confidence I needed to go for them. There was nothing to stop me ramping up work on 'Gleda'. I threw myself into it.

It's a good job I had plenty of energy. There was another challenge I needed to complete in October. At the beginning of the year, I'd started running. Mainly because I'd sold my bike and I had no choice.

Running is not something I've ever really enjoyed. Too many memories of freezing cold cross-country runs in my Grammar School days. But I wanted to get fitter, I needed a goal. So I'd entered the Coventry Half-Marathon.

October 14, 2012 - Half Marathon... Done!

Yay I did it!

A very pedestrian time of just under 2hrs 20min saw me collapsing over the finish line with knees and legs hurting like I've never experienced before. But with an immense feeling of pride in achieving a goal that, at the beginning of the year, seemed an almost impossible task.

The route was a lot hillier than I expected. It wound out of Coventry city centre and out through the lovely countryside around Keresley and Radford.

But it was a huge boost to get the support of so many people lining the pavement cheering, clapping and shouting encouragement. It seems the Olympic spirit is still hanging on after our incredible summer of Sport.

Not that I felt in any way Olympian, particularly as we hit the 8-mile mark and my right knee started wondering why I hadn't stopped. 8 miles was the most I managed to run in training, so I was in unknown territory after that, and I can tell you that it didn't get any easier!

My original target had been to complete the course without walking. But sadly at 11.5 miles I had to slow to walking pace as my knees screamed enough. I soon discovered however that strangely after a few minutes walking they hurt even more, and I had to start running again. A cycle I repeated several times before the finish.

The last 1.1 miles seemed to take forever, not helped by the fact that I couldn't recognise any landmarks to give me hope that the end was close. By now the field had spread out to the point where I was running pretty much on my own. It was touching to say the least, to receive applause and shouts of encouragement that I knew now were directed at me. They lifted my spirits to the point where I was able to keep running for the majority of that last 1.1 miles. And gradually I began to realise that nothing was going to stop me finishing.

Suddenly I was approaching the last turn of the course and seeing the old church that confirmed I only had a hundred yards or so to go. Gail was there behind the barriers amongst the crowds cheering us on, and then I was over the line, job done.

Given that I now seem virtually incapable of walking or standing, I'm very much hoping that a good nights sleep will bring about some sort of miraculous recovery. One that will allow work to continue with sanding sooner rather than later.

My closing comments on this blog post are worth noting.

.....In the meantime, I'll relax and contemplate how building a boat has changed me. How this little weekend jog has confirmed what I was already coming to realise. That I can now set goals that seem impossible, and then work steadily towards them one step at a time, until I achieve them. 'Gleda' has already changed me.

She's made me a better person, she's empowered me to make the right choices in my life, she's made me happier, healthier and wiser. She's done all this despite being incomplete, landlocked in a damp dark barn. What will she do for me when she's afloat? When she's my home, when she's free to transport me beyond those horizons. I can't wait to find out.

I needed persistence and energy for this particular stage of the build. I was filling and sanding the hulls ready for painting. A long, slow, monotonous grind of repetitive physical work.

October 19, 2012 - Mind Games

Another 6 hours sanding today and I'm now a third of the way down the last hull side. Once that's done I just have the decks and cabin tops of the starboard hull to do.

Then I can bring in the jet wash and blast away the blanket of fine white dust that now covers everything in the barn.

This sanding operation is, without doubt, one of the hardest tasks I've had to do so far. It's monotonous, tiring, dirty and noisy. I really dislike being encased in overalls, face mask, goggles, hat and gloves.

It's not a matter of forcing myself to do it though, because I've chosen to do it.

This is an important point, one which I've been applying to a number of things I needed to do recently. If sanding was part of my 'JOB'. If I was employed and paid to do it then, of course, I'd do it. But I'd resent doing it, I'd moan constantly about doing it, and I'd probably make a lousy job of it.

But I'm not employed to sand things, I could choose not to do it if I really wanted to. Maybe I could pay someone else to do it or ask some friends to come help me (not sure how long they'd stay friends for mind!).

Here's the thing though.

I WANT to build a boat.

I WANT to do it on my own.

I WANT the feelings of satisfaction and pride that will come when she's launched.

If those things are going to happen then the sanding needs to be done. And needs to be done well, so with the aforementioned WANTS in mind it's easy to CHOOSE to do it myself.

More than that I choose to do it well. And, having rid myself of any negative feelings about doing it. I can, to some degree enjoy it. Knowing that the work I do now will pay dividends when I come to put some paint on.

I did get a short break from the sanders today as some of the timber for building the beams arrived. So many jobs!

November 4, 2012 - Beaming Cold!

I only managed a 2-hour session today, the weather is at it's worst right now, what do I mean?

Well, for me when it's just above freezing. It's raining, the sky is covered with thick blanket cloud, and there's a cold wind blowing

I really feel it. I'd actually prefer much lower temperatures and a bit of sunshine. It's neither one thing or the other, it's just horrible.

Still, it is what it is and this is the UK in November. It's to be expected. I just have to crack on and remember that I'm working on my means of escape from the next one!

What I wanted to do today was to glue on the second layer of 18 mm ply to the centre beam web I put together yesterday. This I did, although not without a slight cock-up when I applied my epoxy glue to the wrong side of two of the pieces! I blame the cold!

Eric asked an interesting question in the comment he posted last night:

> *Do you ever think about the work you're doing and how critical certain jobs are, and what the consequences would be if the part failed? Not to be morbid, but that's some pretty serious work you're doing!*

To answer that question, yes.

I always keep in mind that these bits of wood I'm glueing together will be all that keeps me and all I hold dear from, to come straight to the point, a watery grave.

It's not being morbid, it's being realistic. One of the main reasons

I'm building a Tiki 38 is because of its sea keeping abilities and safety record. I believe someone once said of Mr Wharram that 'he designs boats for conditions that the majority of owners will never experience'. Ultimately that's the starting point for me.

James Wharram is a genius. I have complete faith in the design that he and Hanneke came up with. I've now had that faith re-affirmed after sailing with Jacques on 'Pilgrim' and hearing him talk about the strength of the boat during his Atlantic Crossing.

I know that all I have to do is follow the plans, use good quality materials and use them properly.

So much of the work done on a Tiki 38 is hidden, it would be possible to take shortcuts and nobody would know, but to do so would be unthinkable.

There's another big barn outside the one I'm building in. I often look at its 30 ft grey wall and remind myself that 'Gleda' could one day be riding ocean waves easily that high.

I usually apply a bit more epoxy after that!

The point is that when 'Gleda' is launched I'll know every inch of her. I'll have complete faith in her, I'll know I did a good job, to me that's one of the joys of self-building.

December 23,- 2012 - Designer Galley

A useful couple of hours today finalising the basic layout for the galley. Gail's input was really useful.

It was the first time she'd spent any amount of time down below. So it was pleasing to hear her say that she was pleasantly surprised how much room there was to move around. We spent some time talking through where things would be stowed, and between us we've come up with something that will work well.

We both agreed that it was sensible to do as little as possible for now, to just concentrate on the big stuff.

Things like dividing up the cupboard space and adding little shelves here and there, can wait. Far better to do these things once we and all our stuff are aboard.

We'll find out soon enough where things need to be then.

What I didn't find out until later was that Gail had got upset after leaving the barn. All the while she was down in the hull helping me with ideas she'd had only one thought going through her mind.

'How can I possibly live in such a small space?'.

She happily admits that her visualisation skills are poor. I didn't give it a thought. Probably due to the fact that for me the hulls were already a home. I'd spent so many hours in them, dreaming, imagining, visualising.

Later on, as the galley started to take shape, she was able to start seeing the reality. Today, after four years living aboard she loves it. As she's said many times. 'How is it possible for an empty space to seem bigger when it's been filled?'.

I closed the year out on an optimistic note.

December 31, 2012 - Farewell

So that's that then, my last work session of the year completed.

I'm not one to spend much time looking back. But it's worth recalling how 2012 went. If for no other reason than to highlight how sometimes things just don't go the way you plan.

When I started this project 6 long years ago I planned to launch 'Gleda' in May 2012. That idea had to be scrapped during 2011 when I did next to no work on the boat, as I struggled to find my path after escaping from the corporate hamster wheel.

At the start of 2012, I was still struggling financially. It took all of January and most of February to get myself sorted and moving in the right direction again.

The sale of my Land Rover paid for some fresh epoxy supplies, and on 23rd February with 1856 hours on the clock, I got started again. Little did I know that before long 'Gleda' would once again be neglected.

I chose to take the opportunity of building horse jumps for the London Olympics, work that took up all of May, June and July. Looking back I now realise that I lost 5 months building time during 2012.

That goes some way to understanding why I've only done 449 hours of work on 'Gleda' during the year.

I've no regrets though. I did what I did to ensure the survival of the project. I'm still far from secure, but I'm in a much better place and I'm now in a position to make up for lost time.

Despite the shortage of hours, 2012 saw me complete the hulls structurally and get them ready for painting. I made a solid start on construction of the beams, and I've started the interior fit out.

Since October I've been working steadily and consistently and will continue to do so.

In summary 2012 turned out to be another watershed year. I started it fearful and a little despondent, I'm ending it excited and optimistic. 2013 will be epic!

2013 YEAR SEVEN (1066HRS) - FULL ATTACK

*M*y mood at the start of 2013 was the same as it had been right at the very beginning of the project in 2006.

It seemed as if I'd finally got myself into the best possible shape to get the project done.

Free of a JOB and all the crap that comes with it. The ability to earn money when I needed it but still with the freedom to choose how I spent my time. Plus an almost ideal work environment and access to tools and equipment.

This was it. This was the year 'Gleda' would float.

I was stoked.

I wanted to get started on the hull paint but being January it was inevitable I'd have to wait for the right temperature. In the meantime, I cracked on with the galley fit-out.

Pleasingly I didn't have to wait long. On the 4th, after weeks and weeks of rain, the weather settled down. A positively balmy 12°C (54°F) and dry. I didn't need a second invitation.

Epoxy primer has to be mixed with a hardener. Once it's mixed it has to be used. I'd calculated I'd need 5 litres for each hull and I wasn't far wrong. The paint was quite thick, so to keep control and to get a better finish I opted to use a 4" roller. It took two full eight hours to get one coat on both hulls.

Over the following week, I got an additional primer coat on, followed by the first top coat. I'd opted for yellow hull sides and white topsides. The effect of a few coats of paint was amazing. I'd spent years looking at bare timber and epoxy. Now, the hulls had been transformed.

Once that paint was applied 'Gleda' really did start to look like the finished item.

Richard and the other guys at the barn came to see, said how impressive she looked. I grinned every morning when I first saw her.

There were probably half a dozen occasions during the whole build when this happened. I'd slog away for weeks, even months, with no real visible sign of progress. Then one day, a few hours work would completely change things. Suddenly it would feel as if I'd made a massive leap forward. Getting paint on the hulls was one of them. It felt like I was getting close to the end.

So confident was I, that I phoned the Wharram's and spoke to Hanneke. I gave them the launch date. Asked if they'd like to attend, she said they'd love to. I was buzzing.

January 11, 2013 - Warm Down Below

I'm glad I got the paint on when I did because the weather is on the slide again.

It's been much colder and damper these last few days and the forecast is for even colder conditions with sleet and snow.

We'll see what happens, but I figured I'd make some preparations for it by closing some more holes in the galley saloon area. I've now fitted the long fixed window on the outboard side of the cabin top, the two round forward facing perspex ports and the hatch over the saloon. It's surprising what a difference it's made despite there still being a big gaping hole where the companionway is. It has stopped the cold draughts blowing through, and with a little fan heater going it was getting very toasty!

If the temperatures do take a tumble I can even throw an old blanket over the companionway and I'll be able to work in comfort, excellent! I also fitted a couple of the fixed ports up in the bow compartments and the opening port over the nav station in the starboard hull.

Whilst fitting the fixed ports I noticed that I actually have two slightly different designs, three of each. The external dimensions are the same but internally three of them are slightly more rounded. I bought them all at Beaulieu Boat Jumble about 4 years ago and never spotted it. I'm not fussed though, it just means that the port and starboard hulls will have slightly different ports, and it'll take someone with a keen eye to spot it.

On a completely different subject, the timber for the beams arrived today at long last. I've got it all stowed safely in the barn and it's my intention to add one layer to a beam during every work session until they're done. There are 16 layers in total so I estimate it'll take me three weeks to complete the job.

I took a break mid-month to go to The London Boat Show. It was a fun trip.

January 16, 2013 - Meeting A Hero

I had a successful visit to the London Boat Show yesterday. It was my first time there.

Apart from having a strong dislike of London, I was fearful that there would be nothing of real interest to me there.

I'm at the complete opposite end of the spectrum from the shows main target audience. On arrival, I feared the worst, huge great gin palace motor yachts, displays of Aston Martins and Range Rovers, Champagne & Wine Cellars, luxury brand this, exclusive brand that.

I walked through these displays as fast as I could and discovered another area filled with chandlery and equipment, much better. I decided to do a preliminary sweep noting the stands that I wanted to visit properly. As I was exploring the far corner of the hall I was suddenly stopped in my tracks by a sight that immediately brought a smile to my face.

It was 'Mingming', Roger Taylor's junk-rigged 21 ft Corribee. Sitting there with the sail up and just as she was taken out of the water after his 3000-mile voyage into the Arctic Circle in 2011.

The sight of her brought back happy memories of 'Mor Gwas'. The Corribee is a very close cousin of the Silhouette.

Imagine my further delight when I realised that the man himself was also there, selling and signing copies of his books.

I guess I shouldn't assume that you've heard of Roger or 'Mingming' so here's a quick bio.

As a young seaman, Roger was shipwrecked on a remote New Zealand shore aboard the square-rigger 'Endeavour II'. He then built a 19ft boat called 'Roc' and twice crossed the Tasman Sea in her. He's sailed 'Mingming' some 20,000 miles.

His voyages included a foray into the Davis Strait west of Greenland. A circumnavigation of Iceland, and a voyage to the isolated Arctic island of Jan Mayen. In 2008 he completed the Azores Jester challenge in 21 days.

All of this single-handed in an engineless 21ft boat, amazing.

Roger's voyages are all the more inspiring given his philosophy of keeping things simple. It's a philosophy shared with James Wharram, build it simply, build it strong, make it easy to repair.

After spending a good amount of time looking over his boat. I was privileged enough to be able to shake Roger by the hand and to chat with him for 10 minutes or so. He was genuinely interested in 'Gleda'.

And I was pleased to hear that whilst 'Mingming' is now retired, he is working on 'Mingming II'. An Achilles 24 in which he plans to return to the Arctic Circle in during 2014.

I was chuffed to bits to have been able to meet with one of my sailing heroes. And although I already have all three of his books, I am now the proud owner of a signed copy of his second book 'Mingming & the Art of Minimal Ocean Cruising'.

It'll make a fine addition to the library on 'Gleda'.

I highly recommend all three of his books and it's best to read them in order. The first was 'Voyages of a Simple Sailor', the second I mention above, and the most recent 'Mingming & The Tonic of Wilderness'.

To be honest, even if I'd achieved nothing else at the show I'd have left happy after that, but I was on a mission and I'm pleased to say that it was successful.

I was very impressed with the latest Rutland wind charger. I'm almost certain now that 'Gleda' will have one of these, along with solar panels for charging.

It was good to be able to see the latest LED lighting as well, now no doubts about using those.

I also found a supplier for some nice foam-backed lining materials for the cabin. And I'll shortly be ordering custom-made mattresses and bedding for the main double and guest single berths.

I know there will be some who question spending money on such things, but 'Gleda' will be my permanent home, and comfort and a good nights sleep are essential for health and wellbeing, enough said.

Apart from being able to see everything under one roof, the other benefit of a show like this is meeting folks face to face, getting names and talking. I did a lot of that. And now have contacts with several suppliers who have agreed to give me some discounted prices on orders I place over the next few months.

So, all in all, it was a very successful trip.

Today I was back to earth with a bang. It was minus 3°C when I drove to the barn. It was minus 2°C when I drove back. The forecast is for even lower temperatures tomorrow and then, if they are to be believed, we've got blizzards on Friday and Saturday.

It was hard working today. But I spent some time cleaning up the mast beam and putting a routed radius on the top plank. I then got the first plank glued to the longest beam. Removed the perspex ports I'd put in with the wrong sealer, and cleaned them up (I've now ordered the right marine grade silicon for the job). Lastly, I finished up by making the templates for the custom mattresses ready to send off

The weather forecast I referred to in that blog post turned out to be accurate. Throughout most of January, the weather had been kind and I'd been able to get loads done. Now there were hints that things were changing.

January 23, 2013 - One Of Those Days

Sometimes you just know it's going to be one of those days don't you?

I'd woken at 4 am with a migraine. Then even before my first cuppa of the day I was outside helping Gail and the next door neighbour get their cars off the driveway.

Fresh wet snow had fallen during the night onto the compacted ice, end result next to zero traction. They got away after much pushing and wheel spinning and I was able to get my breakfast before heading up to the barn.

Guess what? I ended up stuck twice, but managed to extricate myself and eventually got to the boat. As I got out of the car at the barn I slipped on the ice, fell, and banged my elbow hard.

There was a pattern emerging.

As I was keen to get the last two beam planks glued I cracked on. Taking all the temporary screws out of the planks I'd glued yesterday ready to sand and apply epoxy. All seemed to be going well. Then as I was coming out of the epoxy shack I happened to glance at the end of the beam, and to my horror saw that one of the joints had sprung.

Ironic, isn't it? Last night I spouted on about how in these cold temperatures the epoxy doesn't reach its full strength. And what had I done but taken the retaining screws out of a highly tensioned joint less than 18 hours after glueing it!

I quickly realised why it had happened on this beam and not the others. It's the forward beam and it has much steeper curves on the ends than any of the others. They'd taken some serious clamping to get the 1" plank to pull down, and I was simply asking too much of uncured epoxy to hold them.

Anyway, I quickly got some big G-clamps from the workshop and got the joints pulled in tight again, panic over and no harm done. Once they were pulled down I put some long stainless steels screws in which I'll probably leave in place.

Once that drama was over I was able to carry on and glue the last two planks, it was still a struggle though, I got epoxy where I shouldn't have, I dropped things, I lost things, I broke a clamp. I confess to getting myself pretty wound up, but I persisted and the job is now completed.

It was probably a good thing that I'd planned a trip down to Cornwall.

It prevented me from getting even more frustrated. I was excited. When I'd spoken to Hanneke a few weeks before, I'd arranged to go and visit them at Devoran. It would be the first time I'd met with them. But this wasn't to be just a pleasure trip. I was on a mission. We needed somewhere to launch 'Gleda', and I wanted it to be Falmouth.

February 4, 2013 - Launch Site Confirmed!

Well, what a week! It's always a joy to be back in Falmouth, but this time proved to be even more pleasurable.

It's always been my dream to get 'Gleda' on the water somewhere in the Falmouth area. But a lot has changed since my days there on 'Mor Gwas' all those years ago.

I was fearful that the ever creeping development of the marine leisure industry would have destroyed all the special places I once knew. That the costs of launching and keeping a boat anywhere around the Fal would have skyrocketed above my means. That folk wouldn't want anything to do with some numpty from up country with a home built boat.

I'm very pleased to report that my fears were, for the most part, unfounded, and that I can therefore confirm that 'Gleda' will be launched on the River Fal!

As it turned out I was somewhat spoiled for choice when it came to suitable locations to launch.

I needed four things

1. *A yard/space accessible to a 40ft articulated trailer.*
2. *A yard/space big enough to allow final assembly of the boat (40 ft x 25 ft)*
3. *Crane and/or slipway to the water.*
4. *A mooring or mud berth for a few months.*

I now have a shortlist all within a few miles of each other, but at the moment Mylor Yacht Harbour is at the top of the list.

I'm very excited that I now know where 'Gleda' will be going when she comes out of the barn. And it's an added bonus that Mylor is just around the corner from the JWD HQ at Devoran.

So we now know where, but the big question is when!

Well, I'm aiming for the back end of May or the beginning of June, and I'll be working as hard as I can to make it happen.

There's a lot of work to do and it may be that I'm being too ambitious. So it's my intention to make a final decision about the launch date at the beginning of April. By then I'll know for sure what's possible.

I have some other commitments over the next few days. But I managed to squeeze in a couple of hours work on the beams today and I'm planning to do the same tomorrow.

After that, I'll be diving in full time!

As you can tell from my words I was buzzing again. What I hadn't mentioned was the meeting with James and Hanneke.

Gail and I spent two hours chatting with them in their office by the water. Even though we'd not met before, for me it was like meeting old friends.

I guess that's because the Wharram boats and philosophy had occupied some part of my mind for nigh on thirty years.

Ever since seeing 'Ika Roa' and 'Imagine' back in the 'Mor Gwas' days.

Gail was more apprehensive. All of this seemed very strange to her. Walking through the ramshackle building shed. Taking off our shoes. Entering the little Japanese styled office decorated with photos of James and Hanneke sailing naked. Then meeting the people she'd heard me talk about so often.

Early in the conversation, it came up that Gail had never sailed, and that she was apprehensive about it. James put her at ease immediately. He's said many times that he believes women are mentally stronger the men at sea. He told Gail that she'd surprise herself. That she'd help me more than she might expect. He's been proved right many times since.

Perhaps the best example I can give of Hanneke and James's differing character is to relate the questions I was asked.

When I mentioned I'd sailed with Jacques on 'Pilgrim' Hanneke was keen to know how well she'd performed. How close to the wind did we get? How did she tack? What speed did we get?

James however just looked at me with a twinkle in his eye and a smile on his lips and said: " Yes, but how did she make you feel?". I thought back to that telephone conversation with Gail while I was sitting on 'Pilgrim'. The answer came easily; "alive again".

Once back at the barn I threw myself into the work and got the two hulls connected for the first time.

February 11, 2013 - Another Landmark Reached

I may be tired and aching all over, but I'm very happy with today's work.

It may be temporary but 'Gleda' is for the first time looking like a completed boat and I have to say she looks amazing.

I couldn't have expected things to go any better. And it's a huge relief to know that all the time spent ensuring I built the beam troughs accurately has paid off.

It's hard to believe that it was August 2008 when I built them.

First job this morning was to move the beams outside the barn to give me room to work. It snowed last night and was still snowing a bit this morning. So it was the first and, I swear, last time that these beams will have snow on them! (It wasn't).

Once I'd cleared the space I got busy with the tape measure and laser square to mark out the hull centre lines on the barn floor. I took a lot of time over this as I wanted to minimise having to move the hulls again whilst trying to position the beams.

The hull centre lines are 4.6 m (15 ft) apart. Initially I was worried the barn might not be wide enough, it was, and I still have some working room down the outside of the hulls.

I used some white spray paint to mark the lines roughly and then made more accurate marks with a permanent marker.

Once that was done. I was able to bring the fork truck in and carefully lift each end of the hulls bit by bit. Working the cradles over to their correct positions on the centre line.

I've known for ages that the hulls would have to be moved apart by 1 m (3 ft) or so, but once I'd done it I was staggered at how far apart they seemed.

After a cup of coffee I braved the snow and marked the hull centre lines on each beam and then, heart in mouth, it was time to bring in the first beam and drop it in.

At this point, I must give a big shout out to my mate Malc, without whose help I could not have done the job. It was hard physical work simply moving the beams into a position where I could get the fork truck under them. I don't know how much each beam weighs but the two of us could only just lift one.

We carried the first beam into the barn and laid it on trestles. I picked it up with the truck and carefully drove it forward over the cabin tops.

There was just enough clearance, but I was very close to ripping down the strip lights and polythene tent roof! Once over the beam trough I lowered the beam down and to my utter amazement it dropped in as sweet as a nut, one down three to go.

The centre beam dropped in nearly as sweetly. But I could see that the aft parts of the hulls were just a little close together. So we made some slight adjustments before I measured and cut the shorter mast beam.

This beam is the only one that doesn't span the entire width of the hulls, but rather sits in a well.

I was mighty pleased to find that the distance on my hulls matched the distance on the plans to within 25 mm(1").

Once the mast beam was in position that just left the aft beam. This one required a little more jiggling but again it dropped in without too much effort.

Now I know that all is well I'll be able to take my time on each beam. Positioning it absolutely spot on, making the spacers, and lining things up perfectly. Having the beams roughly positioned just makes it so much easier to see what needs levelling and adjusting.

Once the job was done I spent quite a while just walking about under the beams and leaning against the barn wall staring. Just taking in the fact 'Gleda' has once again been transformed.

February 20, 2013 - Spaced Out

It's funny how this boatbuilding lark goes sometimes.

There are days when you arrive ready to crack on, with a clear plan, eager to make the day as productive as possible. And then it all just slips away for no apparent reason.

You keep going, you make a little progress, but you come away at the end of the day disappointed and frustrated with what you've done.

Today was not one of those days. It was one of those where you arrive feeling a bit tired, unclear what you're going to do, and not expecting much at all. You make a start because that's what you have to do, and before long you feel better.

Things start to flow, you pick up momentum, everything you do just works, they are great days and you wish there were more of them.

This morning I thought I'd keep things easy.

I thought I'd make a start by drilling and countersinking holes in the lashing strake spacer blocks I made yesterday. I flew through the job, and so I thought I'd just screw a few to the hull and see what they looked like, I fixed a couple, then a couple more, and I just kept going.

Before I knew it the day was done and I had all 104 (I underestimated yesterday and had to cut some more), screwed to the hulls.

They need a bit of adjustment before I mark around them, take them all off again, prep the hull sides and then glue and screw them back on permanently. So there's plenty left to do before they're finished, but I'll be well chuffed if the rest of the job goes as swimmingly as today.

Normally by the end of February, the worst of the winter weather is over. It wasn't the case in 2013

February 21, 2013 - Bitter Weather, Icy Work

I had intended to try and continue the momentum of yesterdays good work, but the weather had other ideas. It's turned bitterly cold again. The temperature is hovering around freezing and there's a stiff Easterly wind blowing making it feel more like minus 5°C. Unfortunately, Easterlies tend to blow right through the barn making it far too uncomfortable to work sensibly.

The forecast says this is going to continue into next week, which means my work rate will inevitably slow down. I've really had enough of winter now.

To escape the chill I decided to move back into the port hull and continue work on the galley, in particular, the icebox. I'd left the cabin in such a state that I first had to spend some time clearing up, but then I set to making a mess again by cutting up 3" dense insulation foam. I've used a plastic kitchen bin to form the icebox set into two layers of 3" foam insulation, with all the gaps filled with expanding builders foam. I cut the bin off flush and once I've made a frame I'll be able to make the lid which will also be insulated with the same foam, and set into the worktop. It should work a treat.

The weather for the rest of February kept me below, working on the galley mainly.

We also made another trip down to the West Country. Shortly after the last trip, I'd had a call from Mylor Yacht Harbour withdrawing their offer of a mooring.

Despite me having been clear 'Gleda' was a catamaran they said they'd made a mistake. The mooring available was only suitable for monohulls. They were happy to give me yard space and put 'Gleda' in the water, but then I'd have to clear off.

I began to wonder if I'd been a bit premature announcing Falmouth as the launch location. I needed those critical things. First a yard with shoreside crane where we could spend a week reassembling the boat ready for the water. The masts could be stepped ashore if the right crane (travel lift) was available. Alternatively, they could be craned in alongside. Once in the water, I needed time alongside to get the engines sorted and complete a list of other jobs. Once properly afloat I then needed a mooring where we could get the boat ready for sea.

The problem with Falmouth was, now that Mylor had changed their minds, I couldn't get all those things together.

The hardstanding space on arrival was very limited. Once in the water, there were no alongside berths to be had.

Moorings in Falmouth were rare as rocking horse manure.

James and Hanneke had kindly offered a short stay on a mud berth up at Devoran.

But the more I thought about it the more I realised that it was my heart pushing me towards Falmouth, not my head.

I'd become aware of a little boatyard on the Devon side of the Tamar River, about 5 miles inland from the city of Plymouth.

I'd spoken to the owner Mike, and told him what I needed. He reckoned they could provide everything. Hardstanding, a crane, an alongside berth while we needed it, and then a swinging mooring in the river. The yard had a nice shower and toilet block, a little chandlery and wifi. It was worth a trip to go look see.

I came back pretty much decided, but other doubts were beginning to creep in.

March 7, 2013 - Highs & Lows

Our trip down to Plymouth was well worth it.

The weather was spring-like. The scenery around Dartmoor and the Tamar River spectacular, and our visit to Weir Quay Boatyard very positive.

If all goes well it seems likely that Weir Quay will be the place where this project ends its long building phase, and starts its long-awaited sailing phase.

I'm holding off giving too much information right now because there are a few hurdles yet to cross, but I'm optimistic I'll be able to tell you more very soon.

The reason I entitled this blog post 'Highs & Lows' is that during and immediately after the trip to Devon I felt very high and excited. But in the time since, I've slumped somewhat.

This blog is not the place to whine, so I'll just say that the financial and mental pressures are mounting right now.

I'm finding it a bit of a struggle to stay positive.

Even the weather seems to be against me, with cold wind, rain, and winter threatening a return next week. I'll say no more here it's just me moaning and I apologise.

Today at the barn I put my head down and got all 14 beam pads glassed over.

I'm not sure if I'll be able to get to the barn tomorrow but I plan to make a start on the main hatchways next.

March 10, 2013 - Driven Below

In three weeks time, the clocks change to British summer Time, but right now that looks like someone's idea of a joke.

The temperature today hasn't gone above 1°C (34°F) and there's a bitter east wind blowing right through the barn making it feel far colder.

I looked back at the post I made on this day last year, and I was working in 16°C (61°F) with a clear blue sky and bright sunshine!

Anyway, I know when I'm beaten, so I retired down below and started tatting round in the galley again.

I've sanded, filled, sanded and applied a second coat of white primer undercoat to quite a bit of the galley area. I still have some epoxy filleting to do on the outboard side, so that will have to wait for another day.

It looks like this weather could be in for the week, so I'll continue down below whilst it lasts.

Hopefully, the water tanks and water system bits and pieces will arrive tomorrow, that will give me plenty to do.

Other deliveries during March included a full set of sails from Rolly Tasker in Thailand. And the custom-made mattresses I'd ordered at the London Boat Show.

These goodies went some way to helping me see the end of the project , but all in all I was starting to feel down. The weather really wasn't helping.

March 24, 2013 *Snow Go*

Hi folks. Just a quick line to tell you that I'm still here, but that sadly building progress has ground to a halt once more.

The weather has been truly horrendous for weeks now.

Heavy snow again this weekend, a strong bitter wind that has blown the snow right through the barn, and it's been well below freezing.

March 2013 in the UK is going into the record books as the coldest for 50 years.

On top of this, I've had to choose paid work over boatbuilding for the past week. Both of these situations are likely to continue for the next few days at least.

I'm now becoming fearful that my self-imposed deadline for getting 'Gleda' out of the barn may be impossible.

March 28, 2013 - Jet Stream Blues

According to the meteorologists it's all down to the jet stream.

It spent last summer farther south than it should have, and as a result, we had one of the coldest and wettest winters on record.

It seems it liked it down south as it's decided to move out of its usual Northern residence and return there. So now we're getting cold air from the north east instead of warm air from the south east. Net result, we are locked into freezing temperatures.

Drifting snow that fell five days ago is still lying on the ground. There's a slight thaw during the day as temperatures go 1 or 2 degrees above, and then it all freezes again.

This time last year we'd had weeks of warm sunshine, now they are saying this cold could last well into April.

The doom-mongers are pointing to this jet stream relocation as proof of climate change.

All I know is that we're getting a stark illustration of what the UK climate would be if this was to become the norm. It makes me all the more grateful to be building a means of escape.

There's no escaping the effect it's had on the build, I'm well behind where I planned to be.

I'll keep pushing as best I can and see where we are in a few weeks, but right now it looks as if I'll have to make some changes to the plan.

It wasn't just me making excuses. For the UK it was indeed confirmed as being the coldest March since 1962. March was also the coldest month of the 'extended winter', the first time this had happened since 1975. There was still lying snow on the ground on the 1st April.

A few days later I made the decision.

April 4, 2013 - Chasing A Mirage

I wrote the other day about my feelings that this year had yet to start.

It seems a ridiculous thing to say because we're already into the second quarter. However, the continued winter weather has only served to reinforce this feeling of being somehow in limbo, of waiting for things to happen.

Spring is heralded as the season of new growth. Animals come out of hibernation, daffodils blossom and add a much-needed splash of bright colour to the grey landscape. Buds start to appear on the trees, the warmer weather encourages folks outside to breathe in the fresh air and to feel the warm sun again. This seasonal re-awakening has taken on increased importance for me this year. As it's coincided with a personal reawakening.

All through the winter, I've worked as hard as I could to try and make the coming year the one that saw the start of a new life. The year when I returned to the sea in a boat built by my own hands, the year when I could really start to make my dreams real.

It wasn't enough.

There's an old saying that goes something like, 'failing to plan is planning to fail'. That's exactly what I've done.

All through this project, I've plodded along, head down, doing what I could when I could. With no thought given to the end. It was simply too far away.

Then at the end of last year, I looked up, and there on the horizon I could see it. I could see 'Gleda' on the water, sails set, cutting through the blue water as dolphins danced around her bows. The sight lifted my heart and I quickened my pace with renewed energy, keen to tell the world that soon I'd reach my destination.

In the months that followed I continued to focus on that vision, but gradually I began to realise that for all my efforts, I didn't seem to be getting closer to it at all. And then with a sickening feeling in my stomach the reality hit me.

I was chasing a mirage, it wasn't as close as it looked, it was way beyond the horizon, my journey was not over.

I'd completely miscalculated, I'd failed to plan and now I could see things as they really were.

It crushed me, I felt like a failure. I'd let myself be fooled, I'd been stupid, and worse I'd convinced others that my vision was real. They'd made plans, they were excited, they believed in me. Now I was going to have to tell them that I'd been wrong.

This realisation led to me making one of the hardest decisions I've had to make since I started the project, and it hurt me badly.

But here's the thing, sometimes pain can be a good thing, it wakes you from your stupor, you learn from it and you come back from it stronger, renewed.

The decision is made, 'Gleda' will now be launched in May 2014.

Others wiser than me will have seen this coming, here are some comments from recent weeks.

From Chuck: "Man Plans, God laughs".

From Beat: "Don't rush it, my friend! Work on a boat is much easier on land than on the water!"

From Jacques: "Maybe the deadlines and constraints you put on yourself are too high?"

From Beat again: "You're getting an early lesson in your transition to the sailing life where plans are sketchy letterings in the sand at low tide!"

So this month I will be putting what I've learned into practice by reviewing, taking stock and planning.

For me, 2013 is just about to start, and this time I'm going to do it right. I've learnt my lesson and now I have one more chance to succeed. The 'Gleda Project' was never just about building a boat, the time has come to show it.

An appropriate tweet appeared in my timeline this afternoon. "The best time to start was last year. Failing that, today will do".

As you'll have deduced from my words, postponing the launch was a tough thing to do. I had no choice, I knew that. But I felt like I'd let people down, let myself down.

I needn't have worried about the first. Once again my inbox was filled with supportive comments. As for myself, what was done was done. The pressure had been eased. I could crack on again.

During the rest of April, I got the saloon table made and fitted. Finished all the major interior construction, and started painting.

Then the Beaulieu Boat Jumble rolled around again.

April 29, 2013 - Beaulieu Booty

We had a great weekend by the sea and a successful day at the Beaulieu Boat Jumble on Sunday. The weather was kind and after the cancellation last year the place seemed to be really buzzing.

It's a huge event and a real challenge to get around, to a great extent it's sheer pot luck if you find what you're looking for, but I did well this year. I restricted myself to buying stuff I really needed and I stuck to my guns with what I wanted to pay, the end result a nice little haul!

The List

- *1 x Manson Supreme 20kg (44 lb) Anchor*
- *6 x Seasoned Oak Deck Cleats*
- *1 x Large Stainless Steel Bow Roller*
- *2 x Fixed Portlights (for deck pod)*
- *1 x Beautiful Stainless Steel Wheel (brand new)*
- *2 x Mushroom Vents*
- *1 x Roll of neoprene seal (for collision hatches)*
- *2 x Heavy Duty Long Length Stainless Steel 'U' Bolts (for bow bridle)*
- *2 x Heavy Duty Short Length Stainless Steel Pad Eyes (don't know yet)*

April 30, 2013 - An Oath To The Universe

It's the 1st day of May tomorrow, That means I have exactly one year to get 'Gleda' ready for launch.

The next 12 months are going to be the most important 12 months of my life. On this, the last day of April 2013 I'm making a solemn oath to The Universe that I will make the following a reality before 1st May 2014

I will finish building 'Gleda'. I will unburden myself of unwanted possessions and unwanted commitments.

This time next year I will be ready and able to make the changes I've been searching for since the summer of 2006.

I've learned some hard lessons over the past years, I've been battered and bruised, I've been ambushed and hijacked, but I've kept going.

Of all the things I've learned the most valuable is this.

I've proved to myself that I'm capable of far more than I'd believed was possible.

I believe I'm capable of yet more.

Plan- Implement - Learn - Repeat

At the beginning of May, the weather seemed to be turning at last. Some warm sunshine lifted my mood and I made good progress getting the crossbeams construction finished off.

Even once all the beam woodwork was done, there was still an enormous amount of epoxy filleting and glass fibre reinforcement to do.

May 21, 2013 - Filleting Marathon

I knew that filleting these beams would be a bit of a chore. I wasn't wrong!

I've mixed up 14 pots of filled epoxy totalling approximately 2.8 kg (6 lb) today.

I've filleted all four beams on one side, and by my calculation, that's about 50 lm (164 ft) of filleting.

Tomorrow I turn them over and get to do the same thing all over again. Joy.

For those that don't know, these silica filled epoxy fillets are run down the edges of all the joints. It's all about adding strength to these vital components.

The weather still wasn't cooperating though.

May 24, 2013 - Blowing Old Boots

It has to be said that the weather is continuing to be pretty damn lousy.

Not only was it cold today with frequent heavy showers of rain and hail, but there was a strong Northerly wind blowing.

Winds from the North blow right through the barn and it made work today a tad uncomfortable. Not only did it make it feel colder than it actually was, but the frequent gusts kept blowing up grit and dust into my face.

Anything not secured down tended to get moved about, and all in all, I got a bit fed up with it.

I persevered nonetheless and made a start getting the tops of the beams glassed. After a sand down I pre-coated with neat epoxy, laid in the glass biax tape, saturated it with resin, stipple rolled it, and then covered it with PeelPly.

It's an operation I'm pretty familiar with by now and all went smoothly. I got the aft and mast beams done before I ran for cover.

May 26, 2013 - Beam Reach

I really stretched myself today and I have an aching arm and shoulder to show for it.

The pain is eased with satisfaction though, because I achieved my target and got the bottoms of all four beams glassed.

That's about 24 metres (78 ft) of biaxial glass tape and PeelPly, applied with some 4 kg (9 lb) of mixed epoxy. A good days work I reckon.

June 9, 2013 - A Sailing Guru's Words

I'm having a weekend away from building due to a welcome visit by my daughter Nicole.

Yesterday we spent some time in Stratford Upon Avon. Whilst browsing the travel section in a charity bookshop, my eyes fell on the spine of a thin book almost hidden amongst the others. I saw the word 'Moitessier' and my heart skipped.

As I extracted the book from the shelf it revealed itself as 'A Sea Vagabond's World' written by Bernard Moitessier.

Its tagline 'boats and sails, distant shores, islands and lagoons' must surely rank as one of the most enticing I've ever read.

A Sea Vagabond's World' is the last book Moitessier wrote. In some senses, it's a technical manual., compiled from the knowledge and experience he gained during his lifetime of sailing and living ashore in Polynesia.

The word 'technical' doesn't really feel right though.

Because above all else Moitessier's philosophy was one of simplicity. As these quotes show; "I'm absolutely sure that people are going to get fed up with sailing technology, and will want to return to the basics". And "There are different philosophies of sailing. Mine is to do everything as simply as possible. So you can set out to sea in the quickest time and for the least expense ".

He proposed the book to his publishers fifteen days before he died in 1994. And the book may have been lost, had it not been for his friend Véronique Lerebours Pigeonnière who took up the baton and got the book published.

I've mentioned before that James Wharram and Bernard Moitessier shared similar sailing philosophies. It's no surprise that they got on so well when they met in the West Indies after James, Jutte and Ruth sailed 'Tangaroa' across the Atlantic in the 1950's.

I spent a few hours yesterday soaking up the wisdom contained in the pages of Bernard's book. It's a unique blend of hard-earned sailing know-how, beautiful quotes and inspirational philosophy. It's a book I will treasure and re-visit often.

Amongst the many gems inside was this quote that could have been written for 'Gleda';

A boat is freedom, not just a way to reach a goal

I'll never meet Bernard Moitessier, but his writings are a legacy beyond value.

I have made a promise to the Universe though, someday I will make a pilgrimage to Brittany in France, to the little town of Bono. There I will visit a corner of the cemetery and leave my own tribute to the man who has inspired me to build my own freedom and to be myself.

June 11, 2013 - Filling Time

My time and my head have been filled with none 'Gleda' related things for these past few days.

It's all good, I have made choices and they were the right ones to make.

At the same time though there's a part of me that feels I'm not doing enough, that I've taken my foot off the gas, that for some reason I'm choosing badly.

Life is always a juggling act.

Particularly when a huge life-changing project is thrown into the mix and bills still need paying, but I simply cannot let things slip too much. It's approaching mid-June, the UK summer is short, I must make the most of it.

Today I got a filler coat onto all the beams, tomorrow I'll sand them and get the second coat of primer on. (I got a re-supply of paint yesterday) I want these beams finished.

June 14, 2013 - Much Needed Colour

Well, it hasn't felt much like June today.

We've had numerous torrential downpours. It's been windy, and after getting soaked whilst trying to fix my car, I ended up shivering and had to retire to the cabin with the heater and a cuppa to warm up!

I love this country dearly, but is a few months of decent summer weather too much to ask?

Right now it seems so.

Fixing the brakes on my car did as suspected suck up most of the day. I find it incredible that I used to spend most of my time working on cars, earning a living as a mechanic by day, and building rally cars by night.

Now I'm looking forward to that day when the only transport I need is a Tiki 38 and a folding bicycle!

Anyway, I'm mobile again now, and I did manage a couple of hours painting the beams.

First I flipped them over, got the Apollo spray kit out again, and finished off with the white top coat.

When that was done I couldn't resist getting the primrose out and painting the end caps and the outboard sides of the forward and rear beams.

June 17, 2013 - Almost There

Another solid session today, although unlike yesterday I ended up doing less than I'd anticipated.

I underestimated the time it would take to drill the 6 elongated locating pin holes. (18 mm stainless pins go through these to help locate the beams in their troughs).

I needed to take care that I marked the positions correctly and then the actual drilling took time.

I first drilled the two 22 mm holes on one side of the beam as far down as my drill bit would let me, a little less than halfway through the beam. Then I chiselled out the centre section before flipping the beam over and repeating the process on the other side.

Once that was done, I swopped bits and drilled out the remaining timber in the middle. I used the chisel and some files to finish off the inside of the holes then sanded off the sharp edges on the tops.

There were five holes to do today so it took some time. As I worked on each end of the beams

I also fixed the UHMW PVC spacer blocks in their correct positions. Again these needed to be drilled, countersunk and screwed down on bedding compound. I've now completed all three of the long crossbeams.

I just have a couple of hours work to do on the shorter mast beam then I can touch up the paint and I'm there.

It's been a long haul, I started work on these beams in April last year, so they've been work in progress for 14 months.

There were periods when they were put on hold whilst I worked on other things, but I estimate it's taken some 450 hours of work to build them.

It feels great to have finished the last major construction job though, (remember I have aluminium masts). There is nothing remaining that even comes close to needing this amount of work, and for that, I'm extremely grateful.

June 19, 2013 - A Long Awaited Coming Together

A landmark day today, the two hulls are now properly connected for the first time.

The cross beams are completed. They are sitting in exactly the right locations, and there are temporary retaining pins locking them in place.

I felt the difference immediately. I've got used to the hulls rocking slightly in their cradles as I clambered in and out of the cabins, or moved around on deck. Not anymore, she feels solid, she feels as one, she feels like a boat.

I took some time just looking at her, basking in my achievement and thinking about all the exciting times ahead..... It's been a good day.

Next up was the deck pod.

June 21, 2013 - Plodding Along

I've had an enjoyable day today, well at least in the sense that I've had fun playing with my modified deck pod.

What hasn't been quite so enjoyable is hay fever preventing me from breathing and seeing properly.

Plus the fact that my left hand seems to be losing its ability to grip anything without causing me to wince. All things considered I'm pleased I managed to do anything at all!

Hopefully a nights rest will get my hand back to fully functioning, and the forecast weekend rain should help the hay fever, so I'll be sorted.

Anyway, back to the deck pod. Since day one I've never really been a fan of the deck pod as shown on the plans.

Sailing 'Pilgrim' back in September just re-affirmed my desire to try and come up with some modifications that would make it work better for me.

I'd always planned to 'turn' the pod so that the watch berth was positioned forward, and enclosed a bit more with an additional bulkhead. Jacques and I also discussed lowering the pod floor by a few inches so as to increase protection and allow for the addition of a Bimini.

These two things were my starting point today. Thirdly I'd thought about building a helmsman's seat that was big enough to contain the big ice chest I bought some time back. So I added that into the equation.

I've never been able to draw things out well enough to really get a feel for a design, so I just cracked on with mocking up the real thing. I ended up with something that's getting close to what I had in mind and here it is:

Basically I've lowered the floor by about 3 inches and raising the watch berth roof about the same amount. I also decreased the radius of the curve so that more height is retained on the outboard sides.

I've lowered the leading edge of the watch berth roof so that it slopes at a similar angle to the cabin tops on the main hulls. I think I've found a good compromise. One that doesn't increase windage significantly. Provides more shelter at the helm, and just as importantly is in keeping with the boats beautiful lines.

Frustratingly I've now run out of 9 mm ply. So I can't do much more for a few days, that said it's probably a good thing as it means I can let my design simmer for a while to make sure I'm happy.

Seeing that mention of hay-fever has reminded me how much I struggled with it.

It was cruel. I'd spend the winter months desperate for the warm sunny weather to arrive.

Then, when it did, I'd spend a couple of months with nose dripping like a tap, itchy eyes and sneezing. It's almost as if I was allergic to the country.

At the time of writing, I've now been nearly four years away from the UK In that time I've had one cold and no hay-fever.

Something else to add to the long list of things I don't miss.

July 5, 2013 - If I'd Just Worked Harder

Here's an interesting fact I realised today.

If I'd worked on 'Gleda' for 8 hours each and every day for an entire year, i.e. 365 days. Then I would have worked the same number of hours as I've now worked on 'Gleda' since December 2006.

So how should I answer when asked how long I've been building?

If I'd just worked harder I'd have been sailing years ago! Obviously, I'm only joking.

Yes, I could have worked harder and faster, but I've always done what I could when I could, and for the most part continued to make progress.

It's interesting though. Because theoretically, it means that if two people worked 'office' hours over the course of a year. They could build a Tiki 38 from scratch and have her on the water the following year.

No use to me, but if there's anyone else out there considering a build it's food for thought eh?

Back to the weather. Having experienced one of the longest coldest winters in years incredibly we had a heat wave.

July 14, 2013 - Hot Hot Hot!

Wow! It's been years since we've had such a consistent spell of hot weather here in the UK.

For over a week now temperatures have been in the high 20°C's (80 F's) and it's fantastic!

I should just say that I'm very aware that there will be readers in some parts of the world who would consider the idea of this being hot as laughable.

I know, Death Valley it ain't, but after a no-show summer last year, believe me it's bliss for us.

Although available build time has been down I've been able to get much more done. Simply due to the fact that with a slow/medium epoxy hardener I can rattle through stages of glassing that would usually be spread over a couple of days.

If the Universe continues to smile on us for a few more months I'll really be able to move things on.

During my last two work sessions, I've continued with the deck pod glassing and now have all the forward watch berth sections finished.

I also made a start on the aft part of the pod. Due to my modified design I'm once again making it up as I go along, but now I'm clear what I'm going to do. Although it's a narrow section I need to make sure it's plenty strong .

July 17, 2013 - Another Long Job Continues

Once again I've been surprised how I constantly seem to underestimate the time needed to complete some of the build stages.

I realised today that it was nearly 100 work hours ago that I started on the deck pod.

Not all of that time has been spent on the pod, but I reckon something like 75 hours has, and there's still a lot to do.

I know that in part it's been a longer job because I went off plan, but nonetheless I still hadn't anticipated it would take so long.

It's ridiculous really, I should have learned this lesson long ago.

It doesn't really matter. It takes what it takes. But I guess I'm just more conscious of it because of my focus on completion. Something that didn't enter my head for most of the years I've been building.

Anyway, more progress today, the forward cabin sanded, primed and first coat of white applied. The aft section glass reinforced and filled and finally the framework for a small corner seat glued in place.

This was a bit of an afterthought as I pondered how to brace the pod side, I figured I may as well make the bracing useful and another seat seemed a good idea. Heatwave continues, 30°C again today.

This heat wave started on 3rd July and lasted until the 23rd.

In the UK it's unusual to have such a prolonged spell of hot, dry, sunny weather with temperatures exceeding 30 °C for 7 consecutive days. That's what we got and it was confirmed as the most significant UK heatwave since July 2006, which funnily enough was the year I bought my plans.

July 31, 2013 - Sands Of Time And Mood Swings

Another slow day today, although this time I hadn't planned it so.

I spent the morning working on the hatch cover I glued yesterday.

Things started frustratingly when I realised that I'd glued in the wrong crosspieces. Meaning that I had to disassemble the frame and start again. How I didn't spot that I'd made a square frame to fit a rectangular hole I don't know!

At least doing so gave me the opportunity to rebate the top of the frame to take the 9 mm ply lid. And to rout a nice round edge on the other sides, something I should have done yesterday.

I also cut the ply top so that I could epoxy it in place when I glued the frame back together again. My epoxy filler application was sloppy, and my mood wasn't good by the time I'd finished.

It's nothing the belt sander won't sort out tomorrow, but I'm annoyed with myself nonetheless.

After that job was done I decided to change tack and move onto another outstanding job. Making the frames for the opening port above the saloon table and the two narrow tumblehome perspex ports.

Pleasingly I managed this job a bit better, but it took me the rest of the day.

Summer departed temporarily today with thick low cloud and persistent drizzly rain. It only served to remind me how time is flying past, and left me in a heavy mood as I thought about all that is left to do with winter approaching again.

Time is tight, money is tight and on days like today the launch seems as far away as ever.

I know it'll pass, I know I'll keep going, I know I'll get there, but I can't lie, sometimes building this boat seems like the hardest thing I've ever done in my life.

August 2, 2013 - Acceptance of A Good Day

There are many things I want to learn more about, one of them is the principle of acceptance.

Not in the subservient sense, but in the sense of understanding that things are as they are, and not wasting time wishing they were different.

What's happened has happened, what is happening is happening, the only thing that we have any control over is what WILL happen in the future.

It may well be that this control is limited, we can't always get the results we want, but we can at least know what we want, and do whatever we can to get it.

When I was struggling the other day I should have just accepted it. I knew the tide would turn and today proved it yet again.

My mind was clear, the work just flowed, I did more in 8 hours than I'd done in the previous 20, I'll accept that with gratitude.

It was timely to get so much done. I've now passed the 3000-hour marker, how much more to go? I really don't know, but what I do know is that it'll be as many as it takes.

Today's accomplishments: Fitted the perspex portlight into the tumblehome over the saloon table. Made, fitted and glued the starboard main hatch coamings. Made the hardwood stainless steel slider mountings and fitted the tube. Made the main hatch cover for the starboard hull.

August 11, 2013 - A Record Run

I've now worked on 'Gleda' for 15 of the last 17 days, 106 hours of work in total.

When I started this run of work 'Gleda' just had holes in the hulls where the hatches would be. Now all the coamings are fitted and all the hatches and hinging/sliding mechanisms are constructed.

Today I got the first coat of white topcoat on them all, which means that by the middle of next week they'll be back fitted to the boat and ticked off as completed.

I've also built and finished two dorade vents, fitted 4 other through deck ventilators, and fitted the last 3 perspex fixed ports.

The bank account is looking a bit sad because I haven't been earning, but I plan to continue this run for another week and see where I am after that.

All in all, I'm feeling pretty good about things right now, the Universe is being kind and this time next year I'll have been afloat for a couple of months.... can't wait!

August 14, 2013 - Enclosed and Weather Proof

It's been a busy couple of days on and off the boat but two good work sessions have seen another significant step forward on the road to completion.

All the hatches, ports and vents are now fitted. And the whole boat has had a second topcoat of paint.

This means that for the first time 'Gleda' can be closed up fully and she could be exposed to the weather without problems.

When she's outside and the conditions are right I'll apply the last coat of paint in proper daylight!

That's not likely to happen for a little while yet, but nonetheless it feels good to have got her to this stage.

It's actually going to be a bit strange knowing there's no exterior building left to do on the hulls. Of course, there are various bits and pieces still to be attached. Like the lashing strakes and rubbing strip, and there's plenty left to do elsewhere, but as I said, it feels good.

I do have a little bit of paint to touch up here and there, but I'll take it easy tomorrow.

The barn desperately needs a good clean up before I move on to anything else.

August 27, 2013 - Ramping Things Up

I've decided that 'Gleda' will be staying in the barn over the winter.

I'd originally thought that I would have to move her outside into the yard, so that I would be able to get the deck pod into position and work more easily on the decks. But after chatting with Richard today it became obvious that moving her was potentially going to create some problems.

Once that was decided I had another look at the clearances needed to lift the deck pod into place, and although it's a bit tight, I think it's possible.

To that end, I spent a very mucky hour bringing down the temporary polythene canopy. It's been hanging in the barn roof since I put it up a little over 6 years ago. Hence the not inconsiderable amount of dust, bird crap and leaf debris sitting on it!

It's served its purpose and now the boat is weatherproof a few leaks and an occasional deposit of guano won't be a problem.

It's actually quite nice to be able to see the barn roof again after so long.

August 28, 2013 - Deck Pod In Place

On rare occasions throughout this build there have been days when weeks, if not months of work have suddenly been brought to a head. And a dramatic change in the boats appearance has resulted.

Today has been one of those days.

With the help of Richard, Malcolm, Luke, Joel and a JCB mini teleporter, we got 'Gleda's' deck pod lifted and into position. It was a tricky operation due to the lack of height and an inconveniently situated roof truss.

It was only the teleporter's ability to lift at an angle that allowed us to succeed, but once in position, the pod fitted perfectly.

Wow! What a transformation. Not only does the boat look completely different but for the first time I can stand between the hulls, 'on deck'. And see 'Gleda' from previously unseen angles.

It's going to take some getting used to.

I have to be honest though. The Tiki 38 deck pod could never be described as pretty. I don't think my modified design is any worse than the standard version, but neither would I say it's any better.

Ultimately the design of the boat is such that any structure on deck is going to stand out.

I remember when Creed O'Hanlon was having his Tiki 38 built in Thailand way back. He decided to do away with the pod altogether to retain the clean lines of the hulls, she looked a lot better for it. Maybe that's viable in tropical climes. The fact of the matter is though that for me head must rule heart. 'Gleda' is likely to spend the first few years of her life sailing European waters, she may well taste the North Atlantic before she heads south. A sheltered steering position isn't a luxury, it's a necessity.

I'm almost certainly going to add a roof to the deck pod as well, so it will be even more obtrusive. I'll get used to it and I'm certain I'll be very thankful for it some dark stormy night.

My solid run of boatbuilding had to be halted at the end of August. EDB had taken on another major project and once again my help was needed.

October 2, 2013 - New Season, New Start

Well, September passed in a blur. I worked 10-12 hour days and 7 day weeks on a fun project to convert an old Massey Ferguson 135 tractor into a replica Victorian steam engine.

We also built, from scratch, three complete passenger carrying carriages. I was responsible for all the 'coach building'. Things like epoxy coated ply panels to enclose the carriages. Construction of the train cab, and features such as the oil lamps, buffers and smoke box door.

Once again we were working to a hard deadline and it was tight. The train was loaded for transport to London at about 3 am, with the paint still wet. By 9 am it was moving visitors around the site of the new Kings Cross station development in London.

As always I felt frustrated at the lack of boatbuilding progress. But at the same time knew that I was preparing the ground for at least another month of dedicated progress on 'Gleda'.

I've got a few bits and pieces to clear up this week, but next week I'll be back in earnest.

Today I just spent a couple of hours mainly reminding myself which bits of boat went where, before making and epoxying some hardwood strengtheners onto the stern ramp.

October 10, 2013 - Aft Platform In Place

Well, the weather today was a shock to the system. 5'C on the way to the barn, barely reached double figures, and there was a stiff Northerly blowing which made it feel even colder.

I've missed the runny nose and cold fingers, not.

I'm thinking I'd best get used to it though because it's going to get a lot worse before it get's better. I've been here many times before but there's a big difference this time; this is definitely my last winter of building.

Today I cracked on cleaning up the aft deck frame I put together yesterday. Sanding back the excess epoxy, and routing a nice edge on all the underside exposed edges.

Once that was done I was able to drop it into position on the boat so that I could cut the 12mm deck to shape. I made the deck up out of three pieces to save ply, and after marking them up got them screwed and epoxied into place.

Before I fixed them I walk tested the platform out to the stern tube. There was only a small amount of 'bounce'. I know that once the epoxy sets it will stiffen up.

*I'll also be epoxy filleting all the underside joints but I'm prepared to add
a few more strengtheners if needs be.*

What I was referring to there was another slight modification I'd
made to the JWD design. On the plans, the aft starboard side area
of the boat next to the ramp is filled with netting. I wanted
something a bit more substantial. So I built an L-shaped platform.
Its forward edge locates into the last main beam recess. The aft
end I shaped to sit over the tubular aluminium stern beam.

October 14, 2013 - A Long Slow Process

*Yet another grey, wet and cold day as I continued work on the aft
platform and the stern ramp.*

*These relatively simple constructions still take huge amounts of time to
complete as they have to be put through all the various stages of
construction and finishing.*

*Having completed the upper side of the aft platform I was able to flip it
over and get the bottom epoxy coated and filleted. I also added a couple
of strengthening timbers to the aft end of the walkway.*

*Apart from beefing up the platform where it sits on the stern tube, it also
means that I'll be able to get a good fixing for anything I want to mount
on there later on. I'm thinking of VHF aerial, GPS aerial and ensign
staff.*

October 20, 2013 - Long Overdue Coming Together

*I looked back in my blog and discovered it was May 2008 when I cut the
rudder sections I've been working on today.*

*They've been leaning against the barn tent for over 5 years! Covered in
dust and pigeon crap, unloved, forgotten.*

*Given that I'll be relying on these bits of 18 mm ply to steer 'Gleda'
through all manner of watery hazards. I really should have treated them
with a bit more reverence! It's testament to the durability of good quality*

marine ply, that ten minutes with the orbital sander saw these neglected bits of timber looking like they'd just been cut.

Another EDB project I'm working on meant that I was only going to have a couple of hours of boatbuilding today. So I put them to good use and got the two layers of rudder section epoxied . A long overdue coming together complete.

October 22, 2013 - Rudder Sculptures

I spent four hours in close company with a belt sander and an electric plane today. Turning big lumps of roughly shaped epoxy covered plywood into something resembling shapely rudders.

After I'd got the edges all faired off I steeled myself to start removing some substantial amounts of ply,in order to create a nice tapering profile to the trailing edges of each rudder.

The building instructions simply state, 'sand the trailing edges down to approximately 12 mm to improve water flow'. Makes it sound easy, doesn't it?

Before I started I set up a marking gauge and drew in some lines so that I could see how much wood I was removing. And to ensure that I took even amounts off each side.

After that there was no choice but to dive in and start planing.

There is one big advantage to doing this with thick plywood though. And that's the fact that the different laminations appear as it's planed, in a similar way to layers of an onion. Once you start these layers act as a bit of a guide making life a lot easier.

Anyway a couple of hours and a big pile of sawdust later I had the job pretty much completed. I'm pleased with the results and once I've rounded all the rudder edges I'll be able to move onto the rudder mounts.

I'm surprised at the weight and bulk of these rudders now they're *assembled. I know the Wharram 'lashing hinges' work, but I still can't help wondering how they survive.*

I got one of the lads to take a photo of me standing with the rudders to give you some sense of scale.

October 27, 2013 - Awaiting The Storm

Well, if nothing else this is undoubtedly the most hyped UK storm in decades.

For days now we've been warned that a storm was brewing in the Atlantic. And that it's coincidence with the jet stream meant that it would be more powerful than anything we've experienced in recent years.

The shipping forecast for the South Coast of the UK issued this morning read as follows:

Southwest 7 to severe gale 9, becoming cyclonic severe gale 9 to violent storm 11 for a time, perhaps hurricane force 12 later

We're well used to autumnal gales in this country, but seeing the words 'hurricane force 12' even mentioned is extremely rare.

For the sake of accuracy I should highlight that we cannot in fact, get a 'hurricane' in the UK The waters surrounding this little isle are far from tropical. I remember the last one we experienced in the UK back in 1987. It's a blessing that they don't expect the winds to be as strong as then.

I wish 'Gleda' was tucked up a creek somewhere with big anchors laid. At least then I'd feel I'd prepared, that she'd be in her element, that I was with her.

As it is she's stuck in a structurally doubtful barn, built of bricks long since without mortar, a lot of rotten timber and some asbestos sheets. The barn is completely open at both ends.

I went up this afternoon and the power was already out. I did manage to top up the epoxy in the holes I filled yesterday but my mind was on the weather. I've done what I can. I've roped the epoxy tent and plywood stock to a solid steel rail. I've made sure loose objects are stowed, other than that all I can do is pray to the Universe 'Gleda' comes through unscathed.

Current predictions have the storm coming through us in early hours of Monday morning and through into the first part of the day. Fingers crossed and I'll update you tomorrow.

As it turned out the superstorm decided to pass farther south of us than predicted, meaning we got lots of rain but missed the strongest winds. It was blowy down south though. A gust of 99 mph was recorded at The Needles on the Isle of Wight.

October 30, 2013 - *Working For It*

> You are never given a dream without also being
> given the power to make it true. You may have to
> work for it, however.

That quote could have been written for this project, all of us have dreams. All of us have the power to make them come true, not all of us are prepared to do the work that's needed.

I think I've long since proven to myself that I'm prepared to work for mine, but that doesn't mean it gets any easier.

I've noticed these past weeks that I'm getting tired quicker, that my patience is less, that I want this boatbuilding to be over.

It's probably got something to do with the onset of winter. I know all too well what that means and the near-freezing temperatures this morning reinforced the memory.

Subconsciously I am still beating myself up over my missed launch date earlier in the year. I keep thinking that if I'd worked harder I could have been finished by now, 'Gleda' could have been wintering in the lagoon at Culatra.

But it is as it is, I can't yet say that the end is in sight but I feel it's close, like the first signs of land over the horizon after a long ocean passage. So I'll keep working on my dream, job by job, day by day, week by week, and I'll get there, I must.

Today I've glassed one side of the rudders. Made and fitted the supports for the side-deck locker lid. Drilled some drain holes in the side-deck locker bottoms, and finger holes in the locker lids. Tomorrow I'll be glassing the other side of the rudders and the tops of the side-decks, if my epoxy doesn't run out.

November passed with me working in the cold on finishing the rudders, building engine boxes, side decks and lockers plus a myriad of small bits and pieces. I was determined to keep going even when my epoxy ran out.

November 8, 2013 - Throwing The Dice

I ordered some more epoxy this morning.

I paid for it with next months rent money I'd set aside.

Reckless gamble or shrewd move? Opinions will differ.

To be fair the dice are slightly loaded in my favour as I have some money coming soon, I'm just not sure when.

There's another significant factor to be considered. When you find yourself with a problem that simply has to be solved then you solve it. I've made the choice to keep working on my most important project now, and deal with any problem that it creates if and when it appears.

The Universe told me I needed to build a boat, The Universe will provide.

For today I just did a couple of hours at the barn and got two good coats of primer on the upper sides of the side-decks.

My epoxy might not arrive until Monday/Tuesday so I'll probably take a few days off and start fresh again next week.

Engine wells and boxes up next.

November 22, 2013 - VIP Visit

Today was a special day, Gail and I had the pleasure of meeting fellow UK Tiki 38 builders, Janine and Adrian Hall.

Janine and Adrian are building 'Kira' down in the South East corner of the UK

They started in 2009 and after an intensive spell of building this summer, now have both hulls structurally complete.

They called in on their way up North for the weekend. They stayed long enough for us to enjoy a pub lunch, chat at some length about Wharram's, and of course make a visit to the barn so that I could show off 'Gleda'.

It was fantastic to talk with like-minded folks who share our dream, and it's lifted my spirits.

They are aiming to have 'Kira' completed within a couple of years. And I very much hope that one day we may sail our Tiki 38's together somewhere, now that'd be something!

As I'm writing this (November 2017), Adrian is still working on 'Kira'. He and Janine visited us in Cartagena during the summer. Work and family demands have continually slowed his build. He'll get there. I know he will. As I wrote 4 years ago, it's just a case of applying bloody-minded persistence. It's physical and mental as these posts demonstrate.

November 26, 2013 - Bloody Minded Building

With daytime temperatures only just above freezing right now, it would be easy to scrub round any building until things warm up a bit.

As each year passes I seem to dislike the UK winter more. But this time there's a difference, this time I know that pushing through, keeping going, and being bloody-minded, will allow me to escape from the next one.

So that's what I'm doing, it's slow, it's hard work, but I'm making progress.

I've put in eight hours over the past two days and now have engine box No 2 fully assembled. I'll fillet it tomorrow.

December 4, 2013 - Washed Out And Weary

I confess to feeling absolutely washed out tonight.

The last two days have seen me complete some hard physical work and my body doth protest.

There's no doubting that building a Tiki 38 solo frequently makes demands that weed out any weakness of strength both physical and mental.

It creeps up on you though. It's not like trying to bench press a new personal best.

Whilst you're working you don't really notice how much you're doing. But the hours and hours of climbing up and down ladders, squatting, bending, lifting, pushing and pulling, all tot up to a serious whole body workout.

I like to think it's keeping me fit and warding off old age, but on a night like tonight it feels like the opposite.

Anyway, the ache in my bones is tempered by the satisfaction of having made some decent progress.

I'm now ready for a change of tempo as I set about sanding, epoxying, glassing and painting all the components I've been working on these past weeks. I have everything set out under the boat ready to start and it's a bit daunting.

December 7, 2013 - Under The Weather Blip

It's been a strange couple of days. Health-wise I felt distinctly under the weather.

On Thursday we had a big blow come through followed by a very cold snap yesterday.

The storm caused damage across the North and East of the country. The East coast was partially inundated with the highest storm surge for 60 years, and tragically two people lost their lives.

Locally we just had a few branches down and the barn is now full of sizeable dry leaf drifts. I hunkered down to conserve energy. But I didn't forgo 'Gleda' completely.

I spent time quantifying and requesting quotes for my final timber order, (nobody has replied yet though). The quote requests are somewhat provisional at the moment as I still haven't made a final decision regarding what species of woods to use

December 12, 2013 - What It's All About

We're locked into a period of dank dark weather right now.

Not a hint of sunshine, everything is damp to the touch, daylight is in short supply. It's the time of year I dislike the most here in the UK, but thinking of next year keeps me going.

My work sessions may be shorter these days but I'm making them count, and as I've said many times before, any movement forward is good movement.

Today I got the side deck tops and engine box bottoms primed, and one set of engine box lids glassed.

December 18, 2013 - Winding Down To A Seaside Christmas

I've only been by the sea for one day this year, and so the thought of being by the sea for the Christmas holiday fills me with joy.

If all goes to plan we'll be in the small Cornish fishing village of Polperro this weekend. Just me and my lady, a wood burning stove, good food and drink, walks on the cliffs, and lungfuls of sea air.

It's been a tough year for both of us, but this holiday marks a turning point.

In a few short months 'Gleda' and the sea will be our home, we will enter a new chapter in our lives, bring it on!

My final work of the year has been to order the timber I need for the lashing strakes, rubbing strakes, tillers, tiller bar, gaffs and decks. I've settled on Iroko, Ash and Western Red Cedar.

I'll get delivery in early January.

So as I wind down 2013, my 7th year of building, here is the best view I can get of 'Gleda' as she is today.

2014 YEAR EIGHT (1524HRS) - THE ESCAPE

*J*anuary 8, 2014 - The End Of The Beginning

So, here it is, 2014. The year when this project changes from building a boat to sailing a boat.

I know, I know, this time last year I was saying the same thing and within weeks my delusion became plain for all to see.

This time it's different, this time my feet are planted on solid ground and my head is clear. This time I will not fail. Come hell or high water 'Gleda' will at last touch the salt water she was destined for.

This year will see the end of my boatbuilding life and the start of my sailing life. I can't put into words what that means to me.

Christmas and New Year were all that I'd hoped for. Me and my lady by the sea, chilling out and breathing in the fresh sea air.

I've learned over the years that the first week or so back inland after time by the sea is a time when I fall victim to the blues. I'm left feeling listless and unmotivated as my body and mind readjust to the lack of ozone and horizon.

There's no point fighting it, it leaves me when it's ready, and I'm pleased to say that it's already departed. Now I can start work again.

Now I can throw myself into the next 3 or 4 months with all my heart and energy. Now I can get this thing done.

January 13, 2014 - A Whole Lotta Wood

I was at the barn for 8 this morning anticipating an early delivery of my timber, it arrived at 4 pm!

I didn't waste the day though, I spent another few hours on the mast case fettling and finishing. There's nothing more I can do with it now until the epoxy has hardened enough to sand. I'll see what it's like later in the week.

After that, I gave the barn and epoxy shack a mega cleanup. As things stood I wouldn't have been able to get near the hulls in a few places. And as I'll be working on lashing and rubbing strakes soon I needed to make some space.

The timber arrived late afternoon in 7 big packages. I got them offloaded and into the barn just before the heavens opened, and it then took me an hour to unwrap and stack it all safely between the hulls.

The Western Red Cedar smells fantastic.

I have other work to do tomorrow. But I'm going to sneak in an hour so that I can sort through all this new timber and check I have everything.

January 16, 2014 - Lashing It Down

I'm not one to blow my own trumpet but I've worked bloody hard today.

I'm aching all over but my arms and shoulders take the prize for achyness.

It's all good though, because my work has been fruitful and I have a warm glow of satisfaction to ease the pains in my body.

'Gleda' now boasts a full set of lashing strakes. I cocked up with the section I fixed last night. I used a length that's needed for the rub rail, so I took it off this morning and started afresh.

So today's tally ran some 40 metres (131 ft) of Iroko oiled, eight ends shaped and sanded, some 200 holes drilled and countersunk, some 200 screws driven home.

It was getting dark by the time I'd finished and lashing down with rain (again).

The last strake went on under the light of my head torch.

The strakes look great. I think I've put them on with a fair curve. But as I can't stand back more than a few feet around the outside of the boat, I won't really see how good a job I've done until she comes out of the barn. But for now, I'm happy.

Rub rails up tomorrow.

Maybe it was the fumes from all the teak oil I'd been using, but I was feeling high. High enough to commit once again.

January 22, 2014 - BIG NEWS, Launch Plans & an Invitation

OK, here it is, no false dawns this time, it's happening.

'Gleda' will be launched from Weir Quay Boatyard at the end of May. There's still a lot of detail to sort out, but here's the plan. 'Gleda' will arrive at Weir Quay in the early part of week commencing 19th May. She'll be assembled in the yard over the following days and then craned into a mud berth alongside the pontoons for rigging. Hopefully, early part of week commencing 26th. We'll have a launch party on the evening of Saturday 31st May, and on Sunday 1st June 'Gleda' will be 'officially' launched.

AN INVITATION - I'd love to share this special time with as many of my friends and supporters as possible. If you'd like to lend a hand the week before launch there'll be plenty to do, you can just come for the party or just for the launch day, whatever you fancy.

Weir Quay Boatyard is on the Devon side of the river Tamar, a couple of miles upstream from the famous Tamar Bridges that connect Devon and Cornwall. Near the historic Naval city of Plymouth. We had a good feeling about Weir Quay the first time we visited, and the folks there have been really helpful and supportive. Even when I had to postpone the launch last year. Not only are they providing facilities for the launch, but they've also supplied us with a swinging mooring for the summer, so it'll be 'Gleda's' first home.

January 26, 2014 - Decks Near Completion

After a day off yesterday I was keen to get back to work on 'Gleda' despite the appalling weather.

Unlike last year when we had weeks of freezing temperatures and snow, this year it's been all about wind and rain.

Yesterday we had a freak hailstorm with 50mph gusts of wind, thunder and lightning, the works.

Today we've had torrential rain again.

The fields are saturated, the ditches are full, everywhere is wet and muddy. It's just relentless.

Boatbuilding is actually an escape, it may be hard, but I know that every hour of work is getting me closer to being able to escape it all.

January 27, 2014 - One Foot In Front Of The Other

My energy and enthusiasm were a bit down today.

Probably because after all the exciting stuff I've done recently, I'm now back to some fairly mundane tasks. Tasks which, although still moving me forward, lack that same visual impact and sense of achievement.

It was just a case of putting one foot in front of the other today.

The first job of the day was to drop down the forward mast case so that I could get a couple of coats of primer on the underside.

As there wasn't anybody around to help I did it on my own. Unfortunately, as I was lifting it down, it slipped, forcing me to move quickly so as to prevent it dropping hard on the floor. I succeeded, but at the cost of a twisted back and a pulled wrist.

It's easy to forget how physical building a big boat like this can be. And equally easy to get a bit overconfident about your own strength.

I'm not as young as I was when I started so I'll have to be more careful.

Anyway, I got a couple of good coats of primer on the mast case bottom, the forward deck supports, and the toe rails I fitted yesterday.

January 30, 2014 - Rain, Sleet & Snow Day

The Met office has just announced that January in the Southern UK has been the wettest since records began in 1910.

Today was truly miserable. Temperatures just above freezing, rain, sleet and snow falling regularly. A cold Easterly wind blowing and hardly a trace of daylight.

Painting and epoxy work was out of the question.

I tried to keep warm by getting a bit physical and lifting the forward mast box and decks back into position. I got help this time to save my back, and once everything was in place I added some additional 2"x 2" treated softwood stringers to the decks to beef them up a bit.

They've made quite a difference and I'm much happier.

I cut the day short and retreated to the warmth. Roll on summer and a life of following the Sun.

January 31, 2014 - Inland Inundation

It keeps on coming, day after day, week after week, rain, rain and more rain, at this rate I'll be able to forget about transport and float 'Gleda' down to the coast.

At least the temperature had climbed a few degrees today, so I decided to get the first gaff glued together.

It was a bit of a messy job with lots of areas to cover and no skimping on glue application, but the jig made things easier, and I soon had it all clamped together.

It's likely to be a while before I ease those clamps off though. The stress on the bent joints will be high, and I need to be sure that the epoxy has cured properly before I trust them to hold.

February 4, 2014 - Bumping Along The Bottom

I'll keep this short as whinging isn't helpful.

The last two days of works sessions have been tough going.

Crappy weather, crappy mood, nothing working, you get the picture.

I was re-reading 'The Alchemist' by Paulo Coelho recently. In the forward, he talks about the fourth obstacle to the realisation of a dream. Namely, fear, and it's subconscious effect of self-sabotage as achievement of a long worked for goal draws close.

Perhaps I'm experiencing just that. It won't win.

February 13, 2014 - Deck Pod Progressing

The paid work I was anticipating hasn't materialised yet, so I've carried on building these last few days.

The weather continues to hamper although compared to many we're getting away lightly.

I joked last week that if the rain continued I would be able to float 'Gleda' to Weir Quay.

The Met Office published a flood map today. Looking at the amount of land underwater it may actually be possible.

The last time the country experienced such extensive flooding was in the summer of 2007. Coincidentally the year I started building 'Gleda'.

So it looks like I'll be finishing her in an equally notable weather year.

On the subject of moving 'Gleda', I've been getting quotes and talking to transport companies over the last week. I'm close to making a final decision, and although it will be great to get this important task finalised it looks as if I'll need to budget some £2000 for it.

With electrical system, rigging, cordage and a host of sundries left to buy, things are going to be very tight, but I'll find a way.

February 26, 2014 - Me And My Bright Ideas

I'm not sure if I've mentioned this before, but working on a project like this is all-consuming.

The hours I've logged might equate to nearly two years of working a 40 hour week. But there's actually much more time than this that's spent away from the build when you are thinking about the job.

Planning, researching, sourcing, ordering etc. I often 'work' on the boat when I'm asleep as well.

I drift off pondering some technical challenge. Then at some point hand it over to the 'night shift' which usually comes up with a possible idea or a solution.

These ideas aren't always brilliant though, and muggins here still has to make them work using two caggy hands and a small brain.

Today has been a good example, I drifted off last night wondering how I could manufacture a curved end for the washstand in the heads.

I'd made a pattern using grooved back hardboard but I wanted to do the same with the fibreglass faced ply I'd made the top from.

The 'night shift' came up with the bright idea of using the table saw to cut grooves in the back of the ply so that it would bend. But it turned out to be not quite as easy as that.

After cutting the ply to the right shape, I spent about half an hour on the table saw cutting the grooves, and then tried to bend it. No chance, it was still way too stiff.

I sat down with a cuppa and pondered some more. I figured the only way it would bend would be to remove all the wood in the bent area so that just the fibreglass was left.

The big router was the only way to do it accurately, so that's what I used.

It was a horrible job.

Loads of fibreglass and wood dust flying everywhere, and despite covering up as well as I could, I still ended up itching for the rest of the day.

It worked though, and after some final adjustments and juggling with many clamps I was able to epoxy it in place.

Was it a worthwhile use of most of the day? Maybe not, but on the other hand I'll be looking at it for years to come, and smiling when I remember what it took to make it.

March 5, 2014 - On The Right Heading

I bit the bullet this morning and dived right into the remaining glassing and filleting in the toilet compartment.

After a couple of hours of knee crushing, neck twisting, elbow bashing contortions, I had it done. Thank F for that.

I needed a change of scene after that, so I moved over to the galley and set about finishing the through hull fittings, seacocks and plumbing.

I fitted an elbow to the sink drain so that I could neaten up the pipe run, and then got everything clamped and secure.

Next up was the saltwater inlet. I started with the pump and worked backwards down the pipe run to find a below waterline location that was both accessible and unobtrusive.

I ended up putting the hull fitting through under the lowest kitchen unit shelf. It's out of sight but still easy to get to, I don't like having potential sources of salt water ingress where I can't see them.

Needless to say the seacocks I'm using are all DZR corrosion resistant brass.

Next I moved into the deck pod and worked out a location for the bulkhead compass. The compass was actually a leaving present from the company I worked for about 5 years ago, and it's been sitting in a box ever since.

Once I'd chosen a position, I cut the hole and dropped it into place temporarily.

In these days of GPS it could be argued that a compass is almost redundant. But I think there's something reassuring about using an instrument relied on by seafarers for centuries.

On a night watch its gentle glow and movement can be quite hypnotic. I wonder how many hours I'll spend looking at it over the coming years, and what magical places it will guide me to?

March 10, 2014 - More F In Fillets

Today I swapped sides and started work on the port side forward cabin. There's a little less to think about in this area because it's basically just a single berth.

I've not worked in this part of the boat since way back when. So there were a few nasty surprises when I realised what hadn't been done.

In particular loads of filleting. Although I'd filleted and painted the watertight compartment up in the bow before the deck was glued on. The stringers on the underside still needed doing.

They've got to be the most awkward and difficult place to access on the entire boat.

It took a couple of horrible hours to get the job done and at the end of it, I had epoxy in my hair and aches in every limb.

It was actually a relief to move aft out of such a confined space and fillet under and around the beam trough, and to glass the hull joints.

I'm going to have to bite the bullet and just dig in for the next couple of days, because there's still a lot left to do, not to mention making and fitting the steps.

March 16, 2014 - A Splash Of Colour

Everything seems to be going slow right now, I'm making progress, slowly, the weather is improving slowly, my aching bones have me moving, slowly.

Movement may be slow but it's movement nonetheless and in the right direction. It needs to speed up though, time has not slowed, and there will be a wagon pulling into the yard on 19th May to take the first hull south.

The list of jobs still seems endless and my mind is constantly jumping from one part of the boat to another. Working out what needs doing, what bits I need to buy, how to do things.

The last two days have seen me epoxy filleting, glassing, painting, fitting out cabins and working on the steering amongst other things. One of the more enjoyable was slapping some colour into the toilet compartment, it's brightened things up no end.

Now seems the right time to bring another perspective to this story. If you've read this far you'll know that although I was building alone, I was now sharing life away from the boat with Gail.

With the day that 'Gleda' would finally get afloat drawing closer Gail was facing her biggest challenge. That of leaving the comfort and security of her old life behind and starting a new adventure.

She wanted to start blogging. I set her up as 'Land Girl Afloat', and she's been writing ever since. You can follow her at **www.landgirlafloat.com**

I'll let her pick up the story.

*(**GAILS BLOG**) **March 20, 2014 -In The Beginning ...***

I first met Neil back in 1997 when I returned to Leamington from South Wales.

We were both working for Gerflor, a vinyl flooring manufacturer, in Warwick. At a company event a couple of months after I joined, I got very drunk and lost a couple of hours of my life,

I surfaced kissing Neil.

Prior to this moment, I do remember being on a canal barge where the event started. Telling him that I wanted to see the stars as we see them on the TV over Africa. Or Australia where it looks like glitter has been sprinkled over an inky blackness. Neil assured me that the night sky could really look like that, and was not CGI'd as was my thinking.

Anyway, back to the kissing part.

We had a couple of dates but being the good girl I didn't let things go too far. One day in work, after he had been away for the weekend in Cornwall. He gave me a plastic litre bottle of scrumpy cider and told me that 'I was like a bus'*. WTF!*

Apparently, after many months without any female interest, there were two of us (hence the bus reference). And that he had chosen the other bus. Obviously, I was most put out having lost out to a barmaid.

So much for having morals.

Anyway some years later, after I had left Gerflor and then returned. It transpired that Neil had been in the relationship with bus No2 which had not lasted. We eventually got together again at Christmas 2006.

This time, sod the morals I wasn't about to lose him again. As I tell him, I waited for him for nearly 10 years.

In December 2006 Neil had just bought the plans for a Wharram Tiki 38 catamaran and had picked her name, 'Gleda', and started his blog.

From the very beginning, I knew that Gleda was now the other woman, and that Neil's long-term plan was to leave land and 'Gleda' was to become his home.

At the time this was a 4-5 year plan and I had landlocked Neil for at least this long. So started the longest 5 years ever; oh yeah, it was 7.

*I'm forced to make a couple of corrections. I didn't specifically call her a bus, I was referring to females generally, and it was 5 litres of scrumpy, not 1 litre!

(GAILS BLOG) March 27, 2014 - As One Door Closes

Not unexpected, but I have today officially received a redundancy notice from my job after 7 years.

A bit about me - I have been in full-time permanent employment since I was 17 years old and have only moved jobs when I wanted to move.

First experience of a redundancy situation - not nice.

The original plan, for me to join Neil, was work had agreed for me to take a 3-month sabbatical from the office for the boat launch, and for me to try the lifestyle.

More about me - I don't camp, can't row, have never sailed (as in more than sitting on a boat as a passenger). I like my creature comforts, don't like being cold, like 9 hours sleep a night, I've never been without a TV or mains electric, and I love high heeled shoes.

So my 3 months try out has turned out to be a positive lifestyle change. Do I mean positive? Re-reading the above paragraph, it may take some time to come to that conclusion.

Not having the 3-month deadline will make a difference to my mindset. I always intended to return to work after the 3 months. Then if my adventure with Neil was to continue; hand in my notice.

However, for me, it was a massive hurdle to even contemplate leaving a full-time permanent job. Particularly one that I enjoyed (then).

So on with our plan to change our lifestyles; admittedly Neil is some way ahead of me on that, but I'm catching up (bought a waterproof tub to hold the loo roll)!

April 1, 2014 - Gas Masts

As planned we had a little shopping trip this morning out to the local caravan and camping store. I got all the hose, pipe and connectors I need to plumb in the cooker as well as two new 13 kg propane bottles that should see us cooking on gas for a while.

I have to build some plinths and retaining blocks in the gas locker and run the pipework, so that's all added to the list for later.

It was nearly lunchtime before I got to the barn, and once there my priority job was to get the masts prepared ready for welding.

I'm not entirely sure when the guy is coming to do the work but hopefully, it'll be within the week. It was a bit nerve-racking taking a big angle cutter to the aluminium, but I took my time marking out first and took things very carefully.

The masts are raked aft at 9° and 7.5° I decided to cut the mast tops so that the caps will sit level. It was a bit trickier to do but it meant I was able to cut out the slight damage that occurred to one of the masts during shipping.

Once the mast was cut I notched in the cap gussets and marked up the cleat locations on both masts. I also dropped the aft deck section and stern ramp so I could remove the stern tube, as that needs caps welding on the ends as well.

My two LED masthead lamps arrived today as well, so I was able to suss out where and how they'll be mounted on the mast caps. It should be an easy job as long as I remember to run a lead wire through the masts before the tops are welded in place. I'll do that first thing tomorrow.

April 5, 2014 - I'll Get By With A Little Help From My Friends.

I've touched on this before, some folks think I'm a lone builder, but it's not really the case.

Over the last two days, I've had a lot of help from King, Richard, Paul, and Charlie.

King is in the business of graphics and he sorted me out with some stencils for painting the boat name on the bows. He wouldn't take any payment.

Richard and Paul spent several hours yesterday welding my mast fittings. They had problems with the welding plant and worked till late into the evening trying to sort it. We had to call it a night eventually, but we'll be re-visiting the job tomorrow and I know they'll get it done.

Paul has also made me a new shaft for the steering gear.

Today Charlie has helped me with setting up the wood lathe to turn the mast footing. He's also helping me source a new chain for the steering linkages.

Richard is a constant source of help in many ways. Not least with his *generosity in letting me have scrap, and not so scrap, timber and metal from around the yard.*

When 'Gleda' is launched it'll be in no small way the result of these many valuable contributions.

It's hard to switch off at the moment, my head is constantly buzzing with the many and varied jobs I have underway.

Time is compressing and there's still a hell of a lot to do. I didn't get to sleep till gone 3 this morning and was back at the barn by 8.

April 6, 2014 - A Job Weld Done

In the grand scheme of things welding a few bits of aluminium together isn't a big deal, but for me, today, it seems like one.

I've had two long aluminium tubes lying in the dark damp recesses of the barn for years.

Even after I extracted them a few weeks ago they were still just aluminium tubes.

But today they've become masts for a boat.

Paul turned up this morning and this time the welding plant worked just fine, and in a couple of hours, the job was done.

That's testament to Paul's skill because TIG welding aluminium, particularly when welding thick to thin, is very tricky.

Cheers Paul

April 8, 2014 - I've Had Better Days

I was all fired up to paint some aluminium today. But while I waited for the paint to be delivered I spent an hour finishing off the paintwork on 'Oscar' the dinghy. That job's done now and she looks like she belongs to 'Gleda'.

The paint still hadn't arrived, so I decided to continue with making my modified mast bases. Basically, I'm carving them out of solid oak and fitting hardwood 'keys' that locate into notches in the bottoms of the masts to stop them rotating. I can now see the reason to use the bases shown in the plans, because I've changed the game by using aluminium masts instead of wood.

Anyway, getting them into shape involved using 'Big Bertha', the large circular saw in the woodwork shop.

I've used her many times and always treat her with a lot of respect for obvious reasons. Today though my mind was not fully on the job. And after making a cut and powering down the blade, I wandered round to the other side of the saw to pull out the finished piece. The saw blade hadn't quite finished turning (there's no brake on it), nonetheless I stupidly reached in, and she bit me.

I'll be losing the nail on my right index finger. I came close to losing more than that. I'll probably carry a long-term reminder of my stupidity. I've noted the warning.

After patching myself up and having a bit of a lie down, I carried on until I'd reached a point where I'd had enough. I'll ponder the mast bases a bit more before continuing with them.

Just as I was packing up for the day the paint arrived. I thought I'd get a first coat on the stern tube to see how it went. I got the lid off the paint, gave it a good stir and went to pour a bit into the roller tray. The tray tipped up all over my feet! I now have white crocs and socks.

Like I said, I've had better days.

April 12, 2014 - Preparing For The Last Push

It's been a tough week all in all and my body has taken the brunt of it.

I've continued with some painting when I could and I had a play with the galley stove gas pipe routing today.

But next week I've really got to stop messing about and start pushing.

In 5 weeks time, the wagon will pull into the yard to load the first hull.

In 3 weeks time, we need to be cleared out of our rental cottage, it's going to be intense.

My daughter is visiting this weekend so I'm chilling out and re-grouping.

Because starting Monday there will be no more relaxing until we're at Weir Quay.

(GAILS BLOG) April 20, 2014 - Follow 'Your' Dream (or that of someone else)

My friends will know that I've never contemplated living on a boat, or any kind of small space as a way of life.

But then neither have I said that I don't want to.

It is clear that The 'Gleda' Project is Neil's dream. Not just of the build itself but of the change of lifestyle that moving on board will bring.

That said, I don't have a dream, so I'm not giving up on my own dreams and aspirations, or putting them in 2nd place to join Neil in his. I'm over the moon that Neil wants to share his dream with me.

This 'not having a dream' seems to be unusual. My friends at Forever Living, and Neil himself, seem to find it strange that I don't have that dream/aspiration.

Lots of self-help and motivational material starts with 'what is it that you really want?'.

I just don't know - superficially I'd like to be thinner, a real blonde, and be able to raise just one eyebrow.

I've listened to some fantastic stories on what motivated those on their 'Forever' journey. And they are successful and willing to share that with others. I have noticed that a lot of these are 'for the future of their children'. I did wonder if that was it. As I don't have children, do I not have the same motivation to achieve.

But achieve what exactly?

After some thought, I realised I am in a comfortable; comfortable but happy and contented place. I am happy with my lot and not been disappointed by not achieving a dream/aspiration.

I used to think that more money was my motivator. But not enough to motivate me to work harder at my Forever, Pampered Chef, Avon businesses, where I know there is money to be made if you work at it.

Over the last couple of years, I have realised that money is not what I want to strive to achieve. Yes, I'd like to be comfortable and not have to worry about where the money for the next rent or bill payment is coming from. But also I know that more money does not equal more happiness.

I haven't owned a property since my early 20's (not that I owned it then, the bank did). And although I like stability, having a mortgage on another property has not been on my list of wants for many years now.

However, there is no way I'm sitting back in my contented happy place and letting this opportunity of sharing Neil's dream pass me by.

I can see that there are great experiences to be had. And who knows, it may turn out to be that it is the dream/aspiration that I don't know I have, or maybe I'll find it on the journey that we take.

At worst I anticipate remaining happy and contented with my lot - doesn't sound too bad.

April 22, 2014 - Starboard Cabin Fit-Out Day

I pushed hard today and got the last pieces of structural furniture in place.

I've added two more decent sized shelves alongside the double berth, and fitted fronts to the highest ones. I've also fitted the hanging locker louvred door, although I'll be taking it off again to sand and paint.

It's taken me six days to move from an empty hull to a fitted one, and it'll probably need the same again to fillet, sand and paint.

I'm happy to have got to this stage though, and I think this space will work very well.

April 23, 2014 - Doing All I Can

That's the theme right now as time ticks away and the pressure starts to ramp up.

I had trouble sleeping last night as my brain fizzed with thoughts of moving out of our rental cottage, lists of stuff to buy at Beaulieu, getting 'Gleda' out of the barn, all the jobs left to do before I leave, the journey down to the coast, re-assembling the boat, moving on board, launching, will Gail be OK, do I have enough money.

It's all a bit intense.

At the same time though I'm super excited. I know that all these stresses are just my lizard brain resisting change, and it's me that's instigated the changes!

I've just got to take each day as it comes, doing all I can. In a few months, things will be a lot simpler and we can start to build the new life that this project has been all about.

My lack of sleep left me struggling a bit today but I still made some progress.

I got the water tank in place. I fitted a transparent watertight inspection hatch in the bulkhead between main cabin and toilet compartment.

I can't afford a sender and gauge for the water tank. So this hatch will allow me to visually check the level from the toilet compartment without having to lift the bed mattress and tank compartment lid.

April 25, 2014 - Sting In The Tail

It has to be said, today was a bit of a drag.

After a disturbed night thanks to a migraine, I spent the entire work session in the cabin sanding.

I've grown to dislike epoxy filleting, but I dislike sanding even more. The face mask is uncomfortable. Even with safety glasses, the dust gets in your eyes. And they still haven't invented a sander that doesn't blow right in your face at some point.

Not only is the work itself a chore, but it then leaves a huge mess to clean up before you can do anything else.

At one point I caught my foot on the cable for the work light and pulled it down smashing the bulb. And as I moved through the cabin I realised that there is far more filleting left to do than I realised. Not least the stringers under the aft deck.

It's going to take me at least all day tomorrow to get the cabin anywhere near ready for paint.

It seems I'm not out of the woods yet.

Oh, and the weather's been shite, persistent rain all day and much colder.

April 28, 2014 - Life Changing Days

As we enter our last weeks of living ashore many things are changing.

The days ahead will bring new challenges, new routines, in fact, new everything!

Over the years I've tried to keep this blog up to date on a daily basis, but this will also have to change I'm afraid.

Internet access for me will be occasional until I arrive at Weir Quay. Even my mobile signal is dodgy in the barn so I'll be going dark for a while. I'll update when I can though.

And as I've said before, once things have settled down afloat there will be a constant stream of far more interesting things to blog about.

On Saturday I had to do some paid work and today was the same. It may well be my last for a while though so the income is much valued.

Monday May 5th, 2014 - Journal Entry

Well, it's not exactly what I thought it would be but here I am spending my first night aboard 'Gleda'.

She's not afloat, she's not even outside, she's sitting in the barn right where she was built.

We handed back the keys to Cottage 3 this morning after 3 happy years. A new chapter is starting but there's some work left to do yet.

I miss Gail, she's staying with her Mom. But in a few short weeks, we'll be able to start the adventure properly, together.

May 6, 2014 - Still Here, Working Hard

Hi Guys, Apologies for the lack of updates over the last week, but as I said, things were going to get a bit crazy.

So here's a quick summary of what's gone down while I've been offline.

We've moved out of our rental house, and now everything I own in the world is sitting in a barn alongside the boat.

It actually feels great to have offloaded so much stuff and to have removed a big expensive layer of responsibility.

I spent my first night aboard 'Gleda' last night. I confess it was not what I had imagined when I first started building but hey, needs must. I slept very comfortably in the port forward single cabin. I was plenty warm, and somewhat lulled by the sound of rain splashing down on the barn floor from the leaky gutters.

Considering that the whole boat is a worksite right now I was pleasantly surprised how well everything worked, and how comfy I was.

Things can only improve as the weeks go on.

279

I've just about finished the starboard main cabin and completed a host of smaller jobs. I'm back inside bricks and mortar tonight but the next 48 hours will be spent onboard getting ready to move the hulls out of the barn at the weekend.

I'll do my best to post a load of photos and details then.

Anyway much needed sleep beckons now, but I wanted you to know that all is well and moving along on schedule.... laters.

Wednesday 7th May 2014 - Journal Entry

I've felt a bit down today.

Mom is in hospital after a fall. She's damaged her shoulder badly. Part of me says I should be closer to help out.

So I think it's just a combination of things, not least that 'Gleda' is a complete mess.

Actually, that's not true. The main cabin is pretty much finished now.

I unpacked my books and put all Gails stuff in there today. I even have clothes hanging in the locker. The galley/saloon is a different story.

Everything is dusty and messy. The varnish on the hatch coamings is still tacky even after 24 hours. It was irritating.

It brought back memories of when I first moved onto 'Mor Gwas' in Gosport all those years ago.

I shouldn't complain, I know it. But ....

Thursday May 8th, 2014 - Journal Entry

A tough day today. The weather has been crap, very overcast with persistent rain.

I woke at six and was working by seven.

I spent all day in the galley/saloon area painting. I stopped at seven having had only a short lunch break.

With the galley out of bounds, I set the microwave up on deck and zapped a ready meal Jalfrezi curry, washing it down with a dumpy beer. I know how to live.

I rang Dad to see how Mom was doing. She spent most of the day in theatre. A five-hour operation to rebuild and replace the shoulder socket joint. He's going to cancel the hotel they'd booked. They're not going to be at the launch.

I'm beginning to wonder if they will ever get to see the project I've poured so much of my life into.

May 11, 2014 - Where's The Boat Gone!

Well, it's been a crazy week and a crazy last few days in particular.

I'm exhausted but elated, and I can't write much tonight but here's a quick summary.

The cabins are all finished for now and most of our stuff is aboard. But the big news is that today 'Gleda' finally left the barn she was built in.

She is now residing in a muddy farmyard waiting for the wagons which will arrive in a weeks time.

Yesterday I grafted for 12 hours straight to clear the barn ready for the move.

Moving the hulls was tricky. Height restrictions meant we couldn't sling her under the hulls. We had to lift her at the stern under the rudder skegs and at the bow with strops 'strangled' around the bridle mountings.

I knew I'd built her strong, but I also knew this was not the ideal way to lift a boat.

I needn't have worried, she took it all in her stride. Richard and Malc drove the trucks with skill and precision.

Each hull was squeezed through the narrow entrance into the yard, moved along past the other barns, then turned and positioned parallel to the track along which the wagons she'll be transported on will park.

It'll be a far easier lift next time.

I still have a list of jobs I need to complete over the coming week, but they're all easy by comparison,

I'll do my best to update a bit more frequently next week.

May 12, 2014 - In A New Element

A week today 'Gleda' will be on the road south.

It still seems surreal, and I'm still working 12 hours a day on a list that never gets shorter.

But the deadline is set, what isn't done at the barn will be done at the boatyard.

Every time I walked out of the barn today I smiled. I smiled because I was looking at my beautiful boat over on the other side of the yard.

More specifically the hull that since its birth I've never seen from more than four feet away.

It may be a muddy farmyard but it's under an open sky, she's got one new element above her, and soon she'll have her natural element below her.

Today I've been mainly cleaning, prepping and painting. The weather is forecast to settle and warm up midweek into the weekend. I may even work outside :)

The empty barn seems full again as I finish stuff off, but bit by bit it's being moved over by the hulls ready for transport.

By the way, I've stopped counting hours worked. I'm going to round off total build time at 4000 hours.

From now on I'm fitting out and that's likely to be never-ending!

Thursday 15th May 2014 - Journal Entry

Tonight will be the first night spent aboard 'Gleda' outside.

The last couple of nights have been spent at friends, housesitting.

It was great to be back with Gail but we were still in someone else's house, and for me at least 'Gleda' already feels like home. I want it to feel the same for Gail.

As I said to her the other night, "It may be a small space, but it's our space".

I made a meaningful step forward with work today when I got the name painted on the bows. It seemed the right time to do it, and it's a symbolic step to confirm the identity of this beautiful boat I've created.

I found myself standing and staring with pride. There are some builders working on site at the moment.

One of them asked me yesterday if I'd 'refurbed it'.

It felt good to answer "No, I built her from scratch". Even for me, it seems hard to believe.

He just said "Wow".

May 17, 2014 - The Big Move Next

Just a quick update tonight.

I've been working flat out and now everything is pretty much packed up and ready to head south.

The wagons are due in Monday lunchtime, and after loading we have a 200-mile road trip down to Weir Quay, arriving Tuesday morning.

It's been incredibly hard getting everything ready to move, remember it's not just the boat that's moving. It's everything we possess.

Despite being pretty ruthless with getting rid of stuff there's still a frightening amount aboard 'Gleda', probably too much.

But it'll all be sorted in due course, we just need to get down to the yard and get organised, it'll be fine.

Sunday 18th May 2014 - Journal Entry

If all goes to plan this is my last night at the barn and my last night in the landlocked Midlands.

These years of work have brought me here.

Now I must trust the Universe to help me bring my efforts to a successful end and, to deliver 'Gleda' to her natural home and the start of our new lives.

I am excited, a little apprehensive, and slightly scared of what the coming weeks will bring.

Tomorrow I just need to pack everything into the boat properly, secure it, and then wait for the wagons.

Gail will be here about eleven, and once everything is loaded we'll be away.

She's booked us into a Travel Inn for 3 nights so we'll have a breathing space to get sorted.

These are life-changing days and it feels good to be alive and challenging myself.

May 19, 2014 - She's On The Road!

It's the end of an incredibly emotional and stressful 18 hour day so I'm keeping this short.

'Gleda' was loaded onto the wagons this afternoon and is now on the road.

We're in the hotel not far from the boatyard and we'll be there to meet her in the morning.

It's been a momentous day.

HERE'S A VIDEO OF 'GLEDA' LEAVING MANOR FARM - Or search YouTube for **'Wharram Tiki 38 Catamaran 'Gleda' Transported'**

PART III
ESCAPE

BACK TO THE SEA

*We are tied to the ocean. And when we go back to the sea,
whether it is to sail or to watch – we are going back
from whence we came...*

— JOHN F. KENNEDY

THE BOATYARD

May 20, 2014 - 'Gleda' Is In Weir Quay

I've got to be honest. The novelty of seeing my precious boat hanging from various strops, chains and cranes. Being swung about and manoeuvred this way and that. Being set down and lifted again, and generally being put through what a boat wasn't built to be put through, has worn off now.

After an overnight stop en route, 'Gleda' arrived at Weir Quay this morning and, after some 4 hours,everything is now sitting safe and sound in the boatyard.

Loading yesterday went pretty well, although the port hull was a darned tight fit on the low loader trailer. The hull had to be turned 180° in the air so that the stern could slot in between the rear ramps on the trailer.

And fitting the pod up on the front platform was quite challenging too. All of the above was completed on the warmest day of the year so far. The temperature hovered around 25°C all day, unbelievable!

It took all afternoon to get everything loaded but at about 4.30 'Gleda' was on her way.

The wagons made it down to Avonmouth near Bristol before pulling in for the night, and they were at Weir Quay for about 10am this morning.

We always knew things would be a little tricky at Weir Quay.

There are a few miles of twisty narrow lanes to get to the yard, and once down by the water there's a tight turn and only a narrow lane out front of the yard.

There was no way the wagons could be backed into the yard, so we had to park up across the gate and crane 'Gleda' off from there.

To make things easier the guys brought the wagons down to the yard one at a time, leaving one parked up in the village of Bere Alston.

I ran 'escort', driving in front to make sure anything coming the other way got pulled well out of the way before the wagon came through.

Once at the yard Mike and his team got to work lifting 'Gleda' off the trailer and into the yard.

Even getting the last empty trailer back out proved challenging, as 'Ferret' the driver had to reverse back down the lane. Then back in Bere Alston we crossed paths with a large funeral party, there were cars and tractors parked everywhere. 'Ferret' indicated to me that in some places the clearance he'd had was somewhat akin to the thickness of a cigarette wrapping (I'm paraphrasing!).

Anyway another long stressful day draws to a close with another significant milestone passed.

Tomorrow if all goes well we'll get the hulls positioned correctly and start prepping to drop the beams in.

Unfortunately the weather has turned for the worse, and torrential rain is forecast for Thursday, so we'll have to see how we go.

Not experiencing the long-anticipated stress-free relaxed boating lifestyle just yet!

(GAILS BLOG) May 21, 2014 - It's all new to me

...... Well, it will be soon.

After a meeting at work Monday morning, where it was confirmed that my last day in employment will be 19 June 2014, I packed up my little car and headed over to Wroxall for the last time.

The car I have left with Mum. As she said, "I may have lost a daughter but I have gained a car" — not sure she feels hard done by though.

How does Landgirl Afloat feel to be nearly on board her new home of 'Gleda'?

I'll tell you; excited, anticipatory and a little bit scared. Luckily the first two outweigh the other.

I'll let you read Neil's posts on the physical movement of the boat, but I have to say even as the camerawoman, it was heart pumping.

I don't watch sport as I can't stand the anticipation. So watching everything Neil owns, (his possessions are inside) and my new home, being lifted up by a bit of string (so it felt), was gut-wrenching.

There were some moments when the battery had run out on the camera so I wasn't required to film, where I could turn away and not look, but I did watch most of it.

Neil seemed remarkably calm although I bet he wasn't feeling that way inside.

Now down to the last couple of days before she actually goes on the water and we move in.

All well real now.

I checked out the shower room at the boatyard. It has a hairdryer (good), a shower (naturally), a gap under the door for draughts! and a heater, (also good).

Not sure how getting to it will work though. Do I get rowed across by Neil in my robe and crocs carrying my soap bag and towel?

Do I just swim across in my cossie? Not shower? Mmmm.

A few days or so before I need to try that one.

The hotel we are in for now has an ensuite 10 steps from the bed. No sea to cross and it is lovely and toasty warm with a flushing loo and running hot water.

All a bit daunting, but as I said above, very excited.

Friday, May 23rd, 2014 - Journal Entry

Well, here we are. Gail and I sleeping aboard for the first time in the double berth.

Today we spent all day trying to make sense of the boat. Gail worked hard and got both main cabins sorted. I got really stressed with what seemed like lack of progress but actually, we've done well.

I got the pod windows and roof on, got electric to the boat and got all the tools sorted.

It's been hard, it is hard, but we're getting there.

May 24, 2014 - Adjusting To Boatyard Life

It's a long time since I spent time in a boatyard, they're unique places, their location, their atmosphere.

Weir Quay already feels unique, the location is beautiful, the atmosphere is laid back and friendly, it's a nice place to be.

That said these last few days have been hard. We're living in two separate boats until the beams can be lifted in next Wednesday.

The weather hasn't been brilliant.

Just getting organised so that we could live aboard in reasonable comfort, never mind actually get started working toward the launch, seems to have taken ages.

I'm incredibly proud of Gail for the way she's thrown herself into organising things, whilst at the same time adapting to what for her is a completely alien environment.

She's kept a level head even when I've started to get wound up with frustration. All because I can't find anything, and the rain has come on again, and I feel like I'm not making any progress.

If I'm honest I underestimated how long it would take to get sorted and settled.

Today is the first day I've actually done any work on the boat, and that's been limited by the rain.

It pains me to see my boat looking more like a gypsy encampment than the beautiful sailing machine I know she is.

On that subject here's a heads up for those friends and family planning to come visit next weekend.

Right now it seems unlikely 'Gleda' will be on the water by then.

She should be assembled with decks and pod in place, we may even have the masts up, but that's a long shot.

In other words, if you're expecting a 'champagne on the bows as she slides down the slipway' event please don't. You'll be disappointed.

If I've learned anything building this boat it's that you can only do what you can do, and piling on too much pressure isn't helpful.

We still want next weekend to be a celebration of what's been accomplished so far.

We're living aboard our new home, we're on the coast, we're nearly finished, we'd like to celebrate.

I'll keep you updated.

May 26, 2014 - A Life-Changing Week

This time last week 'Gleda' was somewhere on the road heading south, and we were in a hotel room exhausted after a long stressful day.

Today 'Gleda' is sitting peacefully in the boatyard, the sun has shone all day, and I've been working away on the lashing strakes and rub rails, chatting to folks in the yard and generally feeling pretty relaxed.

We ate our evening meal down by the river watching the comings and goings, and enjoying the gorgeous views.

All in all, a good day.

I talked about adjustment in my last blog post and I'm only now beginning to realise how much life has changed for us.

The last month has been so hectic. Moving out of our cottage. Storing and disposing of so many possessions. Getting the barn cleared. Moving the boat 3 times and so on. There's been no time to think.

It's taken a full week for the reality of our new lives to begin to take root.

All the comments I received after my last post really helped, thank you.

Today I felt a warm glow of satisfaction when I looked at 'Gleda' in the yard.

Yes, she looks like a gypsy encampment, but she's here, we're living aboard in comfort, it's just a matter of time now.

Tuesday 27th May 2014 - Journal Entry

I've spent the last few days sorting out a myriad of things.

More rope and blocks ordered, more money spent.

The weather hasn't been great, wet and windy. 'Gleda' still looks like a gypsy camp, folks are going to start arriving for the 'launch' tomorrow.

I'm feeling like I've let them all down.

My morale was boosted with the arrival of a young lad by the name of Jake Woodnutt.

A longtime follower of the blog, he contacted me about a week ago asking if I needed any help. Of course, I said yes.

To be honest I'd pretty much forgotten about him, what with everything else that's been going on. Anyway, he arrived this afternoon. He did so in style, sailing his little Wharram Tiki 26 'A Roamer' upriver from Plymouth.

Unbelievably he'd sailed single-handed from his home in the Channel Island of Alderney, especially to help.

It was a maiden trip after completing a huge restoration of 'A Roamer'.

His Mom & Dad had built her twenty years before, but the boat had been forgotten and neglected until Jake decided to bring her back to life.

We didn't know it at the time but Jake's unexpected and welcome arrival was to be the start of a long friendship.

(GAILS BLOG) May 28, 2014 - Landgirl Adjusts

For such a massive change in my lifestyle and what I thought I would be happy with, I'm pleased to say that I have, so far, felt really positive about this move.

Living in a small space, sorting out our chosen possessions (still had too many, some leaving us), having to climb ladders to move anywhere - I have been fine.

The weather, much the same as anywhere and anything else has an effect.

It is currently raining. So I am sat in the salon (dining area to non-boaties) typing this with the hatches shut listening to Neil and Jake positioning the beam pins. (steel rods that hold the beams in place which hold the boat together; pretty critical).

And don't feel quite so positive as shut in.

Last night we met my best bud Maria and her crew in Tavistock for a meal.

Must admit that when we left them to go back to their holiday accommodation. (they changed their plans from Greece to Devon to be at the launch). I felt quite overwhelmed that although I'm coming home for a couple of weeks shortly, when I'm back to 'Gleda' and we get rid of the car, I will really be living the different life we have been talking about.

A life where friends/family/convenience shops & restaurants are not just a drive, short or long, away.

Mum & Bry came down today for nearly a week. Bry has offered to help, and there will be lots of painting to do.

Again, seeing them was lovely, but when I next leave them in middle of June, when will be the next time?

Next big adjustment for me is when 'Gleda' gets put on the water.

At the moment it is like caravanning. The boat is steady and I don't need to worry about getting to land to shower (as previously mentioned).

When 'Gleda' is on her mooring however, I think there may be a sense of isolation which will be helped with me learning to row.

Rowing - now that's another worry. Whilst I am confident that I can learn to row, the fast flowing tide in this river is something of a worry for an inexperienced and weak rower. I'd feel much more confident with an engine (as well) but currently, that is only on the wish list.

I may look to see if we can hire one*.

The other night, Neil opened the hatch above our berth (bed) so we could see the stars. Yes, soppy sounding and as romantic as it sounds, seeing the stars from bed was always on my personal wish list.

Now just need a clear night without any light pollution, so I can see them as in an African sky.

Looking forward to spending time with friends and family at the launch party at the weekend when we are joined by more.

Here's hoping for a sunny weekend.

*We bought a second-hand one soon after.

May 29, 2014 - Two Become One Again

Yesterday was a big day.

Despite a busy schedule, Mike the yard owner took the time to crane in the beams and deck pod.

By mid-afternoon we had the two hulls joined together for what I very much hope will be the final time.

It was a long, physically tiring job, and a job that simply had to be done right.

One of the unique design features of Wharram catamarans is that the cross beams are attached to the hulls with rope lashings.

On a Tiki 38, there are also 18 mm stainless steel pins fitted through the beams that act as locators. But it's the lashings that hold the whole boat together. It's imperative to get them tight.

Jake and I came up with a technique that involved pulling the round turns as tight as possible using physical force.

Then using a ratchet clamp to pull the two sides of the lashing together while we made the frapping turns and tied off. It worked perfectly.

Unbelievably the hulls actually moved in their cradles as we pulled everything tight. I couldn't have done it on my own.

Without Jakes help, 'Gleda' simply wouldn't be as she is today and I'm immensely grateful.

Today we greased all the beam pins and fitted the hardwood retaining blocks.

As things stand it looks as if 'Gleda' will be craned farther into the yard on Monday afternoon so that I can fit the stern tube, ramp, aft platform and rudders.

If all goes well she'll then be put into the water on Wednesday.

I confess that lifting the complete boat by the beams is something I'm not looking forward to, but it's got to be done.

Apologies for the short post, I'm pretty bushed tonight, but I'm very happy to be sleeping on an assembled boat.

June 2, 2014 - Overwhelming Days

Right now I can't even begin to get my thoughts together enough to attempt a meaningful summary of the past week's events.

Never in my life have I experienced such a prolonged period of intense emotions.

It's going to take some time for me to absorb and process what these life-changing days have meant to me, and all this before 'Gleda' even hits the water!

I've already made mention of Jake. He worked like a trojan for 3 days, and I simply wouldn't have been able to get 'Gleda' assembled without his help.

Folks in the yard asked how long I'd known him. They were incredulous when I told them we'd never met until now. And that he'd sailed that little Tiki 26 out on the mooring singlehanded from Alderney. Just to come and help me.

Frankly, I find it incredible too, and there's even more to the story than I can relate here tonight. Jake, you're an amazing young man and both Gail and I will be eternally grateful.

Jakes arrival was just the prelude to what seemed an endless series of amazing events.

It was brilliant to see so many friends and family turn out to celebrate with us.

But what blew me away completely was the fact that folks I'd never met made long journeys to come along.

Jon Sutton from Pershore. Ian Bamsey and his lovely family down from Exmouth. Then on Sunday Craig from Southampton, followed by Stuart and his partner Zaya. South African, Kiwi and Mongolian respectively, a very multi-national day!

On Saturday night we had 26 people on deck enjoying a drink and chatting in the lovely warm sunshine.

I just couldn't believe that only a few weeks ago 'Gleda' was still in a barn in Warwickshire, and Weir Quay a long way away.

There was a tinge of sadness that others couldn't be there.

My Mom and Dad because of a nasty fall Mom had a few weeks ago. My brother Andy because of work commitments. Although he still managed to get a telephone call through to the boatyard from Burma to wish us well.

Richard, Jane, Malc and Charlie from the farm, and many other friends and supporters.

They were all with us in thought and we look forward to welcoming them aboard 'Gleda' soon.

To all those who were with us in body or spirit I give my thanks.

The weekend will stay long in my memory.

There's been a different kind of intensity today, 'Gleda' had to be moved as a complete boat for the first time.

This involved using the crane to lift her by the beams and then using the yard boat trailer to manoeuvre her farther.

The crane lift went well although my heart rate reached it's highest level of all the lifts we've been through so far.

Unfortunately, the second stage didn't go quite to plan. There was a slippage of the timber beams we were using to span between the beams.

She moved sideways, resulting in some damage to the inboard side of the starboard hull. It became pinned against the top of one of the hydraulic rams, and took some serious pressure on a very small contact point.

The ply wasn't penetrated but rather crushed. I feared the worst, but was amazed to discover that inside the hull there was just a little bit of splitting on the upper lamination of ply.

I've got the damage filled and glassed tonight so no problem there, but we've still got a way to go down the yard before we can splash.

I'll be very pleased when that happens because these lifts are stressing me out now.

Fingers crossed that tomorrows lift and Wednesday's launch goes more smoothly.

Ok. that's me officially knackered out, once again thanks to everyone, and I'll be back with another update soon.

June 3, 2014 - Landlocked No More

I'm utterly shattered, I can't write much.

It's somehow fitting. Just like the rest of this project, the long-awaited final transition from land to water arrived unplanned and unexpectedly.

I'll give you all the details as soon as I can, but late this afternoon 'Gleda' was craned out of the yard and into the basin here at Weir Quay.

It was low tide and the basin is filled with mud and river debris, it's not glamorous but neither is it dry land.

I'm typing this at 9.15pm, high water is less than an hour away.

Through the saloon portlight, I can see only water. The tides are decreasing as we've passed springs, 'Gleda' may not float tonight, and if she doesn't it'll be a few weeks before she does.

I don't care, no more wagons, no more cranes, no more boat lifts, with Mother Natures help she can make her own way from here.

There were some tears shed this afternoon, it's been a long long haul, but we've made it, there's no stopping us now, this is just the beginning.

Sleep well all, I know I will.

June 9, 2014 - Neaped

I can't believe that this time last week 'Gleda' was still sitting in the yard.

It's been a strange week.

It started with the stress and emotional high of watching 'Gleda' being craned into the mud. Thank you so much for all the fantastic comments.

Then just a few days later, I found myself suffering from a kind of postnatal depression as all the buzz and excitement died down.

Gail left to complete her last two weeks of work and I found myself alone onboard listening to the rain hammering on the coachroof and wondering how I was ever going to get the project finished.

The invoices for transport to the yard and cranage into the mud arrived within a few days of each other.

Scary quotes for the standing rigging pinged into the e-mail, and the list of gear still needed keeps growing.

I guess I thought the hard part was over but I should have known better.

As always though it's friends and family that picked me up.

The thought of all the folks that came to the launch party. Along with the goodwill and energy they brought with them, will be a source of fuel for my final drive to finish this project.

I've not been idle these past days though. I dug holes in the mud and got the rudders in place, although the bottom lashings will have to be done on the slip as I can't do them under 6" of muddy water.

The engine boxes and wells are in position, and I've got quite a lot of painting done.

The standing rigging was ordered today for delivery early next week. 'Gleda' and I have been neaped for a week now, but the tide has turned,

I reckon she'll float on Thursday, that'll be good.

June 11, 2014 - Rigging Ready

Yesterday was a bad day, the weather was rubbish, a strong breeze blowing up the river, thick cloud all day, and frequent heavy showers.

I didn't do a fat lot other than cycle up to the village for a few supplies, then sit below studying the plans, thinking about all the work left to do, and spending more money online ordering up essential bits and pieces.

The phone rang late afternoon. It was the riggers in Plymouth to tell me that my standing rigging was ready.

They'd originally said it would be next week at the earliest, so it was a nice surprise.

I decided to head into Plymouth this morning and pick it up. As Gail has the car up country I biked it a couple of miles down the lane to Bere Ferrers and caught the train into town.

It's the first time I've been on a train in years and it was fun. There's a railway bridge over the River Tavy which makes the route far shorter than driving.

It's a scenic route, you also get good views of the Naval Dockyard at Devonport.

It was a twenty-minute walk down to the riggers and a longer one back to the station. I'd kind of underestimated how heavy 100 m of 6 mm stainless wire plus fittings is, and I'll be aching tomorrow!

At least back at Bere Ferrers, I was able to hook the lot over the handlebars and push/freewheel my way back to the yard.

I spent the afternoon on deck marking up the eight shrouds and forestay, then greasing and adding the protective PVC pipe to the mast loops.

While I was doing it the tide came in at it's highest since 'Gleda' went in the mud, I thought she might float but no. I'm beginning to wonder if she's stuck!

For a while there though she looked like she was afloat. There's another couple of feet of tide to go yet before it peaks, so I'm hoping Thursday will be the day, we'll see.

June 13, 2014 - Short But Sweet

It's been a good day.

Tonight 'Gleda' floated free for the first time.

It was for less than an hour but it was nice while it lasted!

I was able to warp her free of the muddy holes she was stuck in and pull her gently about 20ft further down the quay where the water is slightly deeper.

After all those years of sitting in cradles, the weeks of movement by fork trucks, teleporters, wagons, boat lifts and cranes. It was magical to just pull on a piece of rope and have her gently glide towards me.

I cracked a beer and sat on deck feeling her move beneath me, and watching the bows gently bobbing against the backdrop of the blue Tamar.

A special moment, I wish I'd been able to share with Gail.

In other news, I had a surprise visit from Steve Turner this morning. For those that don't know, Steve is probably the world authority on Wharram's.

He's built over 30, and he's a marine surveyor specialising in multihulls.

He was visiting the yard to survey a monohull, and before he started he came aboard 'Gleda' for a cuppa and a chat.

In some ways, Steve is responsible for 'Gleda' being built. Because back in the days when I was living on 'Mor Gwas' up the Penryn river. Steve sailed up one day on his big Wharram 'Imagine' to visit Tim and Heather Whelan on 'Ika Roa'.

The sight of those two incredible boats left an indelible mark that ultimately led to this project.

It took over 30 years, but to have Steve aboard was special.

Incredibly Steve still owns 'Imagine'. He told me that he's in the throws of re-building her after she was seriously damaged when some cowboys lifted her in the boatyard.

Steve is based just down the river at Millbrook so hopefully I'll be able to catch up with him again later in the summer.

It's been another scorching day, and in between chatting and keeping hydrated I have actually done some work.

I got the masthead lights wired in and tested, and got all the standing rigging fitted to the mast. More on that tomorrow.

June 20, 2014 - Sticks Up!

This morning saw another landmark in the project when we finally got the masts stepped.

Everything went pretty smoothly and once I'd got the shrouds roughly lashed in place I was able to stand back and for the first time see 'Gleda' looking like a sailboat. I'll probably wait until 'Gleda' floats again before I tighten the shroud lashings properly.

And in the meantime, I'll just try and get used to the transformation these two bits of aluminium tube have made.

Incredibly it's near enough six years to the day since those shiny tubes arrived in a big crate all the way from Canada, it's been a long haul.

The remaining days of June were spent working on a seemingly endless list of jobs.

Engine boxes and controls, rudder lashings, tillers, standing and running rigging, painting, electrics.

Once again I'd wildly underestimated how much work was left to do. So much time, so much money.

'Gleda' had been in Weir Quay for over a month and hadn't even floated properly yet.

Physically and mentally I was struggling. Frequent migraine headaches, pulled muscles in my chest, neck and shoulder. Constant stress and worry.

Gail kept me sane. Already she was becoming my rock. I'd wondered if she'd be able to cope with life aboard. She was doing it better than me.

To my mind we should have been sailing by now, once again I felt like I'd failed.

But however I felt there was only one thing I could do; keep going.

July 1, 2014 - Two Tikis, Two Good Friends

It's been a while since my last post, sorry about that.

Truth be told there didn't seem to be a lot to tell you.

We had a spell of wet and windy weather that pretty much brought progress to a grinding halt. Then, when the weather improved, I seemed to be tatting about all day without a great deal to show.

To be honest I've been through a bit of a low patch.

I'd thought that we might be sailing by the end of June, but just didn't recognise the amount of work needed to make that happen.

I should know better than set targets but without them, I'm afraid things might drift too much.

My new target is the end of July. That should be doable and it needs to be. Summer here is all too short, the longest day has passed, if we've got three good months left we'll be doing well.

The last few days have been better. I've made some progress and I've decided to work on the three major outstanding groups of work in sequence.

First the engines and controls. Second the steering system, and last the running rigging.

If I can get the first two cracked over the next few weeks then we have the opportunity to get 'Gleda' out of the mud basin around the 14th/15th spring tides.

I really want to get 'Gleda' out on the mooring and properly afloat.

I've got no reason to complain though, Gail and I are happily living aboard our boat in a beautiful location and with the freedom to follow our dreams.

I know there are many out there who would love to be in the same position.

I've also been reminded once again that there are some generous supportive friends out there helping us along.

This week two gifts arrived in the post from different places but with the exact same thought.

The first was from Jake Woodnutt on Alderney. It was a beautiful little Tiki pendant, and as Jake said: "every Tiki should have a Tiki aboard to bring good luck".

Today another package arrived. This time from Olivier Roux in Geneva, and inside was another Tiki!

Apart from building a Tiki 38, Olivier is also a skilled artist and engraver, and the pewter Tiki he sent was made and engraved by him.... Wow!.

What's even more impressive is that Olivier used the same font for the word 'Gleda' on the reverse side.

I'm incredibly grateful to both Jake and Olivier for these thoughtful gifts. I'll treasure them always, and 'Gleda' and her crew are now assured of good luck and protection wherever they may roam.

Today I've been fairly productive and got the engine control recess in the pod finished. As well as all the blocks and cordage in the starboard engine well.

These Tikis are working already :)

THE RIVER

*J*uly 14, 2014 - She's Afloat........Properly!

> *It's been a frustrating week one way and another. But today all of that was forgotten.*

Because on this morning's high tide, under the beautiful blue sky and with hardly a breeze, 'Gleda' finally broke free of the land for good. She floated serenely out into the river Tamar and was finally and properly afloat for the first time.

It's seven years and seven months since I cut that first piece of plywood back in the landlocked Midlands.

There were many times when I wondered if this day would ever come. If seven really is a lucky number then we chose a good day.

It didn't happen quite as I'd envisaged. We were pulled out to the mooring by the yards workboat, but you know what? I don't give a fig.

We're on the water and it's salty! That'll do for me right now, and we're opening a bottle of fizz tonight to celebrate.

Tomorrow I'll start work again with new energy.

Engines, steering linkages and running rigging will be the focus over the coming days. I really want to be sailing by the end of the month.

Tonight we splashed Cornish champagne on the bows and drank to the many years of adventure ahead.........Cheers!

July 22, 2014 - First Week Afloat

Well, we've been on our mooring for just over a week now and generally the weather has been kind to us.

That said we had a pretty rough night last Wednesday. A strong breeze got up during the night and when the tide turned, the river got quite choppy. '

Gleda' decided to lay beam on to the waves. The mooring buoy kept going under the boat, and the Zodiac with outboard still attached, tried to destroy itself against the rudders.

Let's just say that getting in the dinghy and getting the outboard on deck left me wide awake at 2 in the morning.

That little escapade didn't really help with a shoulder/neck strain I picked up the day we got afloat.

I thought it would just clear itself up. But eventually, Gail pushed me into visiting a Doctor for the first time in about 10 years.

The super strong painkillers he prescribed are at least allowing me to sleep better and to keep working. But I'll be much happier when I can stop taking them and get back to normal function.

Today it has been roasting hot with little wind, so I took the opportunity to have a play with the mainsail. I'm still waiting for a lot of the running rigging parts to be delivered. So there was no way I could actually get the sail rigged properly. But after so long waiting I just couldn't resist hoisting it up there to see how it looked. I've got to say it looked just fine.

Can't say the same of the cover though, I'll have to take another look at that.

Day by day 'Gleda' is slowly transforming into the sailboat she was built to be. And I'm still aiming for the end of the month to get her moving.

Numerous seemingly small and insignificant jobs have been ticked off, and each one brings us closer.

A slightly bigger job ticked off today was getting the forward netting in place. It took ages to get right but it's strong (I've bounced in it), and it's added to 'Gleda's' increasingly purposeful look.

July 31, 2014 - Still Moored

Hi all, still here, still working, still not sailing.

Things are moving in the right direction but far slower than I'd wanted.

There are a few reasons, it's harder working on anything when you're on a boat moored out in the river. No shore power, restricted workspace and weather dependent. Just keeping the boat stocked and comfortable also takes time. With runs ashore for supplies, water and showers etc.

It's been difficult to get all the running rigging components sourced at the right price. And although I've now got most of it aboard, there are still a few things like mainsheet blocks that even the manufacturers were out of stock of.

Fingers crossed everything will be here next week. For nearly three weeks now I've been working with a very painful neck/shoulder. Trapped nerve, strained muscle, who knows.

It's getting better slowly, but movement is restricted and painkillers are regularly popped.

I've had to go back to the drawing board as far as my chain drive steering connections are concerned. I just couldn't get enough travel to move the tillers through the full motion.

I've got to revert back to something similar to the plans using a drum, but that means changing the wheel shaft bearing system I'd already fitted.

Gail is heading back up country for two weeks next week so I'll be on my own again, the weather forecast for the coming week shows rain every day. It's going to be a bit of a grind.

Despite all the delays and frustrations, I'm stubbornly moving forward though.

Every day brings us closer to the day when 'Gleda' will be free to leave this mooring and move downriver under her own steam.

Thoughts of heading south to Portugal are still my main motivator.

August 7, 2014 - Under Way At Last

A big day today, I 'drove' 'Gleda' for the first time under her own power.

My first attempt didn't go well. I'd wrapped the steering rope the wrong way around the drum so that the wheel acted like a tiller i.e Turning the wheel to port turned the wheel to starboard.

Then because there was too much slack in the system the whole thing fouled up, and I had to revert to using the tiller anyway.

The wind increased, blowing against the tide, and picking up the mooring on my own proved challenging, to say the least. I lost the boathook and it took 8 attempts before I was able to secure the boat again.

I re-grouped after lunch though, re-routed and adjusted the steering, made up a temporary boathook and tried again.

This time everything worked perfectly and I spent half an hour motoring up and down the river making sure everything was OK.

As the engines were well run in, due to having used them to charge batteries for a few weeks, I opened up the throttles and got 7 knots against a strong tide.

It felt great. I picked up the mooring again without trouble.

I've been working my way through the running rigging and sails this past week, and this morning I was able to get both sails up for the first time.

There's still quite a lot to do but I'm optimistic that I'll be able to do some sailing trials at some point next week.

The weather forecast for the weekend isn't good with the remnants of a Hurricane likely to give us some unseasonal conditions on Sunday.

The summer just seems to be hurtling by, but I'm doing all I can to get 'Gleda' finished and sailing just as soon as I can.

TO THE SEA

*A*ugust 23, 2014 - *Sea Trials Underway*

On Tuesday we left our mooring at Weir Quay and motored down the river Tamar. Out under the Tamar bridges between Devon and Cornwall, past Devonport docks and the Torpoint ferry, and out into Plymouth harbour.

It took the best part of three hours to reach our tranquil overnight anchorage close inshore to the village of Cawsand.

Early the following morning we weighed anchor and headed out past

Rame Head on route for Fowey. With a planned minor 'fly by' of Polperro to wave at some friends who were staying there.

Given that this was the first time I'd been able to raise the sails properly I guess it was somewhat fortuitous that the wind was very light.

But it didn't take long to satisfy myself that actually everything was working pretty well.

We caught a gust off Rame head that saw the log whizz round to 8.5 knots, and I got quite excited. Unfortunately, it didn't last, and for the rest of the 20 odd mile trip we had next to no wind, and what little we had was right on the nose.

We were motor sailing by the time we got to Polperro but the sails came down shortly afterwards.

We pulled into Fowey after some 7 hours and 21 nautical miles. We could have walked it quicker.

As expected the harbour was absolutely packed because it is Regatta week.

It was a tad nervy manoeuvring 'Gleda' through all the moored craft, and to add spice a dinghy race had just started so I had them to contend with as well!

The Fowey Harbour crew were fantastically helpful though. They found us a berth rafted up alongside another cat moored to the temporary pontoons they put in place for the summer.

We've been here for 3 nights enjoying the action. There has been constant activity on the water, and on Thursday night the RAF Red Arrows aerobatic team put on a stunning display.

We were able to host some friends for the display, and a good time was had by all.

Tonight there's a torchlight flotilla through the harbour followed by a fireworks display.

It'll be a nice end to our stay in Fowey.

Tomorrow morning we set sail for Falmouth.

We should get some wind this time although once again it'll be on the nose, so we'll find out how 'Gleda' goes to windward.

The forecast for Monday is lousy, so I'm planning to find a spot up the River Fal somewhere to hunker down for a couple of days.

I'll update you when I can but so far so good, we're cruising

(GAILS BLOG) September 5, 2014 - Long Overdue Update

Firstly, sorry for the delay in putting up a new post, mainly due to connectivity, well lack of.

Since my last post I have been 'up country' for a couple of weeks to sort family issues. Leaving Neil alone on the boat, in what turned out to be rubbish August weather.

We have started sailing, meeting some deadlines and marking some milestones.

While I was in Leamington I collected a wind generator for 'Gleda'. Wind power seems much more likely than sun sat on the River Tamar in Devon at the height of a UK summer. You wouldn't think so, but there you go; the good old British weather.

When I got back to Weir Quay with a car full of stuff, including the genny, Neil had motored 'Gleda' down to the pontoon to pick me and my stuff up.

It was the first time that I had been on her moving under her own power. Such a thrill.

Weather that afternoon was poor so spent most of the time unpacking and putting stuff away.

Putting up the wind genny the next day was exciting in a terrifying kind of way. You know the kind of way that you'd be happy not to have to experience again.

Imagine, a heavy moving wind turbine on top of a long metal pole, at the very back of the boat where there is nothing to hang on to. Above a tide running fast with waves and the wind trying desperately to start the thing spinning at warp speed.

Then add someone (me). Who has never used a drill. Being responsible for pinning in position two legs that hold the pole in place. Knelt on a narrow plank whilst Neil tries to hold the heavy pole in place without it a) falling back on to the boat or b) falling into the river.

After quite some time of heart-stopping drama (trust me it was at the time), we now have a wind generator which has been put to great use.

The following day we headed into Plymouth for some final bits and pieces from the chandlery before we set off for Fowey.

About 3 pm Tuesday afternoon we set off down the Tamar towards Plymouth. We motored down on the tide and our first landmark was heading under the Tamar Bridge.

More than once, in fact, many times, Neil and I had been crossing the Tamar Bridge in a car saying that one day we would be on the water below - well we were.

That night we anchored in Kingsand & Cawsand bay which was really pretty. But a bit hard on the nerves through the night as every little sound had me wondering if we were dragging the anchor. We weren't.

We then headed around the coast towards Fowey. Not much wind so not much sailing was done, so we ended up motoring around.

Next milestone was sailing past the cliffs in Polperro. Where friends, Maria & Ian with my goddaughters, Rachael and Laurel, were on the cliffs to wave us past. After many holidays in Polperro again we had stood on land looking out to sea saying "'one day".

We then headed into Fowey. Bearing in mind that this was Fowey Regatta week, the day before the Red Arrows were due to perform, and is notoriously busy in the summer months anyway. As we headed in, there was a sailing dinghy race taking place across the river.

Neil did brilliantly negotiating his way slowly through this mass of sail (little did he know it would be good practice for the week to come).

Again, this was still only day 2 of sea trials and testing her steering capabilities and sails etc. We had a great few days in Fowey. Not least that there are shower and laundrette facilities.

On the day of the Red Arrows, Maria, Ian, Rachael, Laurel and Maria's brother Nick and family joined us on board to watch the Red Arrows. Not only a fantastic display but another milestone.

4 years previously we had seen the display from a RIB on the water, and had said how great it would be to watch from the deck of 'Gleda'.

Added to which I got to share the moment with my best friend too.

We finished off our stay in Fowey by seeing the firework display at the end of Regatta week, then headed across to Falmouth.

We sailed to Falmouth. Neil seemed pleased, although there was some tweaking he wanted to do. I made tea.

Neil's parents saw us sail into the Carrick Roads at Falmouth past Pendennis Castle.

Another milestone for Neil, as Falmouth is a special place for him and his sailing history.

We spent a good few nights up the River Fal, out of the way of the delightful August winds. Unfortunately, we couldn't keep out of the way of the rain.

We did however during this time anchor again in a creek, for one night only, the wind got up and Neil particularly had another disturbed night.

We also did some more sailing in the Carrick Roads.

Apparently better than our sail around, but still some tweaking to be done.

This was the week of the Tall Ships in Falmouth where they welcome over a dozen tall ships (it's kind of in the name) along with thousands of visitors. It has to be said that seeing some of these ships on the horizon in full sail getting nearer was great.

Mercedes, one of the ships came into Falmouth flying a huge skull & crossbones and fired her cannon. Pendennis Castle fired back. It was just like Pirates of the Caribbean but without Jonny Depp (of course, I have my own pirate).

Neil's daughter Nicole joined us the morning of the Parade of Sail. Which is when all the tall ships parade from Falmouth harbour across the bay to a race starting line off the Helford River.

We were moored in St Mawes harbour by this time, yet another milestone. We had spent a few short breaks at The Idle Rocks Hotel in St Mawes and again looked out ....

Getting to Falmouth for the Tall Ships was a deadline Neil had in the diary since they announced the date at least a couple of years ago.

I have to say the Parade of Sail was fantastic. Not just to see the huge sails of the tall ships. But the literally thousands of sails all around them as people headed on to the water for the best views (which was where we were). You could also see the thousands of spectators on the cliff tops watching.

At one point we inadvertently found ourselves in amongst the tall ships, sailing against them. Neil kept his nerve and managed to manoeuvre, under sail, through them despite the wind dropping and causing him near heart failure.

That could have been a front pager - hand built catamaran takes out 100-year-old historical ship. Actually more likely to be the other way round given the size of them.

The next day the three of us set off and sailed back to Fowey.

Our sail from Fowey back to Cawsand Bay was a challenging one.

It took 8 hours into a Force 4 Easterly with a nasty chop. For the first time, 'Gleda' pushed her slim bows into the waves and we had spray flying over the decks.

I was determined to sail though, and tacked her back and forth past Polperro and Looe and onwards towards Rame Head. I was nervous of course. Alive to every creak and groan. Watching, listening, learning. My nerves weren't helped by an almighty crack that saw the foresail sheet start to flog.

It took seconds only to realise that the mainsheet U bolt had broken loose. The oak retaining block in front of the mast had split. It was easy enough to make a temporary fix and our progress wasn't slowed much. Another job added to the list.

The wind dropped as we came abeam of Rame Head and with the light fading I conceded defeat and dropped the engines for the last few miles to Cawsand Bay.

After a peaceful night on the anchor, we woke to a foggy morning. We sat in the pod for breakfast and watched the sun breaking through. The foghorn of the incoming Plymouth - Roscoff ferry adding to the atmosphere.

We upped anchor and motored into the Sound and headed up river. Past the docks, the warships and the submarines. Dodging the Tamar ferries. Through the moorings at Saltash, and under the bridges. Then into the beautiful wide expanses of the Tamar proper.

It felt like we were coming back home after the holidays.

After picking up our mooring we went ashore for showers, said hi to Mike and the lads, tidied the boat, fitted sail covers, snugged down again.

I was pleased with how things had gone. Apart from a few easily sorted issues 'Gleda' had worked perfectly. Gail had been great, my confidence in handling the boat had come on leaps and bounds.

I should have been happy and excited but I wasn't. Those damn dark clouds were gathering in my mind once more. It seemed that every time I thought I'd shaken them off they reappeared.

As I tried to sleep they filled my head with gloom. My bank account was all but cleared out. I couldn't see how we could get to Portugal or, if we did, how we could survive. I feared that we may end up spending winter in the UK, in the mud and the rain and the cold. If that happened I could see Gail growing to hate the boat and the lifestyle before we'd even started.

I could see her leaving, I could see myself being alone again.

Fear and doubt, my seemingly constant companions.

I should have fallen asleep in aglow of satisfaction.

Instead, I fell asleep angry with myself.

Sunday 7th September 2014 - Journal Entry

Today started badly. Gail got upset and angry with me. Because, as she quite rightly said, I hadn't thought things through and planned properly.

This was prompted by me finally having the courage to express my fears that we may not be able to get to Portugal, and that we'd have to spend winter in the UK

She see's this as meaning separation as she can't imagine living on 'Gleda' through the winter months.

She's right. I don't want to think about it either. I fear I'd struggle myself.

The fact is that Portugal will cost thousands, I have no money. There are also issues around red tape, whether Jake can crew for us or not, the right weather window. The list goes on.

So much to sort out with time and resources desperately short.

I thought that when the boat was launched things would get easier, instead of which the opposite happened.

In my heart I know I've done all that I could. I've worked so damn hard this year.

It's been non-stop pressure. Physical and mental. Could I have foreseen everything that's happened? No. Could I have planned better? In hindsight yes. But I know myself. I had to put the blinkers on, take each day as it came and keep moving forward.

It's all I could do.

The rest of the day went far better. It was a special one. After lunch, we took 'Gleda' down alongside the pontoon so as to receive some VIP guests. James Wharram and Hanneke Boon came to visit along with two of their friends, Peter and his partner Liz.

I was more than a little apprehensive about having such distinguished guests aboard. Given the morning's highlighting of my own inadequacies and failings, my self-confidence was low. What if James grilled me too hard? What if Hanneke spotted things I'd done wrong?

I needn't have worried. OK, Hanneke did ask to be shown the boat in detail, and did suggest a few things I could modify, but both seemed impressed with my efforts.

James is 86 years old now and a little unsteady on his feet. But his mind is as sharp as ever, his enthusiasm undiminished. His energy recharged me, reminded me why I'd started the project, reminded me what was possible.

Peter, who I'd never met before, was equally supportive. James had told me Peter was a writer and a sailor. It's probably a good thing I didn't find out until later that he is in fact, a very notable philosopher, historian, biographer, travel writer and poet.

In my innocence, I mentioned to Peter that I enjoyed blogging and writing, and that I planned to write a book someday. He would no doubt have heard that comment so many times before, yet he was I'm sure genuine when he told me 'keep writing' Neil.

We got back to our mooring about 6:30 and to my annoyance managed to run over the mooring pickup buoy, severing the rope and slicing the buoy.

It's been an emotional day of lows and highs. I feel drained. But tomorrow is another day and I must renew my efforts to improve my mindset and get things working.

Saturday 13th September 2014 - Journal Entry

This will be our last day at Weir Quay.

It's been fun and it's been testing. But the place delivered. It got "Gleda" sailing.

Now it's time for a new chapter in this adventure. I spent the day finishing off jobs.

I wired in the decked lights, fitted some reading lights over the bed and secured the gas cylinders. Once I'd taken off the sail covers that was it, pretty much ready to go.

The plan is to drop Gail ashore first thing (so that she can drive the car down to Falmouth) and then drop down river on the morning tide.

We've said our goodbyes. We're as ready as we can be.

I spoke to Jake tonight. He'll be standing by to crew for us from 1st October. I still don't know how in the hell I'm going to make this happen but I'm committing.

FALMOUTH RETURN

*S*unday *14th September 2014 - Journal Entry*

A tiring day but an incredibly satisfying one.

I dropped Gail ashore just after 9 and an hour later had slipped the mooring for the last time.

The forecast was for fresh to strong Easterly's 20-25 knots. So after an easy motor downriver, I was expecting to get bounced around some once we got into Plymouth Sound. I wasn't disappointed.

The swell was running close to 2 metres and things got lively pretty quickly.

Being single-handed and with no autopilot I had the devils own job getting the main up. I just couldn't get the sail reefed. If I left the wheel for more than a minute 'Gleda' would come off the wind and I'd have to leap back into the pod to regain control.

Just to add to the excitement a Mayday came over the radio. A yacht had lost its mast close by the Eddystone Rock. The voice on the VHF sounded desperate. Within minutes the Plymouth lifeboat came blasting past me heading out.

They must have looked at 'Gleda' with her sails flogging and wondered if they were looking at their next shout.

With reefing proving to be so difficult I opted for plan B. I decided to haul the full main, leave the foresail down, and just run with the jib up forward.

It was a good move.

Once done I turned downwind, got the engines up and set course for Rame Head.

All the activity had made me queasy but my stomach and nerves soon settled and I began to relax and enjoy the ride.

Gail had made up a flask, some sandwiches and a box of goodies. The hot coffee went down a treat.

As we passed Rame making 8-9 knots I was grinning. 'Gleda' easily rode the swells foaming up from astern. I saw gannets diving, a school of porpoises crossed the bows.

I thought back to the last time I'd sailed this same route single-handed. That had been more than 30 years before aboard 'Mor Gwas'. Once again it was just me, my boat and the sea. It was emotional.

With the wind over the stern and the sun shining the sailing was easy.

Unlike our previous passage, the landmarks came quickly. Polperro, Looe and Fowey flew past.

By late afternoon Gull Rock lay astern and Pendennis Castle lay ahead.

Soon afterwards I was turning into the Carrick Roads and getting the sails down. I'd thought to anchor near St Mawes, but the wind was funnelling down the Percuil River and the anchorage looked lumpy!.

So I motored farther up past the castle and tucked into St Just Pool near the beach. Here the high hills sheltered the anchorage. There were a couple of other boats sitting nicely on the hook.

It didn't take me long to join them.

Once settled the kettle went on and I knocked up something to eat. I slept soundly that night.

It was a lazy start the next day. After breakfast I got the dinghy sorted and motored round into the creek on a mission.

Not long after we launched in Weir Quay, I'd had a visit from a young couple called Ben and Alex.

They came down in their camper van to have a look at 'Gleda' on their way to Cornwall where, they told me, they were buying a house.

During the conversation, Ben mentioned casually that the house was on the Roseland Peninsula near to St Just, and that it came with a mooring in the creek.

When I told him we'd be heading that way later in the summer he said we'd be welcome to use it.

A few weeks before leaving Plymouth I'd been in touch with Ben to see if the offer was still open. He said it was. The house was now theirs, they'd moved in and were looking forward to seeing us. There was something we needed to know though. The 'mooring' wasn't really a mooring. Rather it was the right to keep a boat in a small drying inlet called Messack Creek. The water was shallow and the creek tiny ,but he reckoned 'Gleda' could get in there.

Now I was here I wanted to check it out for myself.

As it turned out I didn't get time to do it before Gail turned up. We got permission to park her car at Pascoe's Yard and I dinghied her aboard.

We had a pleasant afternoon.

The sun shone, the water was calm. I scrubbed some Tamar mud off the hulls and then had a swim.

Later that evening as Gail and I sat below having just finished our meal, there was an unexpected knock on the hull. I stuck my head out of the companionway to find Ben and Alex alongside on stand-up paddle-boards.

They came aboard for coffee but couldn't stay long as darkness and tide were falling. I lent them a head torch to get back.

Their visit was a cool reminder that we'd now entered a new world where friends and neighbours could turn up in the strangest of ways.

Before they left we arranged to meet the following morning so I could take them sailing. It would also allow me to better recce Messack Creek.

The next day I took the tender round to find Ben, Alex and her Mom, Binky, waiting on a little shingle beach tucked into the creek. It was certainly an idyllic spot.

Completely sheltered from all winds and surrounded by green fields and trees. The 'house' they'd bought was actually a big old farmhouse at the top of the hill. The only access to the creek was to walk down the hill through the sheep field.

They said Gail could park the car at the farm and we could use the outside tap for water. I said we'd drive around the next day and make a decision but for now, it was time to go sailing.

With all the extra crew aboard it was easy to get underway. We even sailed off the anchor which was nice.

We headed out past Zone Point and into Falmouth Bay. The wind was still blowing over 20 knots from the East, just as it had been a few days before. St Just Pool and Messack were so sheltered we'd no idea.

The sea was lively and we had an exciting sail for an hour before heading up to the head of the Carrick Roads to anchor off Trelissick House.

Annoyingly it took three attempts to get the Manson to bite. Another boat that followed us in had the same problem and I made a mental note to cross the place off my list of possible overnight anchorages.

Despite being a bit breezy we had a pleasant lunch on deck. After a gentle reach back to St Just and dropping our guests back ashore, the sun which had been absent all day finally broke through and Gail and I sat quietly on deck with a drink.

It had been another fun day.

But as we sat there enjoying the evening sunshine there was a lot on my mind. It was mid-way through September. There was still a lot to do to prepare for a Biscay crossing and to get to Portugal. We had to be ready by 1st October, and then we'd realistically only have a few weeks in which to get a weather window. It was already late in the season to leave. The easy option would be to stay. But I'd set a goal way back. 2014 would not only be the year

'Gleda' tasted salt water. It would be the year we left the shores of England. Part of me said wait, part of me said go. The part that said go held sway for now.

I'd given blood sweat and tears to get us this far this year. I wasn't ready to give up while there was still a chance. I simply had to find a last reserve of energy and make it happen.

Despite the turmoil in my head, I overslept the next morning. We had a bit of a dash to get ashore and drive round to Messack Farm for our meet.

The farmhouse was amazing, with stunning views across the Roseland. Ben was at work but Alex took the time to show us the path down the field to the creek. Across their back garden, through two gates. Down a steep grassy field full of sheep. Then through another little gate and a short wooded path before popping out onto the shingle beach where I'd picked them up previously.

The remoteness added to its magical quality and everything looked fine. I said I'd walk around at low tide the next day just to check the bottom, but that if there were no problems I'd bring the boat round on Friday.

As we drove away I once again thanked Providence for helping out.

We'd arrived in Falmouth with really no idea where we'd be. Yes, there are a few anchorages in the Roads and farther up the Fal, but as with all anchorages they're not always tenable. Marinas and moorings in Falmouth were very expensive. We couldn't afford them.

Now we had a safe, sheltered place to stay for as long as we needed it, for free.

With one problem solved I addressed the next one; Money. I

made a call to my financial advisor and established that from April the following year I could access my pension pot. The rules had changed recently and if I wanted, I could draw up to £10,000 per year tax-free. He advised against it of course. Drawing money so soon meant my pension would be substantially reduced in later life. I knew it was sound advice but I didn't care.

All I cared about was the now, being alive and able to make the most of it. I'd worry about how to live in old age when and if I got there.

Getting Marc's confirmation that I could access some funds was huge. Gail had received a decent redundancy payoff when she left work. With a guarantee that I could pay her back the following year, she was happy to use some of that money to fund us over the winter. The financial barrier to Portugal had been lifted.

There was still much to do. We were still adjusting to this sea gypsy lifestyle, but I was feeling more alive than I'd done for years. We were doing things daily that not long before would have seemed a crazy pipe dream. We just needed to keep appreciating them and easing into the change.

MESSACK CREEK

$\mathcal{T}$he following day we got 'Gleda' round into the creek.

I laid a couple of anchors in the mud and ran lines off the trees. It took a few days of re-positioning to find the best place for her to dry out level, and then we started to settle in.

Days were spent working on the boat. I scrubbed the hulls between tides and got another coat of antifouling on.

Gail made up some canvas enclosures to make the pod more sheltered.

I started working through the list of stuff we needed for the crossing. I bought 220 m of leaded line and a sea anchor. I hadn't said anything to Gail but I knew what could happen crossing Biscay in October. I wanted to be prepared.

Actually, Gail hadn't yet committed to coming. It was a big ask.

Some weeks before I'd invited Jake Woodcut to come crew for us down to Portugal. Having a young, fit crewman aboard would be a huge asset. To our delight Jake has jumped at the chance

I'd told Gail that with Jake as crew she wouldn't need to do anything. Part of me wanted her to come. Part of me wondered if that was wise. Was I risking putting her off sailing for good?

We often drove round to Falmouth or Truro for supplies and to get online. With every trip more was crossed off the list. More charts. A spare GPS dongle for the laptop, extra fuel and water containers, lots of tinned food, anti-slip paint, sailmakers palm and needles, radar reflector. We also ordered a larger more efficient fridge as the one we had wasn't working. It seemed never-ending.

Despite the work, Messack became a haven. After a manic day of charging about it was calming to get back to the boat and just appreciate our surroundings.

I collected cockles from the mud at low tide and Gail made a delicious starter for our meal.

There was a little grassy knoll on the shingle beach perfect for having a BBQ. Once the food was cooked I added some twigs and made a little fire.

Gail and I cuddled up around it as darkness fell. To my amazement, Gail told me it was the first time she'd ever sat around a campfire.

Nicole and her Mom came to visit one evening. They parked at Pascoe's, I picked them up in the dinghy and ferried them round to our little hideaway.

We drank wine, lit the BBQ, and just soaked it all up.

Sitting on deck in the mornings was a delight. Herons and Egrets stalked around the boat. Now and again a Kingfisher would fly past. Its vivid blues and scarlet flashing in the sun.

But time was passing. By late September we could feel autumn creeping in. The evenings became chilly. We woke to cold and condensation in the cabins. This was what I feared Gail would hate.

The pressure was building. My journal of 25th September gives an illustration.

After a trip into Truro for supplies, gas and petrol, I got stressed on the way back to the boat. I don't know why. I'm just tired I guess.

I'm worried we're spending too much money, I'm worried about leaving, I'm worried about staying. I don't know.

My head is pounding and I don't know.

After using the farmhouse wheelbarrow to ferry two gas cylinders, 30 litres of petrol and 30 litres of water down the hill I was washed out.

I put my head down for a bit and woke feeling better.

After working on the boat some more this afternoon I once again felt tired and achy.

Tomorrow is a stay on board day and I'm planning to get a lot done. The weather is still holding up and I have to make the most of it.

Gails Decision.

There was an elephant in the room though.

A question left hanging in the air that had to be dealt with.

Was Gail ready to commit to the passage south?

She made her decision. No, she wasn't.

I'd been honest with her. It was getting late in the year to cross Biscay. The chances of hitting bad weather were higher.

Her sailing experience was limited to our passage from Weir Quay to Falmouth and back. That had been comfortable coastal sailing in the summer. This passage was going to be very different.

She'd seen how I'd been preparing the boat. Lifejackets, DSC Radio, Safety Lines and Harnesses, A sea anchor to stop the boat surfing down big waves.

Part of me wanted her to come. She'd stuck by me through so much already, she'd given me strength and support when I needed it trying to get 'Gleda' sailing. But I was scared too. I was scared I'd push her too much, frighten her, put her off sailing for life.

That would be it. She wouldn't be able to stay and I wouldn't be able to leave.

So when she said she wasn't coming, that she'd head back up country and wait until I was in Portugal, my feelings where mixed. Part relief and part dread. There was enough to worry about on this trip without having her in the mix. Jake and I could just concentrate on sailing the boat.

But I dreaded not having her around, worse I dreaded her changing her mind completely and never returning.

I was tempted to call the trip off and stay together, but that might be an even greater risk.

A UK winter on an unheated plywood boat might be just as effective in killing her enthusiasm as a rough Biscay.

I had no choice. I had to go, 'Gleda' had to go.

Sunday 28th September 2014 - Journal Entry

A solid days work today and the boat is now ready.

I sorted the sea anchor bridles and lashed down the warp buckets. I'm praying we don't have to use it but I have confidence that it can now be deployed easily and quickly.

Gail made a new flag for the man overboard buoy, again something I hope we never had to use.

I finished fitting the reefing pennants to the mainsail, stowed all the stuff like paint and tools I've been using these past weeks. Then did a water run up to the farm.

I'm pretty whacked. Jake has his flight booked and arrives on Wednesday.

The weather window looks like it will be open. The clock is now ticking and by this time next week, we should be in Spain.

I'd be lying if I said that there was no trace of anxiety. The last time I tried it didn't go well. No, I'm under no illusion that it's no small thing to cross Biscay and sail down the Spanish and Portuguese coasts.

But I've done as much as I can, it's what 'Gleda' was built to do, and it's the culmination of all that's been done since May when we moved out of the barn.

We have a berth booked for the winter in Lagos marina on the Algarve, and I'm really looking forward to chilling down there.

It still seems unreal. These past weeks have been so hard.

But I committed and once again Providence has delivered.

I'm on the brink of laying the ghost that's haunted me for three decades.

This has been a long time coming.

THANK YOU

So, all that remains is to say a big "thank you" for buying and reading my book. I hope you enjoyed it.

I know you'll have seen this same request in many other books you've read, but I'm going to ask just the same. Could you please take a minute or two to leave a review? It's really important for me to hear what you thought about it. Good or bad I want to know. I'm striving to improve my writing and your feedback will help me do that. Thanks.

Alternatively you can email me neil@neilhawkesford.com

DON'T FORGET YOUR FREE BOOK!

(Just visit www.neilhawkesford.com)

Printed in Poland
by Amazon Fulfillment
Poland Sp. z o.o., Wrocław